I dedicate this book to any man or woman who's been hurt by love, lost love, found love again, and to anyone who's still searching for love. I pray the courageous words spilled on each of these pages serves as a reminder that you are never alone in the way you feel. Love is patient. Love is kind. True love is out there for each of us to find or even better - waiting to find us. Out of the 100 love stories shared along this journey, one of them is just like yours.

Hannah! Thank you so much for supporting me! Love ya :)

100 Days of Dating

Kiana St Louis

Our Stories.

First and foremost, I want to take the time to truly thank each and every one of you for believing in me, supporting me, and giving me the uplifting strength to turn my pain into passion. Cutting myself open and sharing the inner parts of my love life with the world has been the scariest thing I've ever done… and believe me guys, in my 24 years, I've done some pretty wild things! But it took more than courage to admit and push through the reality that I've loved someone with all my heart, only to find they didn't really love me back. It took support, provision, and constant prayer from my friends and family. I couldn't have done this without them.

My best friends allowed me to pour into them time and time again without questioning why I was there or why I felt the way I did. They loved me when I was broken and helped piece together new and stronger parts of myself. Along with prioritizing individual happiness and making it our duties to love ourselves infinitely, this journey has taught me the importance of humanity and connection. Everybody needs somebody. The best part about being human is meeting other humans – loving them, encouraging them, and growing old with them. While my story doesn't end with your typical fairytale prince and princess, I can truly say I am my happiest self, inside and out… and that's because of you.

The purpose of 100 Days of Dating was to unify my thoughts, and not only help myself, but help us all to understand we are not alone in the way we feel at any age. I interviewed 100 people to show that we've all been through heartbreak, we've all known unimaginable love, we have all fallen at some point in our lives, and by grace we've all gotten right back up. I share my story in hopes of releasing my pain and connecting with anyone who may have also felt the same way I did. I was in awe of how willing both my male and female friends were to join in and share their experiences.

100 Days of Dating

I was even more tripped out when people I didn't even know reached out to me after discovering my blog series wanting to be a part of these interviews. It was then I knew, this project was bigger than me. These stories weren't just page turners, they were courage. Our stories bring hope that love is real, love is worth having, and that more importantly, we're all capable of experiencing perfect love.

To every name in this book and to every story shared, I thank you with every part of me for your bravery. Thank you for believing in love. Thank you for reminding me to believe in love. I can't wait to see what each of our futures hold.

Peace & Love,
Ki

100 Days of Dating

Written by: Kiana St Louis
Cover Art by: Deidre Darius

100 Days of Dating

Kiana St Louis

DAY ONE: HEALING

LOVE.

We say the word often in so many different contexts. We *love* our parents. We *love* shoes. We *love* TV shows. But what does it mean to *be in love*? What does it feel like when you truly love someone not for who they are in the eye of the public, not for their talents, not for the things they say to you, but because of who you are when you're with them? What does it feel like to love someone because of the passion they give you, or the genuine kindness they show you when the weight of the world rests on your shoulders, and insists on sharing the load? How does it feel when someone seemingly loves you as much as you love them?

But, more important, how do you move forward when the pain you endured beyond description was *because* of that same love?

Crystal Taylor, 25, has not only felt this pain, but has proven to be one of the strongest young women I know as she struggled with these conflicting emotions. As I begin my 100-day journey into understanding dating, happiness, romanticism, marriage, and divorce, Taylor reminds me of what it is like to be blissfully happy with someone. She also reminds me of the sometimes-unforgiving process of happiness - the reality that nothing lasts forever, including love-filled relationships.

In a series of candid interviews, Taylor opened up to me in an effort to give insight on the healing process after one of the hardest decisions she's had to make in her lifetime - letting her greatest love go. As she poured into me, I reflected her words onto this page, and together we created the lyrics to her pain in addition to constructing hope for her future. This is her story.

Tell me about your love life. Are you single? Dating? In a relationship? Married? It's complicated?

I'm…single. I'm newly single. It's not really complicated - it just ended, essentially. There's not much to say about it. It's pretty tragic actually, but to answer the question, I'm definitely single.

100 Days of Dating

Are you single by choice?

I don't know if I would say it was my choice, but it was a choice that was made. I feel like the choice was made for me, and I kind of just had to move with the gradient; because moving against it wouldn't have helped me in the long run. The decision was made clear without being said, on the other party's account - and I just had to flow with it.

Tell me about your greatest love. What did it feel like to be with him?

My greatest love was the relationship I was just speaking on. How did it feel to be with him? It was a great feeling. I had some of the best moments of my life with him. It was a safe feeling, definitely fun, liberating, and very free.

Do you still feel free?

No. With him? With him do I still feel free?

With Yourself.

With myself, no. Right now, I actually feel like I have the weight of the world on my shoulders. I guess I'm just trying to cope with the whole breakup or even how it happened. How abrupt, or I guess how not abrupt it was. I don't feel free anymore. I feel like I stopped feeling free maybe seven months ago. But I was holding on to what *was* and not what *is*.

Do you remember the moment you fell in love? Could you recall what happened?

The moment I fell in love and the moment I said I was in love were two different times. I didn't just jump into it like, "Hey, I love you." The moment I fell in love, we were in the car, oddly, sitting not too far from my house. We were just having a conversation, and I was literally bursting with laughter. Then when I looked up, I saw that he was staring at me, and I continued looking at him. We had this little awkward stare, and I just looked away like 'okay.' In that very moment, we continued to talk, but of course my mind was still wandering. All I could think was, "Man, I really love this guy." I love the way I feel when I'm with him. I love the way I can just be myself. I love who he is. I love how friendly he is. Always great vibes, always *positive* vibes.

I loved how encouraging he was, because I was having a really bad day. But just like that, I guess you could say he gave me a moment of freedom. I felt so liberated in that moment. With just his presence alone and literally us being in that car, it made me feel like I was in another place and time, even though it couldn't necessarily erase the day I had. That's when I realized that I loved him…just realizing he has the power to do that.

You mention there were two different times, what was it like when you said it?

I was super nervous to say that I loved him to his face. It's so funny because about two days before I said it, I was in my room practicing like, "I love you. I love you." But I never said it, because I kept getting nervous when I was around him. Then another time, once again we were chilling in his car, and we had a disagreement. At this point in our relationship, we had always promised each other that even if we got upset with one another, we'll talk it out, we'll have conversations, and we'll always make sure that our communication is on point.

We were going back and forth, and he ended up saying it first. I was like, "Hmm? Wait, did you say…" He was like, "Yeah, I said it. That's how I feel or whatever." Then I was like, "Oh, yeah? I love you too." That was how we said it. In the moment, actually saying it was like, "Ah!" I was screaming on the inside! But it felt good.

Did you say it at all in any of the ways you had practiced before?

No, it was so different because we were joking. Even though it was a serious moment, we were both laughing together like, "Oh my gosh. Ha, ha, ha! I love you too." It was actually funny - it wasn't as uptight or serious as I thought it would've been. I thought it would've been similar to a sit down, like, "Oh my gosh, I love you." and I would've had to wait for him to respond or not respond, but it wasn't like that. It was pretty much a reflection of the relationship we had - fun.

As I'm watching you share the stories of your past, you light up again from those memories. Do you enjoy remembering?

Sometimes I do…but today, no. Today I was deleting all our pictures out of my phone, and I've never really done that before. It was A LOT of memories. I literally deleted 900 and something photos.

Why did you feel you had to do that?

When two people have their lives so embedded within one another's, moving on is so much more difficult. Everything you do, everything you say, everywhere you walk, certain scents, even people, remind you of that person.

If I can control the immediate things next to me to not remind myself of him, I'm going to try to do that. The simple fact that he bought me this laptop annoys the shit out of me, but I'm not going to get rid of my laptop. I'm going to keep using it. But the pictures of him that were on my mirror, I took them down today. The ones in my phone, I deleted them. I deleted our message thread, which is something I didn't actually want to do, but I told myself, "Just delete it, girl."

As you were deleting the pictures and somewhat erasing what it was that you two shared, can you describe what that felt like for you?

It was hard, because when I saw one of the videos, I just wanted to send it to him and call him like, "Nah, what were we thinking making this video?!" He was twerking in the video. It's mad funny. We were in my living room and he had his hands up. I was like, "No, you got to bend over." We were both so skinny in the video, so I got up and started twerking like, "Oh, my God, am I doing it?" I went through a lot of different emotions. So many happy ones, and so many jokey ones. There are pictures of us from our first anniversary that made me laugh. The launch of the business we both created made me angry because I felt like, "Why were we doing long-term things for something that you weren't even certain of?" Stuff like that made me angry.

At one point, maybe for 10 or15 minutes, I wept. There was snot coming out my nose, like really weeping. I didn't even have any tissue on hand. Everybody was in my living room, so I had to use my scarf, which is now in the dirty laundry because there was a lot in that scarf. When I was done though, when I actually deleted the pictures out of the recently deleted folder in my phone, I cried. That's a whole other life, you know? Deleting the recently deleted files is serious stuff. I cried for a half an hour until I fell asleep, which only lasted for five minutes. Then I woke up, anxiously.

When did you tell yourself you were over it?

Today at work after having a conversation with a friend of mine. I feel like there are certain people in your life whose opinion you value and I value what she thinks. So, in having this conversation, I pretty much asked her to give me her full advice. I simply asked, "What do you think I should do?" and she gave me her honest opinion. Beyond just her opinion, we spoke about life and love; and the reality that when someone's not ready, you can't force them to be ready. She just advised me not to wait on something that wasn't set in stone. I guess in that very moment, I realized that the person who I thought I would've been with, or thought I would've loved for a longer period of time or for even a lifetime, just wasn't the same person anymore. That revelation made me realize, yeah, it's about time I walk away from this table.

In the good, the bad, and the ugly, there are always lessons to be learned. What do you feel you've learned throughout this entire experience?

Oh, I've learned a lot. If I were to write down a list of things that I've learned, there would be categories and subcategories, sub-subcategories, and subcategories to the sub-subs. But I guess one thing that I've taken with me from this relationship, and this can go for people who are both religious and not religious, but being equally yoked. Not only in a religious aspect, it's super important when it comes to relationships as well. I feel that in friendships, you can have that diversity, but in a relationship with somebody that you plan on being intimate with, this is super important.

I didn't fully understand the concept of this I guess as younger Crystal, but being older and actually thinking about a life with someone, kids with someone, going on vacation, living with someone, it definitely changed my view on that. Things as simple as me being raised in a single-parent home, and him being raised by his mother and his father brought up so many differences in our relationship. He was used to the male being the alpha in his home, and I was used to the woman being the alpha in mine. You can't have two alphas in one home or one relationship, at that. This was a huge issue in the beginning of our relationship. I didn't know how to just not say anything. I didn't know how to sit down and let him be the man, the alpha, and take charge.

I learned the importance of communication too, but the biggest lesson for sure is knowing when to walk away, even though that's something I'm still learning. That would be the biggest lesson that I've learned throughout this relationship of learning when to be still, when to not say anything, when to not do anything, and when to walk away. Yeah, that's another big lesson for me - learning to be still. That's something I feel like I can take with me in all aspects of my life. My career as a student, my role as a wife someday, as a mother someday, as a friend, as a mentor to someone; when to be still, and the importance of that in all relationships.

How do you feel about dating or meeting new people?

I feel like a week ago, when I was still hoping that this was temporary between myself and my ex, I thought, *yeah, I could talk to somebody, I could date somebody.* But now that the reality that three years of my life has not necessarily been wasted but has been thrown away, essentially, I don't know if dating is going to be a thing for me right now. At least not for the rest of this year. I genuinely feel like courting someone is super important. I don't want to waste my time. I tend to put myself in these vulnerable situations with men who I think are worth it, and I'm not going to talk to someone I don't think is worth it.

I do know that the next person I date or talk to has to be worth it. Even that in itself is a struggle. Honestly, the idea of dating, courting someone new, literally scares me. The pain I'm feeling dealing with this breakup, I'm just not sure I'm ready. I would have to get this cast off first before willingly jumping off a bridge with somebody else again. Right now it's still a matter of healing. I feel like if I start dating someone else, I'd be going into it with only one foot and one arm, which isn't healthy for either of us. I want to be more stable, and I don't know how long that's going to take, because this is a different kind of pain. A new kind of pain.

You mentioned in order for you to make that next step, the person would have to be *worth it*. How would you know? What are the qualifications of being worthy?

I don't know. I feel like that's something that I'm still trying to figure out, because if anybody would've asked me before, I would've said that my ex was worth it. Back then he *would've* been worth me literally pouring all of myself into his cup, feeling empty. But he wasn't. I don't know if my judgment is even a thing to follow right now, in saying if somebody is or isn't worth it. I will say that I'll be praying a lot more about who I decide to date, so I won't move on my own accord at that point.

I feel like I did a lot of stuff on my own in this relationship. While I love him, I wasn't always asking God for guidance. I kind of always felt like that was it for me…that he was it for me. God "knows it". I "know it". But I feel like God will have more of an active part in the next person I decide to court with. I would like have a little bit more guidance, because I don't know what I'm doing.

Do you know what you want?

From a guy?

Yes.

I have a lot of requirements. If I could pick the top three things that I want from a guy right now, I would say *loyalty, honesty,* and *consistency*. The lack of these three things ended my last relationship.

Do you believe in compromise? Maybe if somebody has two of the three?

Nah, I don't. I compromised a lot with my ex, and I don't know if I could do that again. I feel like maybe when I... No. Even when I heal, I'm not compromising on those three principles. That would be like me walking into the same hole again, so no. Loyalty, honesty, and consistency. I'm not compromising on that.

As you continue to move forward, with or without this person or just figuring out your next steps, happiness should always be at the core. How would you describe being happy, alone as well as in a relationship?

Honestly, happiness alone, I'm not sure what that is like yet. It's actually a scary thought for me.

Why? Why are you afraid to be happy alone?

I'm not afraid to be happy alone, but I'm afraid that maybe I won't find happiness alone. I don't know why, but it's a worry.

What is being happy, to you?

I think happiness for me is having a peace of mind. Having a peace of mind doesn't mean that everything needs to be peaceful around me all the time, or that everything needs to go perfectly. Happiness for me doesn't mean not having struggles or roadblocks, but knowing that I'm on the right track. Knowing that I'm working hard, knowing that the people around me are working as hard as I am, and that they're all loyal, and that they're all honest. That's happiness alone.

Happiness with someone else would look like the first two years of my past relationship if I could get that into a picture. I was happy, *uncontrollably happy*. Everybody knew it when I pulled up and when he pulled up. I don't know if he was, but I was for sure. I don't really know how to put it into words, but I was definitely getting his loyalty, I was getting his honesty, and he was super consistent.

Which allowed you to be free.

Allowed me to have a *peace of mind*. I could go to sleep. I could wake up. I knew he had my back and I had his. I was never afraid of anything. If something went wrong, I knew I could call him. I knew that he would be there to listen to me. I knew he would be honest with me. He would tell me, "Nah, you're fucking up." Or, "Nah, you're right. Don't bend. Don't fold."

100 Days of Dating

DAY TWO: CONFESSIONS

MEN.

Often times, as a woman, I find myself confused and always wondering what men could possibly be thinking. When men do or say certain things, I'm left with my head tilted to the side, squinted eyes and a question mark over my head, with only one response - "What?"

However, I was given insight into the mind of one man on day two of this project.

Khalil Waldron, 22, is no stranger to love or heartbreak, but instead acts as a long-distant friend to both. While men and women speak the same language, like slang, we tend to formulate so many different ways of saying the same thing. However, because of that, I believe our meanings get lost in translation. After trying to say the same thing so many times, at some point you'd want to just stop. Like Khalil, I've too been at this place before. But there's something so comforting in knowing you're not alone in the way you feel.

In this series, Khalil and I walk down a path he's tried to forget. As we tear down the walls of his past to build an understanding for his future, love somehow always remains at the core. This is his story.

Tell me about your love life. Are you single? Married? Talking to someone? It's complicated?

I feel like I'm single. I'm definitely single in my idea of a relationship.

When was your last relationship?

What do you define as a relationship?

I define it as being monogamous with someone. Not flirting with anyone else, or entertaining anyone else, because you wouldn't want to. The person you're with is more than enough.

So, having a girlfriend?

Precisely.

2012

Why so long ago?

I don't know. It's just one of those things I haven't done since.

Are you looking for someone?

I wouldn't say *looking* for someone. I like the thought of just going through life normally, then if someone comes along, sure. But I'm not looking for someone.

Are you afraid to be in a relationship? Or do you think someone just hasn't come along?

I feel like it's a little bit of both.

How so?

I guess, just because every time someone comes along, I think they're going to be good for me. Then it just ends up being the complete opposite of what I thought it was. You get excited to a point where you're like 'alright, I'm going to do this,' and then it goes south. Then it's like, damn, why do these things keep happening? Is this what's going to happen every time I go out there? So, I definitely stay away from this stuff.

Tell me about your greatest love.

My greatest love ... that could be between two people, that's why I'm like 'hmm, which one was the greatest?'. So, I'm going to ask you a weird question: What do you define as the greatest? There are so many different things that could be great but that doesn't necessarily make them good for you.

I'll counter question in order to help you answer that. How do you define love?

100 Days of Dating

Love is like a fire. To me, it's this crazy stupid fire that you're in where you aren't thinking rationally. All you can think about is the blood flow of this warm, lustful, heated sensation. So, it's angry, it's fiery, it's passionate. It's like, you just get out of character and do weird stuff that you don't normally do. You're under a spell and it's hot.

So, of the two women, who did you feel that for the most?

I was under an intense spell for both of them, but one hurt me a little bit more than the other.

How did she hurt you?

I guess, when it was over it just hurt really badly. More so than anything before. I never want to feel like that again.

What do you look for in a woman?

Somebody that could put me under a spell. If you can't put me under a spell, you're not going to be memorable in the grand scheme of things. Like artistic muses, they will just be something in my memory.

Have you ever cheated before?

Technically, yes.

Technically?

What would you define as cheating?

Stepping out on your girlfriend.

Yes. Then technically, yes.

Why would you cheat on your girlfriend?

She was far away and I was starting to lose interest in the whole thing because of the distance. I was getting to a point where I had to say 'you're just too far away.' But it was the beginning stages ... and you know I just wanted to experience more sex. That was the only person I had sex with at the time and I just wanted more of it. And that's what it was.

Did you regret it?

Not really. Is that a bad thing?

You tell me.

Not really.

Did you love your girlfriend? Did you care about her at all?

I definitely cared. I think at the time it was what I thought was love. So, at that stage of my life it was the epitome of what love could be.

Did she ever find out?

Nope.

And to this day you feel nothing about it?

Nah. Sometimes when there are girls that I'm messing with and they ask, "Have you cheated?" I'd say 'I didn't cheat because you're not my girlfriend.' If I had a real girlfriend I would never cheat on her.

Do you see yourself getting married?

Yeah, you know what's funny? One of my brothers just told me he thinks I would have three divorces. I'm like, "What the fuck? Why would you say that?" Then I started thinking to myself, "I don't even think I would get married." If I make it big, I wouldn't get married. Because that's somebody who could potentially leave me and just take a percentage of my worth, my earnings, and a whole lot of other stuff that I did.

Why do you automatically think the worst? You could also just be happily married and live forever with someone. Do you not believe in marriage?

I do, but people change, people grow apart. Some people are able to stay in sync forever. That's amazing. Sometimes people get out of sync for a little while to the point where they get completely out of sync, but then they can come back. Sometimes people get out of sync permanently. But it's the thought that makes it so much better. The thought that you would be in sync all the time.

So, you don't think you ever will, right?

Honestly, you never know what's going to happen. Right now, I feel like I can't find the confidence to love anybody that much. That's the thing that I'm saying, loving someone is doing the most dangerous trick in hopes of not losing your life. That's the exhilarating feeling of doing something so dangerous. But I don't think you're to keep it forever. That's why we celebrate love so much, because it's damn near impossible these days. That's what it would be like in marriage.

Kiana St Louis

DAY THREE: SELF - LOVE

VULNERABILITY.

There is such beauty in pain. Whether we choose to recognize it or not, most of the things that make us sad are aligned with the same things that make us happy. Yet, when faced with certain obstacles, especially those of the heart, we tend to fixate on that pain and the reasons for it so much that we become jaded. We tell ourselves that because this pain was "too much to bare", we will never do that thing that hurt us again, or let that person in again, or go to that place ever again. But what about the times those very things, people, and places made your heart smile?

I think some of us have such a hard time being truly happy because a lot of our happiness is dependent on the actions of others. We demand a list of requirements for the position of our lover. And in exchange for those requirements we give ourselves emotionally and physically. I fear we give and expect so much, that we forget what it's like to give and receive to ourselves.

Ebony Lewis, 23, has been a victim of this very exchange. She's also been her own savior. The series of events that has led her to become the Zen, free-spirit she is today, were by no mistake, but instead to teach her the lesson of being open to understanding how and what SHE feels FIRST. To be vulnerable doesn't always have to mean being susceptible to attack or harm. Throughout this interview, she's taught me vulnerability has a dual meaning of being a risk taker with yourself first and then with love. Last night, her words ignited a tingly sensation I haven't felt in a long time - hope. This is her story.

Tell me about your love life. Are you single? Are you married? Are you in a relationship? It's complicated?

I don't fit any of those categories. I feel like I'm a bit of an explorer, because I definitely just got out of a relationship, but I wouldn't say I am dating. When I think of dating, I think of people who are actively trying to find a partner. I'm not in that space. I'm focusing on myself.

100 Days of Dating

Since you're not actually *looking* for someone, in terms of your explorations, have you happened to find anything worth digging into?

Yeah. I think so. It's weird. About three days after my previous relationship ended, which was very recent, I think it's been a month now officially, I ended up hanging out with someone I used to have an old flame with, and it was nice. Since then, I see a difference in the interactions when we hang out. I also feel like I understand him better, especially after dealing with my partner from my previous relationship. I think it's been really good. It's been refreshing. I feel like we have a trust for each other. I don't know if we needed that distance, but I feel like I recognize the bond this time. That's what I like.

Tell me a little bit about your past relationship. Why did you two break up?

He lacked self-love. That's being cliché, but I don't think any type of romance with an external person can work until your first true love is yourself. It's very apparent, especially now that I think back on it. I feel like everything he does is not for himself. At the time, especially during our breakup when we were going through it, I told him why I felt like everything he was doing was an attempt to keep me with him, he'd say things like, "Hey, look. Just stay with me. I'm going to get better," but that wasn't the reality. If I'm your only motivation, once you get me, you don't have it anymore. So, nothing can work and we can't be truly happy and appreciate each other if number one, he's not his best self and I'm also not my best self.

As I mentioned, I'm at a point in my life where I'm focusing on me. I can't save anyone. Yeah, I can encourage you, I can congratulate you, I can support you, but I feel like he was looking for more of a savior. I'm still a little confused. I don't know if he knows he has his problems and he chooses to ignore them, but it's not okay. It was quickly turning into a toxic situation.

We are all selective with who we allow in our lives, and even with being so selective and being careful, toxic people find a way to slip themselves in. It's really scary, because if I wasn't who I am or strong enough or maybe just wasn't as alert, maybe if I was too consumed with some other area of my life, I would have missed it. We would have been six months in, or we would have been living together and then I would have been like, "Oh my god. What am I in?" I think we didn't work because of how he chooses to deal with his life problems. They were very negative and they're more self-destructive than they are positive.

Could you share what some of that toxic behavior was? At what point did you realize that you had to get out?

His main problem was his choice to overly indulge in alcohol. I don't necessarily think he's an alcoholic. In my world, my definition of an alcoholic is someone who depends on it or needs it. I don't think that's something he needed to do, but I do believe it's something once he indulged in, he couldn't control himself, which is very alarming. It was almost like when he would drink he would become a different person, which was also scary to me.

I just feel like people should be consistent. I value consistency. I feel like no matter what I do, I have my habits, I have my vices, and when I choose to indulge in them, I'm pretty much still the same. I might be a little bit sillier, I might laugh a little more, but I'm still Eb and I'm not taking my frustrations out on my friends. I'm not leaving them confused. They all just know I'm good and they know when they hang around me, it's something positive.

I don't know why he'd get drunk and create problems, but he created problems, even with those he cares about. His past housemate situations haven't worked out. Clearly, our relationship hasn't worked out. It was starting to expand into his career life. He ended up losing a laptop and he couldn't even afford to pay for it. He had to rely on someone else, and after the seventh or eighth time he hit the last strike for me.

There was a point where I thought maybe I might have been in love with him. I remember we were at work one day and he was so dedicated to helping me set up someone's computer, he walked to where I worked and he was with me for a while. We were really trying to figure it out and I'm like, "Wow. This guy. He's always ready to be supportive. He always has my back." When I had to apply to jobs, he knew how terrible of a boss I worked for and how much of a negative place I worked in, he was very supportive.

100 Days of Dating

I might have loved this guy, but then he just pulled it too many times. How many times are you going to be rude to me? How many times are you going to disrespect me?

I realized I had to get out when I wasn't even into him emotionally. I wasn't interested in spending all my time with him. A lot of times he would call my phone and I wouldn't want to answer. I found that when we would hang out on weekends, I was kind of watching the clock, when typically, when you're with someone, whether it be a friend, boyfriend, partner, whatever, you don't watch the clock because you don't care, you're not rushing to go anywhere. I didn't even want him to touch me romantically or sexually. As my boyfriend, that's a problem.

You bring up a great point. How important do you think sex is to a relationship?

I think in our day and age, we're all a little bit more liberated, especially women, so we get to have fun, dabble, and experiment. But sex is also a way to be intimate, to bond, and to become closer to your partner, another way of putting trust in your partner. I feel like if there's a lack of an intimate connection there, it can definitely be a bit of a problem. So, I do feel like it's a bit important.

You mentioned earlier that you're liking the rekindled bond of someone who was in your life before. What are your thoughts on bringing light to an old flame?

That's the thing. I don't feel like anyone should bring light to it because it's so weird. Life has so many grey areas. I don't think anything's ever black and white. I also believe in timing. Timing plays a very key role in everything. Sometimes it does take more time to know someone. Sometimes you might think a year is enough, but you need two or three or however many. We also have to remember that people only show us what they want us to see.

I feel if it happens by chance that you reconnect with someone and it goes well, you should think about it. Think about how your body feels, how you feel as a person internally. How does your soul feel? How do they make you feel on the inside when you spend time with them? I think that's what I really realized this time around. There was so much that I just found attractive and that I just genuinely liked.

I can't help but notice your change in mannerisms at the mention of this old/new guy in your life. Do you see something happening with you two that might be permanent?

I don't really know. I like to not expect anything or look for an outcome. I'm trying to, for lack of a better phrase, go with the flow. But I also feel like that can turn into dangerous territory because sometimes guys feel like if you're not expecting them to do certain these things, they won't be serious. Because it's still new and I think it's only been a month since I broke up with the other guy everything is still fresh. When things are fresh and new, it feels fun, it's exciting, but what's going to happen when we hit the summer time? When we got all these pretty girls out, legs out, buns out, everything's out. What's happens then?

I'm just trying to take it slow, but I definitely think so and I don't think I'm misreading. Like I said, I think we're definitely more open with each other now. I think there's a good chance of something really good. I also want to challenge myself because I'm not very good at expressing myself emotionally. But I feel like this time around, I'm not going to look for the perfect opportunity to bring up how I feel, which is what I was looking for before. I wanted it to "make sense," but feelings don't make sense anyway.

What do you want?

I'm all over the place. I don't want to be single. I *definitely* don't want to have a friend-with-benefits, but I'm not placing emphasis or a priority on being in a relationship. I just want someone I can put my trust into, someone that supports me, respects me, and maybe even admires me. I want someone to view me and also treat me like art, which I definitely think he's capable of, but I also just want *consistency*.

I want to know that when I want to talk to you, I can talk to you. When I want to hang out with you, I can hang out with you. When I want to do whatever with you, if I tell you to come over just to chill, just hang out, not have sex, I can do that. If I call you and I want to have sex, I want to be able to do that. I don't want to worry about some other girl hitting my line while I'm away because I shouldn't have to worry. I want to know that when I'm with you, I'm with you and that I don't have to worry about sharing you. I don't want to share. I just want consistency. I don't really care about a title, because at the end of the day, actions always outweigh words. I want to know that when I want you, when I need you, you're there. That's it. Mine only.

Why do you think it's so hard for men to understand that logic? Do you think that it's something that we, as women, can do a better job of communicating?

No, because we are very straightforward. At least I know I am. Maybe I can't speak for every woman out there, but I can say that I'm very straightforward in general.

How are you straightforward but also unable to communicate emotionally?

I just don't like feeling vulnerable, so that's why. If I feel like I'm going to be putting myself out there, communication stops.

How can you request so much from somebody if you're refusing to be vulnerable with them?

That's true.

Why don't you like to feel vulnerable?

It's an uncomfortable feeling. For example, I feel like when you're vulnerable it's because you're raw. You're not filtering anything. You're being straight forward. You're expressing yourself exactly how you feel. What sucks, is when you express yourself and somebody makes it seem like they're genuine and they're not. It's very disappointing and it's very hurtful. Yeah it can make you angry, but I feel like more than anything it's a letdown. It's sad that you could be 100% and honest with someone and they can look you in the eye, or not even look you in the eye, and can still interact with you, mislead you, and not care for anything but their own benefit.

Kiana St Louis

I feel as if that happens with or without vulnerability. People lie to you at work for no reason. Clients lie. Strangers lie.

And I'd still be mad. People can try to say all they want: "I didn't intentionally hurt you. I've never intentionally hurt you." But you have to know that there are consequences to your actions. We all know the possible outcomes. So, if you still choose to go with that decision, you did intentionally hurt me, so that's what makes it hurt. Yeah, it is everywhere and people shouldn't be like that. People need to start living a more compassionate life. It's like, people just think about themselves and instant gratification, so they don't care if they're lying to a co-worker, their friend, or their girlfriend or boyfriend, or wife or husband. They don't think about that - and that's *really* shitty.

Love comes with vulnerability.

Yup.

Have you ever been in love before?

I think so. I read this article where they talked about the three loves in your life. I feel like one they mentioned was your first love or when you're younger. There was this guy in high school named Gerald. Even to this day I feel like we have an undertone of love and respect for each other. He was definitely something like my first love. He was really nice, really cool, and I guess it was puppy love. I feel like in high school, especially your first three years of high school, is it really love or is it puppy love? I feel like its puppy love, but regardless, he's still the first person of the opposite sex that I ever felt that way about.

Did you feel as if you were vulnerable with him?

No. It felt easy, but then when you're younger you don't really worry about those feelings.

What does love mean to you now?

I don't think I ever thought about it. I don't know. I definitely do believe in love. I think there's someone out there for everyone. I think it's a risk. I know that now, which is why I'm more comfortable with taking a risk. I'm more comfortable with going with the flow and just seeing how things go. I'm now in a place where I'm okay if a situation doesn't work out with someone even if I thought it would. First of all, I know who I am. Like I said, that first love, your true first love is yourself. I love myself, so clearly if something's not working out, it's not for me.

If it's not for me I don't need to waste time hoping that it was or trying to make it something. I feel like that's also where we mess up. Potential. I don't have time for potential. Just because someone has potential doesn't mean they'll get there. You've got to find someone that sees something in you. Someone you actually can be your complete and whole self with. I don't think that happens in a year. I don't think that happens in two years. I don't think that happens in three years. I don't ever honestly feel like you do know someone completely. I just don't think it happens, but you can know a good amount of that person and I feel like that's the beauty in it.

I want to be able to explore when I'm in love. What can I explore with you? What can we do together? Can I help you grow? Can you help me grow? Can you accept me no matter what? My flaws, stupid decisions. If I hurt you, are you willing to work it out because you see that much in me? The same for me. If you hurt me, am I willing to give it another shot? Are you serious enough to change? I think that's what love is. Love is patience, dedication, hard work, exploring, and just taking a risk. You just have to hope that the person you're with is who they say they are. Like I said before, people only show you what they want you to see and what they want you to know. You just have to hope that they're being genuine.

Kiana St Louis

DAY FOUR: BROKEN BOND

MARRIAGE.

As little girls, we're trained to believe that marriage is the ultimate goal. Often times, we're taught the importance of having a man in our lives before we're taught our own self-worth, let alone the importance of a career. I don't think our parents mean to jade us in this way purposely, but I'm afraid the pressures of definitive happiness *with* someone makes it seemingly impossible to be happy alone. And if you are alone, you've somehow failed. There comes a point, in order to combat those feelings of failure, people race with time. Some feel that marriage has to come by or before a certain age, so it's not a care of *who* they marry, rather *when*.

But then, there are real life fairy tales. There are true loves and eternal bonds. There are marriages worth having.

And then there are facades. With those facades, I'm reminded again how we can think we know a person all of our lives yet somehow not know them at all.

Patrice Owens, 33, knows this reality far too well. She knows what it feels like to be catered to, loved, held on a pedestal, and admired for not what she does but for whom she is; she knows the joys of a fairy tale marriage. But she also knows the agony of deceit, lies, and fraud. Last night, we reminisced. Patrice provided me access to a space that only her deepest thoughts occupy, and together we found peace. This is her story.

Tell me about your love life. Are you single, dating, in a relationship, married, it's complicated?

I'm in a relationship. It's not complicated on my end, but it's complicated on my ex's end.

How so?

I feel like he purposely forced me to keep a place in my mind for him. I won't say my heart because I believe that that was gone a long time ago. But I do feel he forced me to keep a part of my mind reserved for him until HE was ready to move on.

Do you think that you've fully moved on from your ex?

After today, yes.

What happened today?

Today, I was at work, and we don't really communicate like that. Not even on a close friend level, not unless it has something to do with the kids. Usually, we'll meet up and I'll get Lily, or he'll get Lily, but today was exchange child day. I contacted him this morning about what we were going to do, what time we're going to meet up, if we're going to meet up today, etc. It wasn't a long conversation. It was probably maybe two minutes. At work, I get a text message that says, "They should be there soon. Put a shirt on. That's not for you. My fault."

When I first read that message, my initial reaction was confusion. I was confused because the whole time we've been apart, every time I mention him being with another female, or dating another female, his response is, "No, no, no, I don't want no females around my kids." But when I got that message today, I thought, *Okay, so, you finally let somebody around the kids.* But, then again, I'm thinking he's very childish, because he wanted me to know. It wasn't by accident he texted me that.

I tried to find all sorts of ways to justify it, but that was done purposely. He'd never text me and say, "Oh it wasn't for you, my bad, sorry," in all the years I've known him.

How long have you known him?

It's been now, maybe 14 years.

How did you feel the moment you realized this was something that you no longer could do?

I felt bad. I suppose that's because I knew that the kids were involved. If I were by myself I think it would be a different story. But because I have my kids, I knew that they had no clue about what was going to happen. That part made me feel bad. But after a while, I felt like I had to do it, not for everybody else, but for me.

Doing "it" meaning staying in the relationship?

Right. I could not keep forcing it to work.

So, how did you feel learning he's bringing another woman around the kids?

I was mad! First of all, he was not in the house. Second of all, the kids never met this person before. So how could you let her meet them like this? Just walk into the house and someone is there? That's crazy. You don't do stuff like that. It took me years before my kids met the person I'm in a relationship with. *Years.* And he was telling me all these times the boys never met her. And they come home to her from school. That was scary for me, I don't trust people.

Why don't you trust people?

I don't know, I feel like most of my emotional scars came from people that I trusted the most. So, for me right now, trust is a huge issue.

How does that work in your current relationship?

Oh boy. I think I ignore a lot of things when I know that I'm being driven by a trust issue.

So if your current person says or does something questionable, you won't acknowledge it?

It's not that I won't acknowledge it, I choose what to acknowledge. So, it could be something like ... he works at night, so during the day when I'm at work, he's at home most of the time and he's asleep. For example, if I call him and he doesn't answer his phone, it's easy for me to say, "Oh my God he's cheating on me." And the fact of the matter may be that he's sleeping because he works at night. And in my last relationship, when the shit hit the fan, the phone was a very big issue for me. It was always: "Why aren't you answering your phone?" Are you with that person? And nine times out of ten I was right.

So, that's why I choose what to pay attention to and what not to when it comes to trust. I know that I can easily ruin every other relationship I have because I feel like I've been through every trust issue that you could possibly go through.

With the ex?

Right.

Was it easy for you to let all those years go?

No, absolutely not. Because unlike the average relationship that involves infidelity, my ex never changed the way that he treated me. He never changed anything that he did. It was just that eleventh finger that was hanging around. But nothing else changed. So, yes it was very hard for me because, emotionally, I don't think that anybody else could ever fill the void he did. I'm telling myself, you'll never get 100% of that again, so from this point on, you have to settle for 98. That 2% that's missing, is a lot. So it's very hard. Well it was hard but I'm okay now. I'm good.

Are you good or have you settled?

I think it's a bit of both. I think I'm good because I decided to settle. Does that make sense?

Yeah. It does make sense. Do you feel as if you love the person that you're with now?

I do. And that's crazy because I feel like if I didn't I would probably go back with my ex.

You would still go back? Knowing everything that you do?

Yes. The reason why I would is because that 2% is missing, emotional happiness for me is this big deal. And emotionally, I feel like even though I was already a confident female, he's helped me to get to the level where I've felt untouchable.

I get that. After everything, what were some of the steps you took to heal?

There were so many and I catch myself still taking steps, because I have this question of: *Am I really healed?* Or, am I telling myself I'm healed? So one of the steps I took, was praying like crazy. I became so close to God that I feel like I could just turn to him and he was right there. I fasted a lot. And after my fast, that's when I started to get a lot of answers. So, those are just the first and most important steps I took. The next step that I took was trying to figure out in my mind: *Can I be without this person?* I actually forced myself to hold back a lot because I didn't want to give everything after finding out that you could give everything and still get hurt like that.

So I just wanted to check myself, like what I was doing, what I was saying, how I was feeling, how I was making him feel. There's so many things I did. I cut a lot of people off, because I felt like I was in a space where nobody understood me. Even though they say they did, nobody had ever been through this. Who the hell has been with a person that cheated on them and the person never changed what they did for you? You hear about people getting cheated on but then the guy is not coming home, or changed his number, he's not doing this anymore, and he's not doing that anymore.

This person still did every single thing that got me to be with him in the first place, while cheating on me. How do you do that?

To this day it blows my mind. He never missed a night out, he never missed a holiday. He never missed a birthday. He didn't even come home late. So how did he manage to do all of that and still maintain this so called respect or pedestal that he had me on. That's crazy.

Have you ever asked him?

No, I never asked him that question. And that's something we never talked about. We talked about a lot of things, but I've never asked him that.

Do you really want to know how?

Yeah I feel I do. I do want to know how. Because I feel like if I didn't want to know, it wouldn't be a question that's always in the front of my mind.

So why haven't you asked?

I don't know... I think because I always take it as a thought, it never comes out as a question.

In the conversations you've had before with him, has he been open about the infidelity?

Very. Extremely. Luckily I've had that kind of open communication with everybody I've been with. We have that type of communication in my current relationship. I feel like we tell each other everything, even when it hurts.

Have you told him you feel as if you're settling?

In my current relationship? Yes, I did absolutely.

How did he feel?

He wasn't happy about it, but at the same time he understood because he's very honest about himself and his actions. From us just talking he knows what kind of relationship I've been in, he knows what I'm used to, knows what I like. He knows everything; and he also knows that he doesn't do 100% of those things. So, when I tell him I'm settling he fully understands what I mean. But he feels like he needs time to get there. So, he's not upset about it, but it's kind of offensive to tell somebody that.

He loves me so much that I feel like he respects the fact that I told him at all. He wouldn't have known any other way, I could have just left him there and said nothing. I think he respects the fact that I addressed it instead of just acting on it, even though it's offensive. When I actually told him he was like, "Well damn." His reaction to it was positive, it wasn't negative. He just felt like he needed time.

They say in order for a woman to get over a guy she needs to get under a new one. Was he your rebound?

I don't believe that at all. I feel like that's where a lot of people make big mistakes. When they act on their last relationship like that, but no, I don't think he was a rebound. When I started talking to him, I never thought that we would be where we are today. We were really just friends. I wasn't looking for a relationship.

Are you happier without your ex?

Happier? I wouldn't say happier because my kids are attached to it.

How has it been for them?

I thank God that they're mentally stable. They're okay, they fully understand what's going on. I feel like at one point, they started to be upset with me. My oldest, he didn't understand why I wasn't there. I think he thought that I left them, or that I didn't want to be in their family anymore. It was important for me to go into everything with them from scratch. After I did that, I was like ... they're okay, my kids are okay now. I'm still happy about that. I'm just sad about the fact that we cannot see each other every day.

But they're doing well in school. Their life with their friends is really good. They're well rounded, they're very intelligent. So, as of now I wouldn't say they're being affected a lot, but you never really know. You never know what they're thinking.

So, you've made the necessary steps to move forward with this new person in your life. Whether it be this person that you're with right now, or maybe in the future, what are the three qualities that you feel like they need to have in order for you to be happy and for the relationship to work?

Communication. I am a talker - I will talk from sun up to sun down. I will explore a situation a thousand times before leaving it alone. So, communication is a big deal for me. The second one, I would say, is faith. I don't know why I didn't pick that as my first one. Can faith and optimism go together?

It's your list, whatever you feel works for you.

The reason I want faith and optimism to go together is because a lot of things that I've accomplished in life came through faith. I believe I put in the effort and I let God do the rest. And I feel like if I'm with somebody that's a pessimist, that's going to bring me down, that's going to drown me. So, faith and optimism go hand in hand as a quality that I need.

The third one will have to be honesty. But at 33 years of life I feel like that's unattainable. Because who knows who's really being honest?

Isn't that a shame?

Right. It is and that's why I put my age on it because when I was 20 years-old, I would've definitely said honesty.

But that's a problem. You're automatically compromising something that should come gradually with a relationship. It's hard to be with somebody if at any point you feel as if they're dishonest with you. So how can that not be a qualifier?

Right, you're absolutely right. But, 14 years of damage, of brain damage will make you eliminate a lot of things. It's almost like I was living in a real-life dream-world, does that make sense?

What do you mean?

Ten years ago, my life was freaking perfect. Anything would go, and I got anything I wanted. Anything you could think of. Having a family, honesty, all those things were real. But here we are, ten years later and they're not real to me anymore. So, were they ever really real? Was my life that way, or was it just a façade for what was about to take place? I don't regret anything that ever happened because I had so many great stories, so many wonderful memories, but was it real? Is that still attainable? Are there people out there like that? Are there relationships like that?

I feel it is attainable, look at where you are now. You are in something that you feel is dream-like, no?

Yes, and I get goose bumps when I talk about my relationship now. People are like 'what are you doing?' But I've been so happy inside that I'm like, 'what the fuck do you mean what am I doing? I'm good.' This relationship is kind of interesting because he works so hard to be the perfect guy for me and he's closer now than ever before, which keeps me interested. I'm waiting to see what he's going to do next. Instead of everything just being in front of my face, it's nice to see there's a hidden mystery there.

I've heard before that as women sometimes we have to teach men how to love us.

Absolutely.

Do you feel as if you're teaching him now?

Yes, and I feel like he's learned a lot since we've been together. There are different women in the world, in life, and different women do love differently. Different women want different things when they do find love, and for me, the way I want to be loved is very unique. I don't think I ask for much because I've had it already, materialistically and emotionally. Attention, yes I want all of it. But I know it's not going to happen, but as much of your attention as I can have, I want it because I feel like that's what I do for you. In other words, he loves me and is still learning how to love me. In the end, I need him to love me the way I love him and vice versa. Everything else will fall into place.

DAY FIVE: TRUST THE PROCESS

PATIENCE.

We say this often: Just be patient. But how many of us are truly patient with ourselves, our feelings, or with the things we cannot control? Being in a relationship requires patience. Being single requires patience. Love requires patience.

But acquiring the capacity to accept or tolerate delay, trouble, or suffering without getting angry or upset is no easy task. Creating this space where you free yourself from anxiety, worry, and doubt concerning anything or anyone is both mental and emotional. Something I too struggle with. I've been at this battlefield before, where I want something to be over, to forget someone, or to hear back from some place so badly that I've erased the idea of patience. I just want what I want right now. I've been so overwhelmed with my exhaustion for hurting and for waiting, that someone telling me to be "patient with myself" is more of an insult than it is comforting.

Do you know what that feels like?

Mike King, 25, reminded me of the beauty of the process. He brought to mind how important patience is to any process, whatever your process may be. At some point in your life, you must strive for a different level of comfort ability within yourself. A different level of confidence even in your flaws. At some point, we have to realize that everything and everyone may not be for us, but that does not mean that we are inadequate. I'm not sure if it was the placidity of his words or the casualness of our interview, but Mike awakened a sense of peace in me. Life has had its way with him, yet he still remains not just hopeful but he inhabits patience, especially with love. This is his story.

Tell me about your love life. Are you single? Dating? In a relationship? Married? It's complicated?

Right now, I'm single. There are a few people whose company I enjoy, but I'm super single.

Is it the same people in rotation?

Yeah, it's the same people in rotation. But I've been having a lot of women hit me up more often since I posted a couple pictures.

How is that for you? Do you like being approached by women first?

Honestly? I don't really like it. But it is different just because 90% of the time, guys are the ones running down on girls. But me, I don't want to say I'm stuck up, but I'm a little more monotone with my behavior. I really just be chillin' most of the time.

How do you feel when you're about to talk to a woman? Do you have words that you say to yourself to boost your confidence before you talk to them?

No, it's not really words. Me being the type of person I am, I'm super confident. I feel like everybody wants me all the time. So, most of the time, it's just thinking how am I going to start it up? Or, what am I going to say to spark the conversation? I usually just crack a joke or something. It's really not that hard.

Of the women in rotation, is there one that you like the most?

I wouldn't say I really like ONE the most because I like different things about different types of women. But there is one, she makes me laugh the most, absolutely. Most of our conversations are just chill. They're real genuine. And then, usually when they get deep, I find it kind of dope because in those moments, you feel like somebody's actually opening up to you and trusting you with that type of information.

Have you ever been in love before?

Yes, twice.

Tell me about them.

100 Days of Dating

During the first one, I was a young buck in the game. You could call it puppy love or whatever the case may be. But the second time, she was just dope, and it was awesome. I went to New Orleans for a project called "NY2NO," and it was right after Katrina. We both went down there to help rebuild. But I don't know, we just clicked.

What is "clicking" for you? How do you know when you're really feeling someone?

It's hard to explain and put into words, but it's usually just genuine. It's when I truly enjoy somebody's company, that's a win.

Are you single by choice? Are you not trying to meet anybody new?

I wouldn't even call it single by choice. I'm not in a rush to be a in a relationship simply because they usually just find you. When you're being your happiest self, that's when people come into your life. It's that energy, regardless of whether or not I say that I'm single. When you're just living happily and freely, people want that feeling, so they usually just gravitate towards you.

For me, personally, because of the places I've been and the jobs that I've had, I see the greater value to life. I can't really stress the small stuff because I know there's people out there who are really, going through some stuff. My life is low key.

Love is timeless. It can't be destroyed or deleted, it's like that same energy is just transferred or put into something else. So, say you're dealing with a girl, and she cheats. Love for the guy, might be different from love from that girl after that experience. But it's still defined as love. He might be on some, "Yo, I'm hurt." His love might be bitter while she could've found somebody new and somebody better, so her love might be better than his love at that point.

Has that happen to you? Have you ever been cheated on before?

No, I've never been cheated on. Well, not to my knowledge. That's not even something I would put into the atmosphere simply because it's never happened to me, but I feel like it would be a lot to deal with. I imagine if that happened, you'd have to feel really low. You'd feel really insecure, really vulnerable after somebody told you they were cheating on you or after you found out somebody cheated on you.

Have you ever cheated before?

Nah, I've never cheated. What's the point? If I don't want to be with you, I'd just tell you.

I feel like friendships and the people you're around impact a lot of the thinking behind cheating. How much do you talk to your friends about your relationships?

I want to say more than I should. Simply because, most of my friends are women. Outside of my two best friends, who are males, 90% of my friends are women. So, when I'm confused about what's actually going through a woman's head, these are the people I lean on. Mainly because they have a worldly view or because I'm seeing a situation as black because I'm a male, and they see it white because they're a woman. So, I'd rather get the white perception of what's going on instead of only having the black perception.

Tell me about your greatest heartbreak.

There were a couple just because you never really see it coming. I feel like sometimes, you're just so happy that you don't realize that things are falling apart behind the scenes.

Has anyone hurt you behind the scenes?

I mean, yeah, of course. I had somebody that made me sad. I was sad for a while, but then I realized you can't really force somebody to want to be with you. You really just have to accept the terms of it. And me personally, I'm a psycho. I do weird things to cope with being sad, so even if I knew it was coming, meaning I can see us about to break up, I wouldn't do it simply for the fact that I wouldn't want to break up. I'd question whether or not I made the right decision for the rest of my life. But if she did it, it would've been like, all right, she did it, she was unhappy, and you just have to accept it. At that point, it was supposed to happen because she was unhappy, but me, I couldn't do it because I'd be switching back and forth like, did I really make the right decision? What was going through her mind? That's how it's been for me.

What do you look for in a woman?

That's a tricky question. I like people with pure souls. People who are looking to try and make you better. People who can make me laugh. People who like to have fun.

What are three qualities your woman would have to possess?

Loving. Funny. I guess I would say reliable and trustworthy. We'll just lump those together.

How long ago was your last relationship?

About a year and three months ago. Give or take.

Was it one of those special relationships?

Well, that's the weird part about it. I've only dated three women in my life. I've had countless encounters with women, but I've only dated three women. One of which met my mom. My mom's like a keep safe, so it takes a lot to meet her.

After the break up, were you able to still be friends?

I wouldn't know. I feel like I'm super cordial, but I can't really place a finger on what's going through a woman's head. But I'm always genuine. I'm nice. I can honestly say out of all the women I've ever messed with, I don't have beef with any of them. I've never ended a relationship on a bad term because I'm really selfless in the way that even if we break up or we don't talk to each other, I truly want the best for you. People might say that, but then they'll shade you, like, "oh, she's sleeping with this one guy," or "she's doing this, she's doing that." I don't do that simply because that's just not in me. I can't.

My mom once told me, especially on the bad days where I just wasn't feeling myself, she was like, "Listen, if you can't touch yesterday, why are you letting yesterday touch you?" And it was like, "Damn." You really can't, you can't really fret the past because there's so much more in the future. If you're just stuck in the past, you're never going to be able to grow. You're just going to become stagnant.

Of that relationship, what were the greatest lessons you've learned?

One, you can't force the issue. Things really have to happen naturally in order for you to grow, and for someone to open up to you.

Then, communication is key. I feel like everything was rushed. We didn't really get to enjoy. You know how people will be like, "Oh, we were such great friends beforehand," we didn't really get to enjoy that part of it because it just happened so fast. If we had went slower and got to know each other on a friend basis, it would've been different. But you can't, I can't really have regrets, that's not me.

How would you describe being happy in a relationship?

I would say laughter. Laughing a lot. An open line of communication. It's freeing to just be able to be yourself around somebody without judgment. You should truly be happy to go through experiences and to be able to grow from them. I'm in such a space where everything I've been through doesn't really mean much because I've elevated from the past.

Do you try not to hold on to grudges and just let everything go?

There's not one person I have a grudge towards. You can ask anybody that I've ever messed with or anybody that I've ever dealt with. I can't be a hateful person because people leave for their own reasons. Yeah, you might be sad at the moment, but you can't knock somebody for leaving for their reasoning. If I wanted to leave for whatever reason I wanted to leave, that's MY personal reason. I might have been going through something and I just wanted to deal with it a different way. You can't really be mad, resentful, or hold a grudge with anybody because everybody goes through things differently. The ways you react are just going to be different.

I feel like most times, it's really hard for men to be as open as you are here today. It's hard for them to streamline their emotions. I don't mean to generalize, but I speak only from my experiences. Why do you think it's hard for men to express themselves like this?

For me, especially growing up around my pops and my brothers, there's this fear of being vulnerable. You don't want to be too vulnerable because then you're going to look soft. Then when you're in a relationship, you're supposed to be soft. You're supposed to vulnerable. You're supposed to be open. That's how you let people in. That's to trust women. That's how you feel. It's really hard to reach that point where you're just allowing yourself to be vulnerable because you know what comes with that.

When you're vulnerable, there's the chance that you could get hurt or there's the chance that this might be the best experience of your life. There might be a fine line between getting fucked-over, or finding that true love that you really desire. I feel like for most guys, they think, *Nah, you not going to get me to that point. You tripping. You crazy, thinking that I'm going to be out here only chasing you?*

If I get to that point, God is telling me this is how it's supposed to go. She was supposed to get you to this point of this vulnerability, so just allow yourself. I'm the type of person that's super guarded, so it takes a while to get there anyway. But once you're there, you really have to open up, be free, and just roll with it. Otherwise, you're not going to really be happy because you're always going to be stand-offish. Like, "Should I have opened up to you? Should I have trusted her more?" Once you get to that point of being super vulnerable, you just have to roll with it and then whatever happens, happens.

Have you ever been at that point?

A point where I was vulnerable? Of course. I'm 25. I've been at that point at least twice.

Kiana St Louis

I wish more people opened themselves up to vulnerability. Females are always putting themselves in that space.

Not to sound sexist, but females are natural lovers. They naturally show emotions, it's in their nature. As males, we grow up in environments where if you show too much emotion, they're going to get you. People are going to clown you. People are going to try you just because you're showing so much emotion.

We have to put up this mask and once that mask is up, it's really hard to come down. It takes a really dope person to let you drop that mask. You don't find dope people every day. You don't find people you click with every day. So, 90% of the time that mask is up and you're just guarded. Personally, I feel like men of today's age swing from girl to girl because we think if we're guarded, it's not going to do anything for us. We can get with a girl and leave a girl because we're not really emotionally invested into it. But when you find somebody dope, it's different. It's hard to let go.

100 Days of Dating

DAY SIX: SELF – SABOTAGE

FORGIVENESS.

Forgiving others is always a chore for us, yet it is something we eventually do. Forgiving ourselves on the other hand, sometimes feels seemingly impossible. I imagine this is because we hold ourselves to extremely high standards. We're our own harshest critics. It's easy to get hurt and be mad at someone for hurting us. But when the tables are turned and we're the ones faulted, our inner thoughts can beat our pride to a pulp.

But, why? Why can't we be as gracious to ourselves as we are to others who have hurt us?

Mika V, 32, has found herself at a common battlefield - the struggle between sense and sensibility, head vs. heart, logic vs. love. At this crossroads she is burdened with the feelings of guilt, shame, and regret as she bears the journey of forgiving herself for past mistakes. I believe a lot of these emotions stem too from fear. Fear that she's hurt someone so bad that they'll never forgive her, fear that she's missed her chance, fear of the unknown.

But there has to be a confidence in love and a confidence in self that can trump fear and allow forgiveness. For how can we ever love another if we don't whole-heartedly love ourselves? We may not always have the answers, but I believe the effort must count for something. Mika, your effort counts. This is your story.

Tell me a little bit about your love life. Are you single? Dating? In a relationship? Married? It's complicated?

At the current moment, I'm super single. Emphasis on super. I'm not one of these girls who says I'm single, but has five or six dudes that I'm talking to, deal with, or in between figuring out what I'm doing. I'm actually single.

Have you just got out of a relationship?

Currently no. I've been single for a while.

How long?

It's been years. I don't really count dating here and there, or trying to figure out someone within three to four months to be a relationship.

What do you consider being in a relationship?

Being committed to one person. You're not dating multiple people. You're not figuring things out. You're focused on one thing.

Do you want that?

Yes, definitely.

Do you feel as if you haven't gotten what you wanted because of things that you're doing? Or do you think it's just a lack of finding that with other people?

Last year, I would have said it's because of other people. I'm not connecting with anyone now. I don't know why. Right now in this place I can say that I don't think I was really ready for anything before. Which is why nothing really came my way. I feel like I wasn't in the mental space to be in anything, which is why God probably didn't send me this magnificent person that I imagine to be with. I thought I was ready to be in a relationship but I was actually just enjoying my life. Traveling, dating different people, and experiencing the whole thing of dating. But now I'm actually ready.

What's the difference between then and now? What kind of space were you in then mentally?

The difference between then and now is I don't really think I knew who I was or what I wanted. I had said it, "I want someone to be funny, family oriented, etc." But I was just saying it because I thought that's what I was supposed to do. At that point I felt really pressured to be in something. Because what was always said to me was, "You're single, why? What's wrong with you?" That came from the outside. My internal family would say things like, "you're a beautiful girl, why don't you have someone?" Or, "oh, are you a lesbian? If you are, I love you any way." I wasn't. But I don't think I was really ready to share my space. I thought I was.

I think I was more in a clouded space. Visually, you imagine yourself being with this ideal person. For me, I wasn't willing to give things up.

Do you feel as if you've somehow failed because you're not in a relationship?

I used to. It was bad. I swear, turning 32 has made me feel amazing. Leading up to it, I was scared to get here because there's always the thought of, "Damn, you're old." I felt like I needed to do something. Everyone around me is married. They have kids. So I impulsively bought a car when I was 30, which was my baby. So when 32 came, I was really scared because I knew that I wasn't married, I wasn't pregnant, and I was still by myself.

Once I turned 32, I just realized how grateful I should be and how blessed I am to have amazing people in my life. I should cherish these moments because when I'm sharing my life with somebody, I'm not going to have the free will to pick up and hop on a plane and go to India for a week and a half. Or, jump on a quick trip with a friend to Barbados for a weekend without having to find a baby sitter. I was so fixated on wanting to be in something because I thought that that's what I had to do.

Now in this moment and space, I'm just happy that I was able to experience that. I'm happy knowing that I'm really blessed to be here and I shouldn't be so caught up in society and the perception that I shouldn't be alone or should be with somebody.

I was able to figure *me* out. I'm still figuring myself out. I'm making more space for self-love. Maybe I didn't really love myself enough. Which is why I probably accepted a lot of bullshit and things didn't work out the way I thought they should have.

You mentioned something I feel like we tend to not talk too much about. You said that your family was making you feel like you had to be at a certain place at a certain time. Have you ever expressed to them how what they were saying made you feel?

Yeah, I have. Recently, too. I told them if it doesn't happen it doesn't happen, who cares, accept it. Harsh I know. People were like "No, you're going to get married." But to myself I've thought, *Nah, if it doesn't rock, I'm okay with being by myself.*

I don't really think I'm going to be alone. I'm just accepting that as a possibility I may not find this person, or he might not exist. So, I had to shut it down. I'm okay with me. I'm happy. I think they were more concerned because culturally we're supposed to be, I don't know, *kept*.

The advice I got from my aunts, especially from my uncles, is different to how we live now. A man's supposed to do this. A woman's supposed to do that. Make sure you always clean your house so you can keep your husband. Can't have your room dirty because no one's going to want to be with you. That's the way I was being raised, everything was basically on us. Everything that I was taught or trained to do was for a man.

What were some of the steps that you took to get from where you were two years ago (mentally) to where you are now?

A lot of heartbreak. I felt like I was basically living on autopilot. I was just doing me.

Back then, I wasn't really being who I was, my core self. So when I'm home, by myself, sick, or I need something to be built or whatever, it's only me. I never had anyone that was there. I don't think I really understood what just going with the flow meant or allowing myself to be free. The dating situation did a bit of a number on me. It was chipping away at my self-esteem. I just had to really be real with myself and say no to certain things and people. I had to get it together. You're going to get what you want. Take a shot. Be still. A lot of self-reflecting and reading and self-help books, gave me clear thoughts.

Praying as well. I've been instructed to pray many times and for many reasons. I'm told you'll hear things and I didn't really hear anything but I felt it. I feel if someone is meant to be in my life, they'll be in my life. Anyone I bring into my life must be real and if not then I don't need it.

You mention a part of that self-reflection came from heartbreak. Can you tell me about your greatest heartbreak?

It was in my mid-twenties. And I felt like my heart was at the pit of my stomach. I couldn't breathe. I was literally killing myself by allowing a lot of things that I would never allow to happen. I put myself in awkward situations. Being second best for someone that I thought really loved me. It was a very toxic relationship. We were young. I was really gullible. I think I was probably scared to be alone. So anything he wanted to do to me, I allowed. He was intentionally punishing me for something I had done to him a few years prior. Instead of him being an open, honest person and telling me he didn't want this, or this is not going to work, he just stringed me along and I went along for the ride.

I feel like I had no self-worth. I was so broken and torn that I was just willing to be stepped on and go through whatever to be in this person's presence. You don't even know who you are in your twenties. But I thought that he was it.

It's scary just talking about it now because I would never want to feel that way ever again. I won't ever put myself in a situation like that. I don't feel the way that I felt then for anybody right now. I think that's amazing. That's been a blessing for me.

Even though it wasn't my greatest love, I just took it. I think maybe because I was really broken. There were other relationships that I felt like I failed at. I think that I was literally punishing myself by going through what I was going through with this specific person.

So what was your greatest love like?

I don't know. I had my greatest love when I didn't love it back.

What do you mean?

That's what I'm thinking now. My greatest love was selfless. It was so pure and honest. In my eyes I would say. It was real. I had friend, a lover, and a fucking ride or die partner at the same time. At the time, I don't think I realized what was happening. I think I was just rolling with the punches. "I have a boyfriend. I have a relationship." I was reading about all the glitz and glam of being in a relationship. Going on dates and setting up stuff for my birthday, all the good things about relationships. But at that point in my life, I don't think I was my best self. So, I'd have outbursts at times. I would over extend things. I had this pure bitchy attitude. At this point I'm realizing that. He was amazing. We were young, I but I felt like I connected with somebody.

I really thought that we'd get married and have kids and everything. Honestly, if I didn't run away from that situation, I probably would have had kids and got married. But I wanted to do me. I wanted to be free. I didn't want to settle into being somebody's wife.

So again, I'm going to go back to the culture. Culturally, you're raised a certain way. So, if you date someone also in the same culture, the family is going to see you in that way as well. You cook, you clean, and you do laundry. I always thought that I was a free spirit. I was like, we can just get somebody to take care of this. I'm not going to always be in the house. I can do all that but I never thought that I would want do that for someone. I didn't mind doing that for him, though.

100 Days of Dating

I got in my head and I got scared. I feel like I ruined that relationship. Out of all the guys that I've dated or experienced, he's the only person that I felt really had my heart. I didn't appreciate just having someone to listen to you and care.

Now, it's hard to even have conversations on the phone with people. Everyone's busy and everyone has their life. I have a schedule. You have to compromise and make things work with people. It's not about you. It's so petty, it's so stupid. It's being older. Experiencing that love at such a young age, I appreciate it now. I don't think I could ever tell him that because I'm so embarrassed.

Listening to you now, you sound so filled with pain. Do you regret what happened between you two?

Yeah. I do. I never ever say I regret anything in life because I love life and its experiences. Things happen. You roll with the punches. But this situation, I feel like I do regret. I regret my actions. Because like I said, I wasn't my best self. I didn't even know who I was. I didn't love myself enough. I was so young. I'm older now and I sometimes think: You have a good job and you look good and take care of yourself, what's the problem? Why can't you date? Why can't you find someone nice? What is it? Recently I've been thinking is it because maybe this is the person that you're supposed to be with. You should go find your love. I don't know. I'm crazy. I think things like that. I'm just super emotional talking about this right now.

It happens. It definitely happens. Regardless there was something to have learned. Whether it was to be a learning lesson for him or vice versa.

The crazy thing for me is that I didn't learn until recently. I literally blocked it out. I realize when traumatic situations happen, or things happen in my life that I don't want to deal with, I block it out. I move on, run away, whatever it is. My memories are just crowded. So I have to think hard about a situation.

I found clarity. I've centered myself. And as I think about certain situations and certain people, I'm getting these flashbacks and I've been super emotional lately because of them. I'm like why do I feel this way. I'm literally feeling how I felt in that moment now. I'm reflecting on my past and I think to myself, *you were crazy. You were really crazy. You were just way too impossible.* I feel like now I'm simple, as simple as it gets.

Do you think that you're feeling this way because you have yet to make peace with your past?

Yeah. Someone told me I needed closure. I'm getting closure eight years later. What type of shit is that? Do I need to write a book or do a documentary or something?

Eight years ago. I swear to God I did not think I cared as much. I didn't think about this person. I wasn't stressing over this person. In my mind I told myself I hated this person. And I'm good. Like I don't never need to hurt for nothing.

But we've had our setbacks in the last maybe four years. You know, little hook up situations here and there, but there was never a mental connection. It was like I was physically using my body to do things that I mentally didn't really connect with. And yes I probably had those feelings. We had heart to hearts. I think with two hook ups in the last like five years maybe, there was no connection.

It just was what it was. Now I'm thinking wow why did I do that? I could have gotten my closure then. I could have connected then. What was I thinking? I was a pretty face and a body and that was it. Now, I'm super emotional. I just want to be pure with this person and just give my soul out and say I know what I did was wrong. I'm not asking for anything. I just want to apologize for not being the person that I know you deserved at that time.

100 Days of Dating

DAY SEVEN: FINDING LOVE

PASSION.

I believe passion must be at the core of everything that we do. I couldn't imagine spending money on something I hated or supporting a cause I cared nothing about. I couldn't see myself getting up for work each morning and hating what I do or being friends with someone I didn't care for. As I look at it now, I couldn't imagine being in a relationship someone I didn't have a strong and barely controllable emotion for. Every scenario mentioned requires some capacity of passion.

Yet, we make excuses or ignore when we're *not* feeling passionate about someone: "It's too early in the relationship; we have to give it time; I'm still feeling this out; I'm just seeing where it goes..." Justification. At what point will we realize that passion isn't something that we must hope for when being with someone, but instead something that we must require of ourselves beforehand?

Brandon Max, 22, believes the same. Moving from Michigan to New York City can be somewhat of a culture shock, not just in the way things look around here but in the reality that New Yorkers are no joke. Max has had to maneuver everything in this new space from finding a place to live to finding love. As he gets a handle on what it is that he wants out of his search, he realizes that he is not only motivated by passion but needs that from someone else. Max and I chatted casually over lunch as we fed each other insight on dating that neither of us thought too much about. Even through the laughs, passion found its way into our encounter. This is his story.

Tell me about your love life. Are you single? Are you married? Are you in a relationship? It's complicated?

I'm definitely single. I would say "complicated single" because there's a couple of people here and there that I've been hooking up with but nothing serious.

So what makes it complicated if it's nothing serious?

Just complicated in the sense of trying to not combine these two girls. One's my neighbor and one's her friend. So I try not to mix that up.

Do they know about each other?

One knows about the other, but the other one doesn't. The neighbor knows about the friend. So, that's why I was saying it's complicated.

How is that for you? Do you ever feel bad?

No, I don't feel bad because the neighbor knows about it and she is consenting completely. She's like, "Don't tell Denise." So, there's Clara, who's the neighbor, and then Denise who's her best friend.

Best friend? Woah, that's nuts.

I mean it's her really good friend I guess. I don't know their relationship details too closely, I try to stay out of it. I don't really like hanging out with either of them. So, it's purely hookups. I'll hang out with them when I want to hook up which is terrible. This probably sounds like the worst thing ever, right?

Surprisingly, no. I've heard worse. But why don't you like to hang out with them?

That's a big part of my love life and the reason why I feel like I'm single. I feel like my standards are just too high. My standards are so fucked up. They're both pretty, but it's not even a good-looking thing for me ever. You can't be butt-ass ugly, but you have to bring something else to the table. It can't just be about looks. When we talk or hang out I'm just not interested in what they're saying. Their personalities just don't really click.

What do you look for in a woman? What are your standards?

100 Days of Dating

Not shallow, but good looking enough. Intelligent. They have to have goals of their own. Someone who's passionate, honestly. If someone's passionate about something, I'm a 100% connected to them already. Finding that is so important because I think what I'm lacking is passion. I'm not really passionate about a lot of things, so when I see passion in someone else, I'm thinking, *oh shit. What is this person about?*

So, passion, intelligence, goals, and decent looking. That's what I'd say my qualities are.

Are you looking for a relationship?

Sure, I'm open to the idea. Every relationship I've had has been longer than two years. My last relationship was probably two years ago but it lasted for four years. These two years I've been trying to not be in a relationship, but now I'm trying to figure out if I'm ready again. You hear it all the time, "be happy with yourself before trying to be happy with someone else." You always have to love yourself before you can love someone else.

I feel like I love myself but you can only love yourself to a certain extent. You can sit there and love yourself all you want but you need another human. I think I'm happy with myself enough to find a relationship, but I just want to make sure it's the right person. Plus we're at that age. I don't even know what age we're at but I feel like people are getting married and shit.

That's always in the back of my head, if I date someone this has to be the real thing. People just date people to say that they're in a relationship. They know it's not going to go anywhere and they date people for like two years and then break up. That's just not what I'm about. I'd rather just hook up with someone or see a future with them. It's either see a future with them or let them be.

Have you ever been in love before?

What is love? I'd say yes. Every girl I've dated I've been in love with at a different point in my life. I only date people if I really like them. That's why I've only dated two people.

I've loved. I loved my exes. I still talk to my exes to this day. We're still friends. It's sometimes awkward when we're mad at each other but we're still friends. That's how I think it should be. I think if you have a really successful, healthy relationship you should be able to break up and understand the other person, why they're breaking up, and forgive them. Maybe it takes a while but still forgive them.

You asked me what love is. What is love to you?

I was in love, but I don't think I know what love is. I imagine the feeling you get when you care about someone genuinely. It's when I'm not just asking how your day is for small talk. I genuinely want to know how your fucking day is. That's love to me at least because I don't care about a lot of people, but when I do care you know.

There's a different level when I ask someone that I'm really into, 'how is your day?' So I'd say love is just giving apart of yourself to someone. Love is when I dated this girl Jane and she had a test or something, *I'd* be stressed out. I'd be like, "have you studied enough?" That's why I fucking hate relationships, because I get so stressed out about the other person's life. So did they study enough? I help them study. Their life becomes a part of mine, that's what I think love is. It's when you take on the responsibility of someone else's problems.

Tell me about your greatest love.

I think they were all equal love. I would love someone until I realized that I couldn't love them anymore. My first girlfriend, Diane, I loved her for two or three years and then I realized she was going to be working at the Burger King or at the local town's shop for the rest of her life. She's trying to go to school but not doing well.

I guess that has a lot to do with my relationships in general. Just how the other person is doing in life. I only broke up with Jane because I figured I was with one girl for too long.

I was too young to be with one girl for that long so I broke up with her thinking I'm going to try out the single life. I thought I was going to get all these ladies. Then I broke up with her and think to myself, *Shit I'm not getting half as much as I thought.*

Can't say that one was greater than the other?

Right. I don't know. When I broke up with Jane it wasn't for any reason beside me being selfish. I wanted to be by myself. I didn't want to be stressed about her life. So, I broke up with her thinking I really lost something good. When I broke up with her two years ago I was like, "Fuck why did I do this? Shit was good." Then I started thinking about it and before you knew it, it's too late. I already broke up with her. I had to move on.

Have you ever tried to talk to her again?

Yes. Anytime we're in Michigan or the same town we always end up connecting. She lives in Chicago now. I live here. We're doing our own shit.

How is dating in Michigan verses dating in New York?

I haven't really dated in New York. I've only hooked up in New York. I feel like New York is the best place to hook up. When I came here I was hooking up with girls way more than I did in Michigan. Back home, I would take girls on dates.

Damn, what does that say about New York women?

New Yorkers are like, "Fuck it. I have shit to do. I know what I want."
The last girl I was super interested in was in Michigan and I tried so hard. We'd go on dates, I would do everything, and I would try really hard to get her to like me. Yes she liked me to a point, but we never ended up dating and I moved here. Then when I moved here it was just straight hook ups. I'd meet a girl and then before we know it, it was that same night and we were back at my apartment. That's how this neighbor thing happened. She basically knocked on my door and was like, "Hey let's hang out."

Sounds like you're living the dream. Isn't that a good thing to you?

No, I fucking hate hookups. I'm so sick of hookups. I'd rather connect with one person. I feel like all my friends that are my age will go and talk to anybody who talks to them. They'd be at a bar and if a girl comes up to them, game over. They're going to try to hook up with that girl no matter what. If a girl comes up to me or if I go up to a girl and I'm not feeling her, I'm going to drop it. I'm just not going to pursue it after that, but other people are just so worried about getting their dicks wet.

All my friends are so worried about just getting their numbers up instead of actually meaning something, which is why I feel soft at times. Guys are savages. I just want a girl I can connect with. It's not even always about the sex.

Wow. I must say, hearing this from a guy about guys is crazy! You seem to have this roadmap for what a girl needs to have in order to be with her. What do you think you have to offer in a relationship or to a woman?

I invest myself in their life. I get stressed about their type of shit. I feel like that's something I can offer, actually being there. I should work on a better list of things I can offer, but I'd be caring and definitely a good time.

If you could share some of the things that you've learned, whether it reflects being in a relationship or just dating, what would some of those lessons be?

I think the number one thing that I've learned over my years of being in a relationship is trust. If trust isn't there the relationship will never work. If you ever have to look at your significant other's phone, you might as well just end it right there. 100%. Once you go down that road, there's no stopping.

Another lesson is caring. A big problem in my relationships has been at the result of me saying, "You don't care as much as me." I can't even tell you how many times I've said that to someone. Soft as fuck. I've cared way more about someone than they have about me. But that's just something you can't even measure. How do you measure how much someone cares about you? Don't put an emphasis on that.

Finally, I've learned you need to allow a certain level of selfishness. Let people be selfish. If you're too unselfish and you give up too much of yourself to the person you're in a relationship with, then you've lost sight of you.

So, allowing selfishness. Be open to caring. 100% trust.

It's funny you mention being "soft." I had a conversation with someone recently about men feeling like they have to put on a mask because being soft for a guy is almost unacceptable. Yet, here you are bearing it all.

I think it comes down to the person. You have to love yourself enough to be soft with someone. It comes out as confidence almost because if you're not confident enough to share what you really feel with a person, then what is that? If you can't share your wants with the person that you really like or really love, then that's just bullshit. I don't want to sit there and act like someone I'm not the whole time.

I'm not soft when it comes to everyday shit, but if I actually care about someone then yes that's who I am. I get soft and sometimes I'll be jealous. I'm very open with my emotions for sure.

Kiana St Louis

DAY EIGHT: MANIPULATION

RECOVERY.

It's not always easy to spot when you're being taken advantage of or when you're being controlled in a relationship. Often times, we're so blinded by love, or what we think is love, we're almost willing to accept any and everything that comes with it. I want to say this happens more often in younger relationships. I think we want to be happy and be "in a relationship" so bad that we forget or better, ignore, obvious signs. But the reality is no matter how old you are, just because you love someone doesn't mean they're right for you.

Which begs to question: If not him or her, then who?

Danicia Campbell, 22, has been here before. She's endured manipulation to a point that has separated her from close friends, stopped her from going out, and doing the things she loved. She was so engulfed in the way she felt about the person she was with that she forgot about herself. She forgot about her needs, wants, and genuine happiness. Love can be desperate. There is something so volatile in wanting the admiration of another person; that *want* can play tricks on not just our minds but also our hearts.

Campbell found her way. She was able to break free, but the road to recovery is one with no direction. Campbell and I spoke about feelings that were never put to rest until this interview. Her journey is nowhere near over, however, the joys of healing are on the horizon. This is her story.

Tell me a little bit about your love life. Are you single, dating, in a relationship, married, it's complicated?

Right now, I'm currently single. I am talking to somebody at the moment. It's going well, and it's getting pretty serious. But I'm still very uneasy about the situation only because of my past, so I'm not trying to rush into things with this person.

100 Days of Dating

Tell me about him. Why do you feel confident to take these next steps?

This guy and I have been friends for three years. While we were friends, he was in a relationship and so was I. I was in a relationship for about five years, and we actually broke up in the summer time. Well it kind of ended officially earlier. You know how relationships never *really* end when they're that long? But it originally ended about October of last year.

Since then, he and I became even closer, I would consider him my best friend. When I was having issues in my past relationship, he was having issues with his, and we used to confide in one another. It was then we started realizing that we might have more than just a friendship.

He and his ex-girlfriend broke up. Then my ex and I ended up breaking up. After, we decided to see if this could actually be more than a friendship, or if we were just limiting ourselves to the friendship relationship.

This always felt real though. We didn't have to hide anything. I didn't have to lie and since we were real friends from the beginning, it was easy to talk to him and for him to come to me when he had issues. He never judged, he never said, "Oh, well, you know, you don't need them. You need me," it was never like that. He still expressed how he felt for me but it was always respectful because he knew I was in a relationship and he knew how deeply I was in love with the other boy.

How long have you and this person been talking now?

I want to say we started officially taking each other seriously in November, right before Thanksgiving.

So, do you not consider yourself dating this person? Or do you think there's a difference between "talking to someone" and dating them?

If anybody were to ask if this was my boyfriend, I would say no because he's not. But we do speak every day. Now that I'm not home, I'm in school, every time I come home he makes sure we spend time together. He takes me out on dates. But, we're just taking it slow. It's a little more than a friendship but it's a little bit less than a relationship.

Being with this person almost sounds easy. You can talk to him, and you've opened up this new way of communication. Knowing this, what makes this situation, "uneasy" for you?

I was with my ex for five years and he was with his ex-girlfriend for about three to four years, so there's always that. I feel like we always tend to slip back into where we're comfortable and I've noticed that about myself. If he and I get into an argument I'm always like, you know what? I'd rather just be with my ex because if I'm going to go through the same thing with you I might as well just do it with somebody that I've been doing it for so long with. A lot of the insecurities I have from my last relationship are drawing into this one.

If we argue I always feel like he's going to run back to his ex, and sometimes it's just really mental even though the guy can show me he's really here for me. But in the back of my mind I'm thinking, *she was always able to come back when you guys argued before so what's different now?* I know he's spoken to other girls while he was with his ex, so what's different about me? How do I know that one day he won't pick up and just say "you know what, I'm going to go back to my ex again?"

But he's amazing to me and it's something different because I was with my ex since I was 15 and I'm about to be 23. My ex was all I knew, so I just took whatever he gave me because I thought that's all I deserved in a relationship. Talking to somebody else feels like this is what a relationship is supposed to be. It's supposed to be a 50-50 thing.

100 Days of Dating

I wasn't getting that before and all my friends noticed. But I guess I was so blinded by love or so blinded by the fact that I had a boyfriend, which I thought: *We've been doing this for so long, why end it now? It will get better.* I just didn't realize that my self-esteem wasn't the same, I didn't think of myself the same, my friends didn't look at me the same way. Nobody could tell me differently though.

Do you trust the person that you're talking to now?

I do trust him, but I feel like because of my insecurities it's not 100%. He has never really given me a reason to think I can't trust him.

Tell me a little bit about your past relationship. It seems to hold an enormous amount of weight on not just who you've been with but essentially who you're becoming as a person.

Right. So we met when I was 15. I was young then so I wasn't really trying to get into a relationship. I don't think we officially started dating until I was about 17 going on 18, and in the beginning it was good, of course. You know, that's how relationships always start. I saw him often, he would come over, he would spend time with my family and I would spend time with his.

But as I started getting older, it just wasn't the same. The connection wasn't the same. I didn't really feel appreciated. Some girls, they just want to hear "you look nice today, babe," or "let's do this, let's go out." It was never that. I feel like in the four or five years we'd been dating we probably went on five or six dates. Looking back at it, that's ridiculous, first of all. But while I was in the relationship, it didn't dawn on me that this is not how it was supposed to be.

I went away to school, and he'd always say, "You're changing, you're not the person that you used to be when you were 16 years old" and I'm just like, yeah, I'm growing up. We were going to go through changes and it's either you're going to grow with me or we're going to grow apart. I started to feel like he wasn't okay with the person that I was changing into. He tried to control me. He didn't want me going out. He didn't want me hanging out with certain people. I lost a lot of friends because of this guy. But while I was in it, I thought: *he's just being a boyfriend, so I'm going to do what I have to do to keep him happy.* When I started getting older, about 19, 20 years old, if I wanted to go out, I would always ask myself first- *Is he going to be okay with this?*

There's no reason that I should have been limiting *myself* because of *his* feelings or *his* insecurities. If I'd go out, he would be calling down my phone, he'd be texting me asking why wasn't I home, and accusing me of doing this or that. While in reality, I would only be with the two friends that I have. I used to think: *what is going on?* It was crazy. I promise you, I did not enjoy my freshman year of college when everybody else was. If people asked me to go out, it was always, "I'm not going out because my boyfriend doesn't want me to." Everybody was just like "what?" If you're in a relationship with somebody they have to know how to trust you and if you don't have that trust it's never going to go anywhere. But I didn't see that when I was in the relationship.

So, I started to get distant and started talking to other people to fill the spaces in my heart that he wasn't filling for me anymore. I did cheat on him and I can't even tell him. Knowing that I cheated on him would hurt him even more. I was always worried about hurting him. I never really worried about myself. I always wanted to make sure he was happy whether I was happy or not, and it just continued. I'd give him the last dime in my pocket and I never felt like any of it was really appreciated. He would say he loved me. But I mean that's what you're supposed to do in a relationship. Nothing was genuine for me and it took me a really long time to actually see that.

How did you feel, having made the decision to cheat, and then after cheating?

While it was happening or when I decided to cheat, I didn't feel bad. I felt like I wasn't happy, so I thought: *Why keep suffering?* But then afterwards I would think about it, and I'd just be like damn. If he were to find out I wouldn't even be mad, I would just be hurt at the fact that he found out that I cheated on him.

That's when I realized that maybe this is not who I'm supposed to be with. I thought because we'd been together since I was 15, we could figure it out, take some space, you know? But sometimes space is not enough, because it was never just a space issue between us. We would stop speaking for maybe an hour and he's calling down my phone, popping up at my house, and I'd think to myself, *wait, aren't we on a break?* It was bad at such a young age. It came to the point where he was controlling and he used to play a lot of mind games. When we would argue and he was wrong, he was so good at flipping the script. I would end up thinking, *damn, maybe I did so this* or *damn, maybe I should have did this or that*. In reality I didn't do anything wrong.

He was just so good at manipulating me into thinking other things. Thinking things of certain people, even my close friends. I began to form different viewpoints of them and I had to check myself. When he got me mad or when I've cried over him, they're the ones that are there for me, so I really had to start realizing exactly what he was doing. People will always tell you things, but your friends are always there to tell you when you're changing, and let you know this is not the guy for you. But until you see it, whatever they say, no matter how close of a friend they are, you're not going to see it until you're actually ready. Regardless of how long it takes. It clearly took me a long time.

It sounds like you've done well with filling the voids, especially in terms of a relationship. Is the current person that you're with now filling a void?

I would say no. I really don't have the need or the urge to even speak to other people. This guy and I are not even in a relationship yet, I could be out, courting with others. But I don't even feel the need to do that anymore. We speak literally *all* the time. He shows me that he cares. It's just a whole different feeling and it's actually really genuine when it comes to him.

What advice would you give someone who was in that same situation?

When you're ready to make that change in your life, you will. No matter what your friends or parents say - you know when you're ready to move on. Until then, if you know what you want, go for it. It's hard, it's a really hard process when you know you don't belong somewhere but you keep fighting that feeling. But until you're ready to move on, it's not going to happen. You can let other people in, but you can't let others influence you because nobody's inside the relationship with you. Everybody's looking in from the outside and no matter how much you tell them, they don't really know how you feel. So my advice is to take your time, and when you're ready it will happen.

100 Days of Dating

DAY NINE: INSECURE

TIMOROUS.

Women know the feelings of insecurity all too well. We've been to the place of no return where our thoughts and emotions get the best of us. The place where we whisper our accomplishments and scream our failures. The place where we compare ourselves to others; our bodies, our processes, our goals, where we are in life. We dissect every part of ourselves so much so that there isn't much left. I've been to that place before, too. I've been unsure, I've been unhappy, I've felt like I wasn't enough.

I believe men feel this way too. This is a place we all have in common. But just as the world has set a double standard for women in certain instances, I believe we have set the same for men. We don't allow men to be insecure. It's "weak." How can you be a provider? How can you be the epitome of strength? How can you protect me if you're too busy battling insecurities?

The difference between being a woman in this place as opposed to being a man is how we handle everything. I think women do a better job of handling being hurt and unsure a little better than men do. Our feelings may be the same but our reactions are so different. Call me biased, I speak only from my experiences.

Veronica H., 27, and I caught up over dinner. While she too is no stranger to the place of insecurity, her struggle was not in battling her own but that of her partner. One minute they're happy, the next minute he finds out she makes more money than him, the following minute he's unsure of the relationship. Stuck, hurt, and confused, she's forced yet again to pick up the pieces of her love life. Her views on love and of men have become somewhat distorted due to her continued love escapades. Yet, she still believes and while a bit jaded, is still on the hunt for love.
I wanted to try something a little different with this interview. Veronica is a creative soul, so I want to share her story as creatively as possible. I dedicate this poem to you.

Kiana St Louis

From Men to Boyz

At 27, they say I should have it figured out.
This love thing, this drug thing
But, I'm just an addict with a full clip, a tight lip, and loose hips
Looking for that last hit
I call it my last because I want it so bad.
I want it so bad, I don't want anything after
I've gone through all the disasters, I just want to master
this idea of love.
And just when I thought I've had enough, in walks your sweet
smell, tan face, and attractive physique.
Instantly my knees are weak. No SWV, but I can hardly breathe
I'm in awe of you. I want more of you. I need all of you.
At your 38, this is more than just a dinner date for two,
but instead the beginning of our forever, I assume.
You're open with me, and I with you.
I am the book and you are my pages.
Lost language, I give you my patience.
Wrapped up and sealed, I give my all to you.
But I'm nothing more than a silly girl, I was a fool.
You wanted only a muse.
All the aspects of a woman minus success,
you wanted my thoughts but my work ethic to be less.
I was enough until I was too much to handle,
too much to stand next to
too much to love.
How could you let your insecurities ruin me?
What about what I do makes me too much for you?
What are your standards? Do you measure up?
For you my cup ran over, from you all I wanted was love.
All you wanted was to be a step above.
To dominate, to have the upper hand, you dragged me through this
mess just so you can remain "the man"
I want to be over you.
Over our memories, our lives, your lies.
I question, was it real? My answers lie only in the way I feel.
I hold you accountable not for who you are but for what you've
done,
for ending our moments in the sun.

100 Days of Dating

You wrapped your arms around me, took hold of me, demanded
more of me
but never of yourself.
I hear the beat of my heart against the keys of these letters. I want
to say you've lost, you'll never find another,
but I'm the one hesitant that I'll find better.
No more tears, your challenge is accepted
I will be your biggest regret, the sweetest song you can't forget,
your favorite lost toy, a solemn reminder you are still just a boy.

DAY TEN: LONG DISTANCE

TIME.

Timing is everything. Time has more control over our lives than we do. We race to beat time, we depend on time to heal, we hate to run out of time, and with time, there's simply never enough. There's nothing more certain than perfect timing. The beauty of being right where you're supposed to be with whom you're supposed to be with. It's a feeling like no other.

Jessica G., 25, knows this feeling well. Love and time have worked together in her life to show the results of patience. While distance stands between her and her boyfriend, she has found comfort in knowing that time is on her side. They will see each other again soon, and in the meantime they are putting together the pieces of what their new love will look like. Long distance dating is far from impossible. It takes twice the amount of effort, commitment, and trust, but when you want something, you work for it, right? I can't say that I believe in love as hard as I have once before, but I do believe in allowing time to do what it needs to.

Jessica taught me this love thing comes with no manual and being far or near has little to do with endurance. But sometimes, as cliché as it sounds, only time will tell. This is her story.

Tell me about your love life. Are you single? Dating? In a relationship? Married?

I am currently in a relationship. It's kind of nice to hear me say that, because it's been a while.

How long has it been?

I haven't dated anyone in like five or six years. I know. I was a single lady for quite a while.

How was that, being single for that long?

Honestly, I think it was okay for me. I think I needed that time. My prior relationship affected me in ways I didn't expect. I was very young at the time and I lost a bit of myself without even realizing, until it ended. It took those five or six years to reflect on what happened and really gain confidence in myself again.

After being single for so long, was it hard for you to get into the groove of being in a relationship again?

Yes. The first time I hung out with my current boyfriend, we sat in a park and we shared our first kiss that same day. It was so unexpected because I'm the type to make you wait and kiss on the third date! But here I was kissing him and I was freaking out internally. That first month we started dating, I made weird rules where I'd only hang out with him for three or four hours at a time. In retrospect, it was dumb, but I guess I needed time to be sure that I was ready for a relationship.

In the beginning, did you ever think this could be more than just dating because you felt yourself moving a little bit faster than you would normally?

Yeah, definitely. I think that's why it was so scary at first. I wasn't expecting to meet someone, let alone be that comfortable with the person so quickly. It's cliché, but you know that saying, if you're happy with yourself, you'll meet someone? I totally believe that. I definitely wasn't ready to date anyone for the majority of my single years. I was too stuck in the past and had trouble letting go of that prior relationship. Then I got over it, and I challenged myself like "what am I doing?" Right before meeting him, I got to a place where I was feeling really happy with how I had grown. And then he showed up.

Do you see any of those feelings of self-doubt or insecurity falling into the new relationship?

Yeah, sometimes.

How do you deal with it?

I think because we're dating long distance, those insecurities can creep back in. When he left at the end of last year, that's when all of my insecurities rushed to the surface. I sobbed and told him all the reasons why I was feeling that way and why I was scared about taking this step. I think being upfront about how you're feeling in the moment is what helps – something I have difficulty doing. He's very open with me and so I push myself to do the same. I trust this guy and feel incredibly comfortable with him. He has a way of calming any insecurities I do have.

What is the dynamic of your relationship?

I think it's pretty great, actually. It's really fun. He's very loving and I am too. Sharing yourself completely with someone can be scary but if you've found the right person, it comes naturally. I learned how to love myself and now I'm learning how to be loved by another person.

How do you like to be loved?

I like affection. I like the good morning/goodnight texts. I like surprise phone calls or video calls…things like that. I like when someone picks up on small details of my personality and accepts me just as I am.

How do you reciprocate that love to him?

I think I do the same. I'll send him cute messages so he knows I'm thinking of him, or send a picture of myself one day. I make sure to ask him about his day, about his family. I make sure that he knows that I appreciate him staying up late just to talk to me. Basically, I want him to know that I care and that I'm always there for him, even if I'm physically not there.

What do you think is the key to making your long distance relationship work?

Communication and honesty, for sure.

How have you two mastered not only communicating but also being able to be open with each other?

I think that's what made me nervous about dating long distance in the beginning – because your day to day isn't always going to be exciting, so I questioned how do make sure you're communicating even when you don't have a lot to share? So, we've come up with a few ways to "hang out" with each other even if we're not in the same place. We started a Netflix show together. We started playing video games together, which is something I didn't think I'd be into – but I am! It's fun and we talk to each other as we do these activities. So, in the end we're still able to keep things exciting.

That's really cute! Are you any good at the games?

I get really into them, that's the thing. And then I get competitive.

Do you feel as if you're happier with him than you were without?

That's a good question. I think he brings out another level of happiness in me. He brings out certain things in me that I wouldn't show other people and it's nice to share that. I worked really hard to be happy on my own so when he came around, he added to that happiness.

If you guys were to break up tomorrow, how would you feel?

I'd be pretty heartbroken. I don't give my heart out to many people, so when I do, it means I'm all in.

Is he ever insecure about what you're doing when you two aren't speaking?

He never has, actually. And I don't think I've ever asked him. We're really good about telling each other what our plans are for the day and keeping each other updated. I share those things with him because I genuinely want him to know, not because I feel like I have to.

So, it's like he's never thinking more than he has to, essentially?

Exactly. And he does the same for me.

If you could give advice to someone whose in a long distance relationships or maybe even a woman who's been by herself for so long, what would you tell her?

We've only been dating long distance for a few months now and we're still trying to figure it all out, so not sure I'm the best to give advice on that! But, for someone who's been on her own for a while, I say it's okay to take the time you need. Take time to really love who you are. My prior relationship affected me so badly because I was trying to be this person that I thought he wanted me to be. I changed myself trying to live up to his expectations, and in the end, he still didn't want me. So, I took my time to fall back in love with myself and go from there.

100 Days of Dating

DAY ELEVEN: GOING THE DISTANCE

HIS PERSPECTIVE.

It's always refreshing to learn from the other side - to hear thoughts behind why a few men act the way they do, say the things they do, love the way they do. I've gained more insight from a few 30min conversations, than I have in all my years of dating. Maybe these guys are just super sharers, or maybe I've never asked the right questions.

I had no idea that both Day 10 and Day 11 would be highlighting long distance relationships, however, I find it a bit beautiful. It's rare we get an inside look at both a male and female perspective on something as personal as a relationship. A true bond between two people is not only sacred but a single shared choice between lovers. It's a choice to be monogamous in a society that praises sex and savagery. A choice to be one with someone else. A choice to love. It's one thing to have this bond with the boy next door, but another to create and upkeep a connection miles apart.

Edward Niles, 23, says that might be the easiest part though. When you fall in love with someone that is in sync with you, complements where you lack, or is your perfect opposite, the upkeep should come easy. Temptation happens, yes, and in more ways than one. However, this is something we can expect. The "surprising" part happens with us, when we turn away from temptation because we already know what we have. I think it takes a different kind of guy to not only realize this but stand by it while on tours, shows, and when a million other people are fighting for your attention. But Niles has always been in a class of his own. We chatted briefly about the joys of his love and it came to me like a breath of fresh air. I hope it does the same for you. This is his story.

Tell me about your love life. Are you single? Dating? In a relationship? Married? Divorced? It's complicated?

I am in a relationship.

How long have you guys been together?

For a year and 5 or 4 months.

That's awesome. Tell me about it. How's it going?

It's cool. She doesn't live here though.

How does that work?

I see her when I can. We fly to each other.

And where is she?

She's in Minnesota.

How did you guys meet?

I actually saw a picture of her and then invited her to one of the shows that we had in her city. That's the first time I met her face-to-face. Shit just moves so fast for me most times. So when I saw her I was like, "Oh, shoot we'll be in your city, so come to the show."

Having connected with your girlfriend via social media, what are your thoughts on the role technology plays in our love lives?

I used to think it was weird, but then I realized that social media is all people do now days so it's not as weird to me anymore. It's just like how I would have naturally met people before. It's like if I saw this girl on the street, or this girl lives on my block, it would be regular. And now it's just – oh cool, I saw this girl on Instagram, I'm about to like ten of her pictures and send her a DM. That type of stuff. It's become a normal thing.

Do you ever feel hesitant about the distance? Does it ever evoke any types of insecurities on both ends, either yours or hers?

I don't have anything to be insecure about until I find something. I will give her the benefit of the doubt. I trust her enough to be away and not do anything. And I don't have any other reason to think she had done otherwise.

You have an amazing career, you travel, and do so many great things. Was there ever a point where the external distractions messed with what you both have internally?

No, because for me it's literally just not doing it. It's not hard. Just don't do it. Anything external that's tempting, just walk away from it. It's not anything complicated. You don't even have to be like, "Damn, I want to but, nah" because if you really love the person you're with you don't really have to think twice about that type of stuff.

Do you love her?

Yep.

How did you know?

I don't really know how I knew. I kind of just did. She leaves me stuck a lot and that doesn't happen. It tends to not happen. Stuck in the sense where I'm looking at her and not even saying anything. And not even noticing I'm doing it until she says something.

How would you define love?

I don't know how to define it. I think it's just something you feel. If you know when it's there you will know. There's not even a long explanation for it really, it's just something you feel. When you feel it, you just know.

What advice would you give a guy in your position?

To any guy in a long distance relationship, I would say if you don't really trust a person like that, you shouldn't be in a long distance relationship. A relationship is built on trust period, but it has to be a whole lot more trust, if you're going be in a long distance relationship and really make it work. They're not around you all the time. You can't just see them when you want.

Would you say that the love you have now is your greatest?

I would say so, because I haven't experienced anything greater than this. I would say yes. I probably wouldn't be in a relationship with her if I didn't think so.

Prior to this, were you single and looking? Or did she just change things completely for you?

I'm never really *looking* for a relationship. Even when we got into a relationship I wasn't looking for one. I kind of just fucked with what was going on. So, with her I thought to myself, *alright, cool. I can survive with this person. I can see myself being with this person for longer than a couple of months.* I don't really attach to people like that. So it was cool to know there is somebody.

Can you tell me about your greatest heartbreak?

I don't know if I have a greatest heartbreak. I know some people who have been heartbroken. They don't know how to focus, they don't know how to deal. I've never really experienced that. I've been sad about stuff that wasn't going to work that I wanted to work, but I don't know if I would say that's a great heartbreak.

Have you ever been in love before this time around?

Yes, with the girl I took to prom.

Tell me about her.

I don't know. I like a lot about her. She was one of the very few people who could genuinely just make me smile by being herself. Not trying too hard, to be like, "Oh yeah. I'm going to try and be funny around cameras." That's just how she is.

Speaking of smiles and happiness, how would you describe being happy in a relationship?

Not worrying or stressing out 24/7. In a relationship you're going to have some sort of stress. It's not going to be flowers and sunshine and rainbows all the time but … you're going to have some sort of stress. But if you're stressing all the time, that's horrible. You should definitely get out of that type of relationship. That's unhealthy.

What 3 qualities does your woman have or need to have in order to be with you?

She's goofy, that's one. Two, she presents herself well when she talks to other people and in front of other people. Three, she cares a lot for people almost as much as she cares about herself or me or her family. She generally just cares about other people.

And those are qualities you feel like you need?

Yeah. For sure. Because I'm kind of not like that. I don't think it would make sense for me to be with someone that's exactly like me. I need that. Not saying I don't care about people but she cares more for those she doesn't necessarily know. It's selfless and I love that.

Kiana St Louis

DAY TWELVE: SISTERHOOD

FRIENDSHIPS.

Last week, 10 of my close girlfriends and I took a trip to Cancun, México. In short, the trip was a movie. Yes, 10 girls, one house, and nothing but good vibes. Something I believe is so rare! We didn't argue once about anything. We barely disagreed. And in the off chance we weren't on the same page, somebody would begin to dance or sing and next thing you know, we were on set of the black High School Musical.

But, tonight's piece isn't solely about the trip itself but more so about the feeling these young women left with me. Over the past six years, our friendship has grown exponentially. We are a large group with smaller groups inside of that group, however, we've somehow managed to make it work. I believe this is because at the foundation of our friendship is love and respect. We respect each other's goals, opinions, ideas, and decisions; and while we might not always agree, we never tear each other down. We love one another, far more than words can explain. We support each other, we pray for and with one another, and at the core, we allow God to guide each and every one of our endeavors.

The purpose of #100DaysofDating is heavily routed to my journey in believing in love again. I admit that for the past four months, I've been in a pretty dark place. I'll smile in pictures and laugh at jokes, but the reality is I've been enduring what feels like my greatest heartbreak. Love does that sometimes. It gets you really excited about the possibility of a happily ever after until the excitement wears off. The side effects of this drug thing, I guess. But being with these women this past week evoked a new sense of power in me. It's almost as if I'd been sleeping this whole time and they woke me up. They gave me light.

I didn't go there teary-eyed and confused, nor did I bring up my love life at all. But I didn't have to. I immediately felt calm as I sat on the couch surrounded by love. As we laughed with each other, I was reminded how important support is. I was reminded how important having genuine people in your corner is. I was reminded that as much as you think you're okay, and how strong you think you are, everybody needs somebody. As I reminisce on our getaway, I realize that I have 10 special somebodies.

Sometimes, we take the people in our lives for granted. We're so consumed in work, our plans, and goals that we put off spending time with the people who deserve it. We send our best friends to voicemail with hopes of calling them back. We cancel engagements in hopes of hanging out another time. We constantly put things and people off because we think we'll get to it eventually. We do all of this knowing the reality of how temporary life is, yet we're so dependent on tomorrow. We all claim to want love and are so eager to give it to someone, yet we show the lowest form of love to those who already love us. I too am victim to this.

But when you have a bond with people, just as effort is required in relationships, it is too required in friendships. And I think we forget that sometimes – friendships are relationships, too. Anything that you want to last requires effort and upkeep. Dealing with people is no different. My girls taught me that.

I want to dedicate this segment to them. We've built a sisterhood on love. While it may not be romantic, it's a love that is consistent, a love that is pure, and a love that I can count on. At the end of the day that's all I really want and I am blessed to have found that in them. Every love story is different, but ours is my favorite.
#LivLuvLux

Kiana St Louis

DAY THIRTEEN: GROWTH

MOTHERHOOD.

The bond between a mother and child is peculiar. That love far exceeds anything I've ever known. It's as if you love a deeper version of yourself, at least that's what it is for me. I can only relate by the love I feel for my mother and the Gilmore Girl-style relationship we've formed over the years. The love I have for her is somewhat indescribable. I am in awe of my mother and I've wrapped my life goals around trying to make her proud. I know through my ups and downs, it's her duty to always be there. To care. To love me too. But prior to her getting married, I'd wonder who would be there for her.

Sometimes I wonder what that is like for all mothers. Women who constantly give to their children, to those around them… who gives to them?

Yes, there are some beautiful stories filled with superwomen who have supermen filling that gap. There are men who give to their women thus giving them the strength to keep going. And then there are just superwomen. Single mothers. Going back to that bond and love between mother and child, I know it can be extremely fulfilling, but it begs to question: Is that enough?

Renae Bispham, 24, is a young single mother whom I believe also battles with this question. She pours so much of herself and values into her daughter and I've seen nothing but greatness come out of that. She is a phenomenal woman and mother. But as I watch her take on countless school events or exchange colds with her kid, I wonder, *who will have her back?* Renae and I didn't come to any conclusions nor do we have the answers to every question, but I do believe we brought light to a few seemingly dark places when we spoke the other night. But that's the thing about love, we may not always understand it, like it, or completely agree with our feelings but it's all necessary for growth. I believe this was necessary for her, too. This is her story.

Tell me about your love life.

It's trash. I'm a single girl.

Why do you say it like that?

Because I'm partially excited to be single, but before it used to make me sad. But not anymore.

Do you want to be in a relationship?

At this point in my life, I feel like it would be cool, but I'm still skeptical.

Why?

My daughter … I'm afraid to bring her around someone new, someone she doesn't really know. For example, her meeting a brand new person, mainly because her dad is not in her life. So, bringing a new person around her makes *me* scared. She's seen me with someone, but she was a baby at the time. That used to be the norm, but now he's not around anymore.

When was the last time you were in a relationship?

My daughter's dad. And then there was a guy I was seeing somewhat recently.

How old is your daughter?

Five and a half.

Do you still think about this other guy?

Up until a week ago … yeah. But this past weekend I had a revelation.

What was the revelation?

He doesn't deserve me.

How did you come to that?

I rekindled an old flame that kind of made me feel like 'Stella Got Her Groove Back.' I was so stuck on him, the previous person that was around my daughter, that I felt like I couldn't move past him, ever. I was just so tired ... I thought that something was wrong with me. I'd think: *What am I doing wrong? Why do they keep leaving me? Did I do something? Am I not good enough?*

This "other guy" wasn't my boyfriend because we weren't together, but he was my first adult relationship. I had my daughter young. Her dad and I were young, but this guy, I felt like he was my first take at adulthood. I was so stuck. I thought that he was the one. I just knew it.

The signs were there that he wasn't, as time went along. But I just chose to ignore them because I wanted this to work so badly. Because things didn't work out with my daughter's dad, I think that I wanted to fill that void. Everything just seemed so right. I always prayed and asked God to show me the signs. Put it in my face or mix it up. God would do that constantly and I would still be like "No that's not it. That's not the sign. No, you would show me in a different way." I was battling with God.

As the years went along, it was just so hard. Four and a half years later and I'm just empty. You can still be with someone and feel so empty. I felt empty towards the ending of us parting. I couldn't do this. It wasn't healthy for me or my sanity. So I decided that I didn't want to try this anymore. When he went away, it was easier for us to not speak as much and I started getting comfortable in that emptiness, I guess. It forced me to get over him ... Not get over him, but accept it for what it was at that point, which was hard for a little bit.

Did you love him?

Hell yeah. I loved that man with every fiber of my being.

Would you say it was your greatest love?

I don't think I have found my greatest love yet. It was amazing ... something different, but I don't think that was my greatest. My greatest love won't be one-sided. I felt like what I had was one-sided. Did I love him? With every fiber in me, like I said. I'm a lover and when I fall in love, I fall deeply in love with someone. I don't think he was all of that for me.

Do you regret it?

I don't regret anything that I ever do. One, because at one point he made me happy, and two, because I just feel like there is always a lesson to be learned in everything that you do. Relationships ... Friendships ... Your everyday life. There is always something to be learned. I don't regret it. It was fun. It was amazing. I learned a lot about myself. I learned what I want in a relationship, what I don't want, how I would introduce someone to my daughter. It was new ... I was just scared, but then it was easier because she was a baby. She just got used to seeing that face. I appreciate that situation-ship for teaching me the things about myself that I know now.

Are you comfortable with yourself? Are you comfortable being single?

Now, yeah. After stepping outside of that situation. Honestly, all of this is recent, literally, a couple of days ago. I feel like, "Bitch, you poppin," right now. I have to keep reminding myself that. I was so sunken. I was so sad because I just knew that that was it. I knew that he was it for me and he confirmed something for me. Being with him made me see how much time I wasted with the wrong guy. I just know that if I can give the wrong guy that much love, I can wait for the right one and really make something amazing happen.

What about the old flame you recently rekindled. Do you think this guy is the right one? Or could be?

I don't know. I'm just having fun. But I don't think this is just a distraction. I mean the act of talking to someone new is great, but I don't think me feeling great about myself is solely based on talking to someone new.

Would you say that you're happier without your ex?

It's still fresh. My revelation is still fresh, but I'm not in that sunken place anymore. I can go through the day without thinking about him. I can hear a song and not get sad. Now I just laugh about things. I have these little ah ha moments with myself and I just start laughing. I literally question myself: *Why was I such a dub?* Now, I just feel free and I know my worth. In this stage in the game it's all about knowing my worth - knowing I'm worth it. I tell myself that every day, "You're worth it." Even if this new guy and I don't go past two weeks, I can truly say to myself: "Okay, well that was fun, but I am still worth something greater." I can't wait for the greater.

Moving forward, what three qualities do you require of your partner?

Loyalty. Honesty. For me, I just want somebody to be honest with me. I want my friends to be honest with me. I want that of my parents. I want my daughter to be honest. I want honesty from my lover. I just want people to always be honest with me because I feel like I'm a very understanding person. If you're not happy, tell me. If you're feeling like you don't want to be here anymore, tell me. I just need honesty.

Can I pick more than three?

This is your list baby.

God fearing, for sure. I am not holier than thou, not even close. I just want someone who has a relationship with God. I want to be able to be like, "Babe, I had a rough day." And you say to me, "Let's pray." In our good times or our bad times, I want you to be able to feel comfortable opening up to God with me.

I want someone who loves deeply. Like I said before, I am a deep lover, and I just want to be loved the way I love. I want someone who my daughter can look up to, essentially. Someone like my dad.

DAY FOURTEEN: REALITY CHECK

LOVE IS NOT HARD.

Sometimes, I have to keep reminding myself that. I keep trying to wrap my head around the reason behind relationships not working out the way I've planned. I'll get frustrated with myself trying to answer questions that I've never asked aloud. I've allowed feelings of insecurity to sneak up on my memories and choke my happiness. All in an effort to understand what I've done *wrong*. All in an effort to understand why I've seemingly lost.

Have you ever felt this way? Has the end of a relationship ever brought your mind to this place?

The truth is, we haven't a lost anything. We've done nothing wrong. I realize I've been trying to sell myself happiness instead of actively obtaining it. At the root of many of these interviews, I've learned there is an art to self-love. There is a process in getting there. There is time needed as with all things. I've also realized I'm not all the way there yet and by assigning a due date to my healing, I've almost been slowing myself down in getting there.

This week was a little rough. I needed a quick pause in this series to reevaluate, re read, and see where I almost lost myself. These stories have really been helping me. But the reality check didn't kick in until two of my good friends, more like my sisters, slapped some sense into me. I needed to read this:

Jia

15m ago from Camera Roll

I remember my ex fiance telling me that I wasn't giving him time to miss me and warning me that my attempts to be close to him would "run him off".

I remember being called clingy for hugging him. I remember being convinced that my requirement that he come home after arguments was ridiculous.

I, like a lot of women, believed that I was "too".

Too emotional. Too affectionate. Too talkative. Too damaged. Too worrisome. Too concerned - just to name a few. And I, like a lot of women, put all my eggs in one basket. I committed to this man's potential in hopes that I could mold his view of me by reducing my excessiveness.

I died a little bit everyday with the end goal of being reborn as a woman who wasn't "too", and instead the one who was "enough" for him. So that our house of cards wouldn't fall down.

Ladies: you are only "too" for the wrong man.

So the second you begin to feel inferior for being too much to fit into his standards or criteria, start reevaluating. Because while you're curling your toes, clinching your feet, damaging yourself to fit into shoes two sizes too small...the perfect pair is on display in a store down the street.

Love is not hard. In fact, it should be one of the easiest things we do. It should be one of the most uplifting feelings we feel. We complicate things. I complicate things. But I have to be one with time and learn to embrace healing. This segment was for me. My story is only beginning.

DAY FIFTEEN: SINGLE

IS BEING SINGLE A BAD THING?

People have asked the above question and are quick to answer, *no*. No, there's nothing wrong with being single. No, you don't *have* to be in a relationship to be happy. However, it seems as if after a certain time-period or age in your life, if you aren't in a relationship or haven't been in one there's a hint of skepticism. A side eye. A raised eyebrow. A wonder of, why not?

Caitlin Crews, 31, has probably been subject to this one time or another. A single love is one she is not only familiar with but whole-heartedly accepts. Being single brings about a certain kind of joy and acceptance of self. It's as much of learning period as it is a break from being a part of someone to truly become one with yourself. It's also a time for fun, a time to enjoy the luxury of experiences, and a time to take a chance on yourself. A kind of freedom, if you will. A freedom that is still hopeful for more. Caitlin and I chatted about the ins and outs of a single woman, the difference between dating and love, and the beauty of hope. This is her story.

Tell me about your love life. Are you single? Dating? In a relationship? Married?

I am single. It's interesting because I don't think I've ever had a typical love life, I'll put it that way. It kind of goes back to high school. I'm from a really small town. I went to a small Catholic school. I was one of three black people. The other two people were my cousins. We're somehow related in some sort of way. In a town of 14,000 people you're related to everybody.

Where are you from?

Uniontown, Pennsylvania, 15 minutes from West Virginia. South of Pittsburgh. A small coal mining town. When I was in high school everyone was your friend. I was friends with all the guys. I played sports, I did art. I did everything. And then it was this weird moment where I was like, "Oh. I kind of actually have a crush on somebody." But I'm the queen of not saying it, of not telling anybody.

I went through high school crushing on this person. He was actually my prom date because we were friends. We were really good friends, and I think for some reason that friend thing has followed me my whole life. So, I never had that traditional boyfriend in high school. I didn't date anyone in college. Again, I met this really great guy. He was lovely. I was just really focused on school and I was totally okay with being friends.

I moved to New York at 23 and I was not dating. Never dated anyone. And to this day I've never been somebody's girlfriend. I've had all the elements of that, but a word has never been put to it. And I think it's really interesting when all the emotions I have come up. It's like, "Yeah, that's totally fine." Other times it's like, "No. It's a lonely feeling." It's a sad feeling. I've spent many years being sad about that. Then when I hit 30, my outlook on everything completely changed and my outlook on dating completely changed.

It's interesting because I think there's a huge difference between love and dating. I definitely have been in love with people. I've definitely loved men that I have been with but, in terms of a strict relationship, I haven't had that. And it's weird. People are like, "How do you do that?" Truth is, you struggle with it. There's definitely every element that makes a relationship but of the three [situation-ships] I've had, it was never called that. That's kind of painful in a way too.

I've had some really interesting things happen where I'm dating somebody, and you definitely love them and they love you. You say it, but then it does not go any further. I'm also the queen of staying friends with everyone, which is not always good. Sometimes you got to cut people off and I've recently had to do that. That's where I've had a problem. At the basis of all of it, it's a friendship. It's this thing that works both ways and when that starts to not work both ways, it's when it's got to stop.

Why do you think these relationships have never made it past the friend zone?

That's a hard question of why it doesn't. I think each time had kind of relatively been the same. Either they're not available to be in that relationship or I'm not mentally available, which could be a possibility.

You mentioned that there were three potential people in your life that could have been relationships. What happened? What do you think went wrong?

I never demanded or asked for them to be in a relationship with me. I think when you don't do that after a certain time of a relationship, then, from what I understand, because this is what someone that I did date for a while said, "I never knew that you actually felt that deeply about it."

So, I didn't take it seriously enough. I thought to myself, *you're stupid. How do you not?* And then learning about that person, he was the first person that I dated. I was 23. We met on *OKCupid*. And he was a wonderful human being. He was my first for a lot of things, but he also passed away three years ago.

I was at work and I got a phone call and oddly enough his first girlfriend is one of my great friends. It had been years apart, but she's still one of my closest friends. I remember getting all these weird text messages after meeting a friend for lunch. By the time I got back I was like, "What do you mean where is he?" Something happened with his heart when he was running in the morning.

That was a crazy experience. And he's someone that I was truly friends with after a really awkward relationship. A nondescript relationship. He was the first person to put it into perspective and tell me, "You don't really ever say how you feel about things." And then at that point I think there was a moment, and there have been a few times where I felt I needed to say something and I didn't say anything.

What's stopped you from saying something?

I think it's a little bit of a fear of rejection. That's a real thing. Because I know that on my own or with friends, I'm in control of the situation. That's another thing - I'm in control of how I feel about things, how I respond to things. When you're in a relationship with somebody else you're giving up a part of that control to somebody. And I don't like that.

You mentioned the difference between dating and love. How do you feel about love now?

Well, I think love now is something that I want in my life with another person. I grew up with two parents that have been married for 46 years. They are the best of friends, and sometimes they want to kill each other, which is hilarious. So I grew up with that in mind as a goal.

But, I turned out to be one of those who think, if it happens, it happens. I do want to find love. I do want to spend that time with someone and give love to somebody else. But I also want them to give it back to me in an equal way. I think that's the thing that a lot of people don't ever receive. Or to know when it's done. That's a hard thing, too.

Do the thoughts of being alone forever creep into your mind?

I think so a little bit. I've lived on my own since I was 19. I'm very okay with being physically by myself. But I will say this: I lived in the suburbs of New Jersey for three years before moving to Brooklyn. But when I moved to Brooklyn and was by myself, which was the saddest, miserable, and one of the most depressing parts of life.

There are so many people around, but I'm completely by myself. There's literally someone next door that I can hear yelling at their cat, but they're so far away from me. The act of being alone does not scare me, or rather, physically being alone. But emotionally being alone? Or sexually being alone? That's sad. A lot of the time, I don't want to be by myself. Other times, I need to be.

What would you say your greatest heartbreak was? What did you learn from it?

It's interesting, because the people that I've dated, I've stopped dating, and then have dated again. So, it's never been a clean break of any certain time.

You're preaching to the choir.

I think the first person that I was ever really completely engaged and enamored with passed away, that was the biggest heartbreak. We hadn't dated for a really long time but we stayed friends forever. And he was the person who introduced me to so many types of different music and movies. He's the person who got me to really appreciate cooking. My mom cooked a lot, but he, for some reason, had this great appreciation for cooking and feeding people, and that's something that I love to do.

So when he passed away, I think that was the hardest thing. To this day, it's been almost three years now, I still reach for my phone and even as a friend to be like, "Oh man. Matt would really love this." And I can't do that. So that, to me, was a little bit of a heartbreak. It was definitely a heartbreak. Even post any sort of relationship or physical relationship he was just a friend. So, not having that was really, really difficult.

I still expect the, "Hey, what's going on?" And I can't do that anymore. I think because I haven't really shut off a lot of the relationships that I've had, I think that can also be really heartbreaking, too. Where it's like, *why did I keep letting you back in? There's somebody in my life now, but, why do I keep letting you back in?*

Have you found the answer to that? The *why* to letting them in?

No, I think the answer changes all the time because I make an excuse to why. For the person who's in my life right now, he is an amazing human being. It's not a committed situation by any means, but from a mental standpoint, has always been there. It's more of a support than a relationship.

But he's a very lovely and wonderful person. So, I have had disappointments, but having a true heartbreak is hard because you can't ever have a broken heart if you keep letting people back in. Your heart can be cracked a little bit. But it's hard to have a full break because you haven't shut them off. I think a broken heart comes when you actually shut somebody out.

What would you say that you've learned from your different experiences?

The thing I've learned is, not take a lot of things seriously anymore. And to actually weigh the actual impact in your day and in your future. So, if I say to this person, "Okay, I'm done." For the moment, it feels like shit. But I know that in another month or so, I'll feel better. So, it's a day at a time. And there are going to be people in your life for short amounts of time and people in your life for longer amounts of time. I think it's just a choice of how long they're supposed to be there.

You can't rush people. What song is it? Is it Bonnie Raitt? *I Can't Make You Love Me if You Don't.* You can't. That song is the best song because it's the truth. I can't force you. I cannot force anyone. So one day at a time. Whatever happens, happens. It's kind of how I live life right now in all aspects.

Kiana St Louis

DAY SIXTEEN: BUILDING

LOVERS AND FRIENDS.

I used to let anger consume me when I'd see people happily in love on train, in a store, or taking up space on the sidewalk because they couldn't bear to release their intertwined fingers. It was as if I'd see only a gray cloud while everyone around me enjoyed the warmth of the sun. At one point, my two best friends and I were all some version of single and dreading the idea of love together. We were under the same cloud.

But then one of us got into a relationship. Great for her, sucked for us. Or so we thought, until we fell in love with him too. Suddenly, we were all in a relationship with her. (With limits, of course).

Eniola Alawoya, 23, has had a special part of my heart for the past 6 years. Our odd friendship began in high school but blossomed into an eternal sisterhood that I'm sure neither of us saw coming. I'm protective of my sisters. So, when she realized her casual dating scheme was turning into more of a one-man habit, things shifted for all of us – but for the better. I've seen growth in her as a result of this relationship, more growth than I've ever admitted to.

She's been happy. She's been sad. She's been confused along with a whirlwind of other emotions as part of this relationship. But to me, the most important thing is that she's been loved. A love that has changed her perspective. A love that has changed mine. She exudes a level of strength, passion, and patience that I'm not sure I ever had. But she also gives me hope that there's time to reach that level. There's time to heal from mistakes. There's just time. This is her story.

Tell me about your love life.

I'm in a relationship. We've been together for about three, going on four years.

Why do you say it like that?

I mean, I don't really like to gush and make a big deal about the years and stuff like that. I feel like recently I've been telling more people that piece of information and everybody's reaction is always, "Oh wow, good for you guys." And it's like, ah, okay.

Do you not see value in the length of your relationship?

I definitely do. Obviously our time together means a lot to me and it is significant, I guess I'm always a little hesitant to be so public about my love life.

Why are you hesitant?

Kevin and I were actually talking about this the other day. I think earlier in our relationship, he really made a big deal about being private and keeping things to ourselves. So I guess I'm still in that habit of keeping things low key.

Why did you feel in the beginning of your relationship that you had to keep things low?

Honestly, I didn't feel that way. I've never really been the one to care about it too much. But I'm not the type to broadcast things, I think that's just me, I don't really broadcast things in general. So, I wouldn't broadcast our relationship, but I would never purposefully hide it or anything like that. But Kevin has always been a very private person so he always made a very strange deal about it, or he made a very strange deal about it earlier in our relationship. I think since then he's gotten over it a bit.

On the idea of public verses privacy in the relationship, do you think that he'd feel a way about you having this conversation now? Being that this would be public?

To be honest I don't know, but I feel like he would. Because I did tell him that I was going to have this interview and he wasn't opposed to it, but I guess maybe. He is definitely still the type to feel like I might be revealing too much.

Have you ever spoken to him about it? Why is privacy so important?

We've spoken about it and often times he'll say things like, "Oh, it's not that big of a deal, I just don't like people in my personal space." He actually said the other day, he doesn't know why he always took it so seriously because in retrospect it really isn't that big of a deal. So I think at the time, maybe because we were little bit younger, he maybe had a different mentality.

Have you ever felt like a secret?

I definitely did early on in our relationship. We had started dating in a kind of transitioning phase, becoming a little bit more than just friends with benefits. So I felt like for a little while there was a hint of 'let's not really put it out there yet, we're still not sure what this is.' I felt like for a while I didn't really care that much and I explained to him why I didn't care that much about it and he still cared about it, so I felt like he was definitely trying to hide. I thought he was doing that more so because I figured he had something else going on and he was trying to be free; he was definitely more on the Greek scene when we were in college.

Do you feel like he's your greatest love?

Yeah. I do really think so. I think the love that I share with Kevin is one that's definitely transcended beyond just a romantic love and I do really just love him as a person.

When we first got into a relationship I was still really captivated in that honeymoon stage and we'd gone through a lot. I've definitely grown and changed so much as a person that now the love that I have for him has really developed into the brotherly love. He's my best friend, things happen to me and I'm just like, "I can't wait to tell Kevin," or, "Oh my God, I have to call Kevin." If there is such a thing as soul mates or great love or things like that, he's definitely it for me. He represents a lot.

Do you see yourself being married to him?

Yeah, I do. At this point in my life I don't see anyone else that I would be marrying. I definitely don't say that in the sense of, *who else is it going to be,* but it's more so like I don't see anyone else that I would *want* to marry.

Does that kind of love ever scare you?

All the time. I get nervous that I'm investing so much in this, and leaving myself so open. At the end of the day, I whole heartedly believe that Kevin loves me back and that we are both 100 percent in this, but the truth is, anything could happen. People can change, situations can change people and it just really scares me. Because I don't want to be so invested. I don't want to be so invested and have my heart broken.

Have you ever had your heart broken?

You know, I think I have in different ways by different people, and I think heartbreak is going to happen. I'm not terrified of that happening but I think what I am afraid of is to have my heart broken by Kevin, knowing how much I really love him. I feel like that might be the one that really does a number on me, which would be a different type of pain.

What do you think is the secret behind the success of your relationship?

Want. I think it's that the both of us, maybe not always at the same time, but in points in our relationship, we both *wanted* it so much that we continue to go back, and continue to fight, and continue to deal with something that the other person was doing that maybe we didn't really want to deal with at that moment. But we try to get over that hump because of how much we really *wanted* the relationship.

I think right now we're in a stage where it's the both of us that want it, but it's not always like that. Sometimes I feel like I want it more than he does, sometimes I know he wants it more than I do because I know when I'm definitely not 100 percent in it. But I think we've both been able to feed off of each other in the sense where I want it sometimes, he wants it sometimes, but we both work really hard for it all the time.

How would you describe being happy in a relationship?

Kiana St Louis

I think being happy is when the both of you can find comfort in yourselves. When you guys can just be with each other and be 100 percent comfortable regardless of whatever it is that you're doing.

So, when Kevin and I went to Miami, we didn't really do much. We got an AirBnB, we went grocery shopping, cooked, and went to the beach. But we were so comfortable with each other. We laid on the couch and watched movies and we ate together and we were just 100 percent in our comfort zone *with* each other and it was just the happiest I've been with him in a really long time. So, I really feel like that's what it means to be happy in your relationship. To just be at peace and in place of comfort with the person that you're with regardless of where you are.

DAY SEVENTEEN: COMPROMISE

LOVE IS BALANCE.

I don't think I truly understood this balance until recently. Most times, I'd find myself at this place of confusion because I am constantly thinking of the things *I've* done in a relationship, or where *I* was in life, and what *my* expectations were. I've been confused because I didn't understand why I was ready for someone and they weren't ready for me. I didn't consider this balance. I didn't leave room for compromise.

Ricardo Picasso, 24, has a unique perspective on the concept of understanding. He reminded me that just as women go through our phases, need time and clarity, and set ourselves up for being ready for love, men do the same. And while we might not always understand this process, it is one that is essential for their growth and ultimately the future of our relationships. We're all different in our processes, but the hope for the result is the same. We just want to be ready for love. This is his story.

Tell me about your love life. Are you single, are you in a relationship, married, divorced?

Currently, I'm single. I've been meeting different women as usual, but it doesn't really transpire to anything much more. It's like 'did this, done that' I was going through five tendencies that I'm not really too fond of.

What are some of the tendencies that you aren't fond of?

I just have this big issue with people being themselves. I'm big on accepting people for who they are, but a lot of times, I don't feel like people are always genuine. One minute they're this awesome person, a friend, and then over time you start to see them differently. And it comes to you like: this isn't a friend, this is somebody that I may not really get along with. People start to do things that I don't like.

Are you looking to be in a relationship?

Honestly, yes. I am but I know what I want and I don't plan on settling. Until I find that little key piece, I don't feel like I should settle for a relationship because I do want to take a relationship serious. I don't want it to be like, "Oh well, you know, we're just dating, and oh, it didn't work out." I've done that enough in the past.

What do you think that key piece is, or do you think it's one of those things that'll come to you and you'll just know?

It's a little mixture of the two. I think everybody is different when it comes to what they're looking for. But for me, it is definitely about having that friendship and taking the time to understand my personality. I play a lot but I'm also very serious. So, I may be dead serious and I'll be laughing at the same time, but more or less I'm very serious about my feelings. Respect my feelings as a friend, but also be here as a lover, if that makes sense.

Yeah, I definitely think it does. I mean in all things you need a balance, and I think in love we kind of forget that. In relationships, you wear all these different hats. Sometimes, it's like, "Okay, I'm your girlfriend right now, so I may not be able to be as loose with you as I was when we were dating." But I think people are supposed to be flirty and fun. Sometimes people lose that spark. Maybe that could be a reason why things change or why people change.

That's definitely true. But also, it's a matter of being open and honest about how you feel. It may sound bad, but don't hide your feelings from me. If I did something that bothers you, I rather you tell me it bothers you and we talk about it and we get over it or we don't get over it, but don't hide. I want to see your real emotion. I'm a button pusher. I want to know what buttons to push, what's going to irritate you. I'm going to do things that I know probably is going to get on your nerves just so I can see how you'll react. I want to see how comfortable you get around me. I don't want it to be three years down the line and you're like, "I hated every time you made fun of me about my forehead, I've been insecure about my forehead my whole life." I want you to be open and honest at all times.

It's funny that you require such honesty, when I can't help but feel like a lot of the guys that I've known are the exact opposite. Are you as open with your feelings?

It takes time. It takes a certain level of trust. I try to do it little by little, I like to hang out and date. I like to say something and see how you react to it. Then see if I can be open with you at all, but I may not be as open as I do require. I can admit that. It's just because that's how I am. I'm not going to say I'm timid or I'm shy, but it takes a while for me to get comfortable with people.

Where does that stem from? That hesitancy of being open?

Believe it or not, when I was younger, it was more of an insecurity. It took a lot to accept somebody actually liking me for me. Growing up I was never really the ideal guy, the ideal person that people would be attracted to, so when I did try to express my feelings to people growing up, it was kind of like, "Stop playing. Oh, you not cool," "What're you talking about?" So, it made me become a shell at one point. That took a while to break out of but it's still there.

How long have you been single?

A couple of years. I've been single since 2012.

Has no one come along to fit your standards and hit the key point?

I'll say people have come along, but we weren't on the same page, so maybe they were that for me, but I wasn't that for them. And then vice versa. I feel like there's a little bit of both I haven't really found where it's equal.

Have you ever been in love before?

I haven't been in love, but I have love for someone, a lot of people.

What's the difference?

Being in love is just a certain type of feeling, a certain type of commitment. It's an experience that you share with that person. I'm not going to say that you can't share with anybody else, but it's somewhat unexplainable because you just get different types of emotions. Everybody loves for different reasons. And everybody falls in love for different reasons, but when you love someone it's like you deeply care about that person. You care about that person's health, you care about that person's well-being, and you want that person to do well. Having love is more of a natural feeling. Less commitment, or want, it's just natural.

Have you ever experienced a love or a girl that's gotten away?

I would say yes, but no because I feel like she got away when I wasn't ready. Maybe she prepared me for somebody else so I want to say yes because she was an amazing girl. If we were to interact today, mentally where I'm at now and where she was then, we'd be amazing together but I don't know. I want to say yes, but I also want to say no.

What is being *ready*?

As men, we have certain things that we live by. We're prideful and we can't help it. So, when you're ready you can be ready for different reasons. You can be ready financially, mentally, physically, emotionally. I don't think a lot of people balance those things out. When you're ready you have to be ready emotionally as man. If I'm not ready financially to be in a relationship, I should not be in a relationship. Emotionally, if I don't know which direction I want to take your feelings, I should not get in a relationship. If physically, I'm not satisfied with myself, I should not be in a relationship. This is because once you get into a relationship with this person, their problems will become your problems and vice versa.

When you start to care about somebody, you start to have love with somebody, believe it or not when something effects them it affects you. That's when you know you're ready, when you're ready to share that with somebody, and you're ready to not hurt them because you don't want to be in a relationship where you're just constantly hurting somebody over little actions.

Do you expect women to wait while you get ready?

No. I have, I used to. I used to think the ideal woman was, the girl that you meet when you're younger and then she waits for you to become the man that you are. I used to think that was the ideal woman because I thought that's what women were supposed to do, but I don't expect women to wait until I get ready. I appreciate it if you do, but I wouldn't advise anybody to wait. Because I know me personally, I act off of feelings so I feel you should do exactly how you feel. If you want to wait, I appreciate it. Amen to you, but I would not advise it.

If you could give any advice to a guy who wants to be ready but isn't ready yet, what would you say?

I'd ask them what they are actually looking for. Are you actually looking for a relationship? Are you just looking for someone to talk to? Once you know what you're looking for, know what you bring to the table, and know what you offer. Know your worth and be ready to work at it lot because women are a lot. They're great, but they are a lot. Know your worth, know what you bring to the table, and ask yourself are you willing to compromise?

Kiana St Louis

DAY EIGHTEEN: MEMORIES

THINGS END, BUT MEMORIES LAST FOREVER.

One of my close friends and I caught up this weekend, and of course a hot topic of conversation is always love. While she too pieces together the end of her relationship, we sat laughing as we traded old stories of our lovers. We recalled some of the funny moments we had, laughed at old videos, and smiled at our past. This was the first time in a long time, thinking back on my last relationship made me feel warm. A feeling I almost forgot.

But it was in that moment I realized how far I've come. Where I was February 8th and where I am today, looking back at who I was then and who I saw in the mirror this morning represent two different places; two different people. My memories have a lot to do with that growth. I used to think of us (my ex and I), and I'd try to recall days, conversations, anything specific, a sign as to when I was losing him. I'd think back to try and pinpoint *when* he started to give up. That wasn't helpful. But now, when I think back on us, I'm reminded of some of the inside jokes we shared that I still laugh at. I'll see clothes that remind me of some crazy shopping experience, or simply pass by his stop on the train and remember meeting up to go on some exciting adventure. I remember, and those memories have served as comfort to me.

Let's not get it twisted, I'm not holding on. In fact, I've never felt freer. I just rather smile as I let go, grudges are too heavy to hold. This comfort of my thoughts simply reminds me that while I may not have all the answers, or know who he is anymore, and I may never get closure -- I was happy once, really happy. And it was because of him. I cherish those memories, but more importantly I look forward to making new ones.

Dr. Seuss probably said it best: "Sometimes you will never know the value of a moment until it becomes a memory." I ran across this poem a long time ago in an urban fiction book entitled *True to the Game*, I think it's the perfect fit for this piece and the continuation of my story.

100 Days of Dating

I Reminisce

I reminisce for you

I reminisce the days

I try to forget

But the feelings never go away.

I reminisce for you

I reminisce the nights

For the things we did

And how it felt so right.

I reminisce for the love

For the love that was always there

I reminisce, I reminisce, and I know in my heart

That you really did care.

Even though my mind plays tricks on me

And I can't seem to let you go

I believe it's because you're still loving me

I reminisce, I reminisce

And the memories tell me so.

Kiana St Louis

DAY NINETEEN: A BEAUTIFUL RISK

THE UNKNOWN.

I've figured it out for the most part: Love is a risk. It's a risk to put all of your eggs in one basket. There's a risk in giving someone your heart. There's a risk associated with telling someone you love them and trusting that they truly love you too. People can say anything, do anything, be anyone they choose to be, but the hardest task is believing them.

Not everyone is a fraud. Some people will fight for you. Some people will honor you. Some people will say they love you and spend every day of their lives proving that to you. But when you've been burned so many times before, it's easy to want to shut the thought of love out. It's easy to become a narcissist. It's easy to lock love away and throw away the key. But then, by ignoring chance and avoiding the greatest risk of all, you miss what could be the most beautiful part of life: sharing it with someone else.

Julia Marcel, 24, was no different from that of an officer. A suited uniform and gun to match, standing in front of love's cell. She was determined to keep love detained. She was sure she'd never love again after life had its way with her. But then chance came along, and while she was stubborn, the heart always knows what it wants. We have to stop fighting that. We have to stop playing with our emotions and own up to them. Sometimes, it's the shoe you weren't looking for that could be the perfect fit. This is her story.

Tell me about your love life. Are you single? Are you married? Are you in a relationship? It's complicated?

I'm in a relationship.

How long have you guys been together?

Almost two years in June.

What do you think the secret is to keeping your relationship going?

100 Days of Dating

Communication and openness.

Is it a long distance relationship?

It depends what you consider long distance.

Well, what do *you* consider long distance?

Well, it's not so much a long distance relationship. We see each other when we want to see each other, or when we have time. But, it's just an hour away, an hour to 45 minutes away from each other. But sometimes it feels so much farther.

How do you personally deal, when you have those feelings of wanting to be with that person and can't?

Oh, I hate it. I call her phone so much and always face time her, or I'll just call to hear her voice and then I get over it.

Can you describe what it feels like to be with your lover?

When I'm with my lover, I feel like I'm a whole, like nobody else matters. Not even my best friend, at the moment. [*Do you see the shade? I'm definitely her best friend*] However, it's just such a wonderful feeling that I don't want to end, even when I have to go home, or go to work. It's just like, nah, I don't want to, but I know I have to.

What was it like in the beginning? Was it always as seemingly perfect as it is now?

No, in the beginning I actually didn't give her the time of day. She was very persistent. I started to like how things were going, we'd talk every day, and she would check on me. I started to let the other people I was talking to, go. Then we became a thing and that was really amazing.

When you say you were letting the other people go, there's kind of a risk when it comes to that because it's putting your focus all on her. Were you ever scared?

Of course I was scared. I was scared that I'm ... you know how people say don't put all your apples in one thing? That's what I did, but I felt like I was making a good decision. I was like all right, this is going to be it.

Do you think she is your greatest love?

I would have to say yes, by far. In my previous relationships, I thought that I was so in love. Well, with the first person that I loved, or that I think I loved, it wasn't as good as the second love. The first love didn't really count, so this is the second love, but I feel like it's better than the first love.

Why do you feel like this one is better?

This one's better because we understand each other more. I don't have trust issues. The communication is great, I'm not ashamed, and I don't have to worry about people cheating and all that. So, I guess it just boils down to trust.

You've felt ashamed in a relationship before, or to be with somebody?

No, but I did with her, my current girlfriend. I was kind of uneasy because it wasn't the ideal fit, you know? I'm usually into the preppy and cute. I shouldn't say cute, but it just wasn't what I was normally used to. She was the complete opposite.

Yet, she swept you off your feet?

Yes.

So would you say that moving forward, judging a book by a cover is something you'd never do?

Yeah. I think that should be thrown away, seriously. Because, she had dreads, I hate dreads! I wouldn't even talk to anybody if they had dreads. So, the fact that she had dreads, I mean, she doesn't have it now, but the fact that she had dreads, and I still talked to her, that's a lot for me. That's one of the things on my list: no dreads. So, yeah, you shouldn't judge a book by its cover.

What are some qualities that your partner must possess?

They have to be a go-getter. They have to be smart. I feel like they have to love me a little more than I love them, and they have to make me laugh.

You mentioned that she doesn't have dreads anymore. Did she cut them off because of you?

Well, she thinks she didn't cut it off because of me, but I influenced. I had something to do with that. I also encouraged her to get her license; I encouraged her to get a better job. I helped her get her car. Now we're working on getting this house. She's looking for another job. I'm constantly encouraging her to do better, and she does the same thing for me with school and other things.

Have you made changes for her?

I gave up my nasty attitude. I feel like I got so much better with communicating, altogether. My sisters even said that. She's really helped me. After I broke up with my ex, I had this wall up and I was just talking to whomever I wanted and I didn't have a care. I was kind of a bad girl, but I wasn't a bad girl. She made me break down that wall and she made me trust her. That's another thing she helped me do, I feel like I kind of went back to school for her.

It sounds like the two of you really have a positive influence on each other.

Right. That's how it should be though.

What were some lessons that you learned from taking your guard down and going in the direction that you wouldn't normally go for love?

Not everybody's going to do you dirty, and not everybody's going to do what the past did to you. I've learned that good things come out of the unexpected. If we were to break up, not to say that I would step out of my comfort zone again, but I would definitely give it a shot.

If you could tell her something that you've never told her ever before, what would it be?

Kiana St Louis

When we first started talking, I stopped talking to two other people that I used to talk to for her. I starting talking to them again, but it was just to see if I would ever do anything, or if I would ever cheat on her. But it didn't happen like that. That's how I knew I was getting serious about her. It was then that I knew I was really in this. So, that's one thing that I never told her. That's basically saying that I really love her and I found that out really early, but I never let her know. I was still hard and stuck, and my wall was still up. But she told me even though I had my wall, that she still loved me. I was in awe of that, I felt like that made it easier for me to talk to her.

100 Days of Dating

DAY TWENTY: DEAR SELF,

YOU CAN ONLY GIVE LOVE IF FIRST YOU LOVE YOURSELF

Self-love requires practice. As much as we may want to be more in tune with ourselves, to be real with who we are and what we're about, or to be comfortable being truly alone, like most things, getting there is a process.

Life is well known for causing drama when we don't need it. You can count on life to take people away from you unexpectedly, to surprise you, to challenge you, to uplift you, and sometimes to bring you down. While we strive for balance and understand its importance, the truth is we're human. And sometimes life can get the best of us. It can bring us to some of our lowest points; the points where it feels as if love can't even save us.

Talking to Sara Rodgers, 23, was like conversing with myself four months ago. Her thoughts, pain, confusion, and self-doubt is wrapped in a beautiful facade. Her thoughts of love mimic that of a mirage in the Sahara Desert; a concept she can see but is covered in her imagination. I realized that while these stories are helpful to talk about, talk through, and suggest relation, we don't always have the answers. Not every story is complete with a happy ending, but I've likened to the idea of finding happiness in life lessons. Sara has admitted to being broken, but is far from defeated. This is her story.

Tell me about your love life. Are you single? Are you in a relationship? Are you married? It's complicated?

I'm completely single. You're talking about presently, or like what I've been doing?

Presently.

On paper if I were to tell anybody, I'd be completely single. I'm dating here and there, but single.

What's the difference between what you've been doing and where you are now?

For the past three to four months I'd say, I've been spontaneously dating random guys through the magic of online dating and nothing has been working out. Intimacy is great and so is meeting new people with different personalities here and there. I guess the worst part is that they're all great guys. They're all good, genuine people, it's just I never feel the connection, so I just decided to give it up because I'd rather not give my authentic self to somebody I don't want to say doesn't deserve it, but they deserve something better than what I can give right now. Does that make sense?

Yeah, I think so. It sounds like you're just in an unfamiliar place that you're also trying to figure out.

Yeah. I don't think I'm necessarily ready for a relationship, not to say that I feel like I couldn't be the best girlfriend in the world, I really think I could. I think I'd be that type of girlfriend that'd be like, "Yes, you look good daddy." I could easily boost his ego. It's just hard to feel like, which sounds terrible, that somebody would be worth it. You can date and go out and have a lot of fun and even be intimate, but to put a title on somebody and have somebody put a title on me is the hardest thing. I just can't give that to somebody.

Why is it hard? The title should be the easiest part if you know it's real, no?

I'm a people person, so I like connections, emotional spirituality, things like that; it's not hard for me to connect to people that really like to get into depth about their fears, their emotions. But I think it's the whole concept of, when you put a title on somebody, you're essentially telling the whole world, whether it's your family, your friends, social media, etc. What if it falls apart and then you get embarrassed because you invested all your time in this person? Whether they felt they were going to be your husband, your boyfriend, the person who was going to change your life, you could end up looking like a fool.

100 Days of Dating

I think that's why I do this casual dating thing, where you keep it a secret or it's just between you two, like an intimate relationship or *situation-ship*, that's what I call them. Eventually, it all falls apart and I never really feel any emotional tie to it because I never emotionally invested myself. But the other person kind of opens up to me which sounds terrible, but that's what usually happens.

Where did the restriction of opening up stem from?

It's kind of funny, I was reading a self-help book like three days ago about it. I'd say my dad. I was exposed and trained to believe that I wasn't enough as a woman and I wasn't capable of relationships or marriage because I didn't know how to do the cooking and cleaning, and just be a domestic housewife. To be docile and sweet because I was always aggressive, I was always loud; I was really into books when women weren't supposed to be educated. To my dad, we're supposed to be submissive. Growing up, when I got into my first six-year relationship, I thought it was ideal. I tried to act the way men assume you're supposed to act in a relationship and my personality was too strong. I really tried to tone it down the entire relationship, but then I got older. I got more mature.

I started reading, I started experiencing new cultures, new arts, and being exposed to so many things just made me realize that it's so hard for me to personally limit myself to one person and one thing because I'm confusing myself. How can you ever be enough and how can they ever be enough for you when you're always going to want more? That's my biggest flaw, I'm always going to strive for greatness and strive for more.

So you don't want to be in a relationship?

I don't aspire to have relationships or a marriage of any sort. It's not something that would make me happy. It's one of those things I feel like a lot of women feel they need to be satisfied and having that makes them accomplished.

I'm not necessarily afraid of being alone, that's not something I want, but if someone was to come into my life that was *worth it* and also believed I was worth it -- having patience and taking time to get to know each other, dating, learning each other's flaws, good points, bad points, -- I would try to see where it could go. But at the point that I'm in in my life right now, I just don't see a relationship or something serious happening now.

Describe *worth it*. What would somebody who's worth it look like to you?

It has nothing to do with physical appearance. Even though six-pack abs are great, because I value health, nutrition, and fitness, so someone who takes care of their body and is in tune with health and wellness is a big deal to me. That's definitely on the list, someone sharing the same values that I have, especially nutrition-eating well because I can't be with someone who tries to put me down on things that I'm passionate about. The number one thing that would make a person worth it that I haven't found yet, and I'm not sure is even possible, is to find someone who can handle all of the pain that I've been through and be able to accept it. I want someone to help me grow and build through it versus someone who's scared of all that I've been through and doesn't know how to handle me at my worst and my best.

You mentioned enjoying the secrecy/less public life of just dating. I know personally, that's something I've battled with, especially in my last relationship. I wanted to show him off, I wanted to show us off. Not even just to *show* but I wanted to share with people how happy this person made me, but in the back of my mind, there was always a risk of, "Damn, I don't want to look stupid." Why do you think we automatically assume the worst when it comes to public affection?

100 Days of Dating

We're millennials, so from the days of Beebo and Sconex, Zenga, MySpace, (yeah I'm taking it back), people have been looking like fools. People have dedicated pages toward happiness forever. They'd be together for two days, two months, two years, and then they cry and they're embarrassed because the relationship ends because someone cheated or it just didn't work out. It's like you invested making this whole page, you're editing these pictures, doing the lighting. You're going out on these trips with this person to Greece, California, and then you come back and you just get embarrassed.

I don't know if you've ever seen these memes, but you can find out a person's marital status through what they post on social media subliminally. You shouldn't even be able to determine that, but it's just a society we live in today and I don't ever want to be that person that invested my time. I never want to be like I posted this person's face and not his watch on my social media and he ends up never texting me back or not calling me. I got rejected so many times. I loved hard once; only once in my life and it was unrequited. I guess I'm just never going to try to put myself back out there again.

Never say never. We do these crazy things and we love hard because love is a risk. Love makes us foolish. At what point do we accept that and just continue to learn as opposed to winning or losing?

I think it's all just a matter of putting yourself out there and to keep trying it. Love shouldn't be a game but honey, it just feels like it is. You go out there and try to play your cards. Another thing is, people are just faking it the entire time. No, let me not say everyone, because that's not true, but people put on this façade when it's the honeymoon stage of a relationship. They'll be this good and genuine person. I think it just connects back to what I was saying before. When someone finds out your true pain or your true story or what you've been through or your family background, whatever is considered unholy or not nice, the person backs away.

Kiana St Louis

Do you keep repeating the cycle of people finding out your story or finding out your flaws and get rejected over and over again? You're trying to do this, and then if you get to a point of maybe this person will accept you for who you are. Then you could tell them all the bad stuff later because they're already trapped.

Love is a trap?

I don't want to say a trap, but I think that just accounts to one of my flaws. In a relationship, you have to sacrifice a piece of yourself for somebody else. I understand that could be very controversial, but I do personally feel that when you're in a relationship, you're limiting yourself in some way. Even the little things like something as unconscious as, "I'm not going to wear this dress because I know that it would probably upset him." I want the freedom to be able to do everything when I want. I just don't ever want to be limited.

You mention your flaws quite a bit. What do you think you have to offer that makes *you* worth it?

That's a very good question. I guess right now I'm on the path of trying to discover the whole self-love thing, because it was something I was never really taught. Women often criticize themselves and put themselves down, so for me to even talk about the positives is very hard because I legit don't know. Besides physical appearance, because it's what people tell you. "You're a beautiful black girl." But I'm more than my hazel eyes, my skin, and my hair, but that's all ever people really see when they look at me.

I do believe that I'm patient. I have a good heart. I'm a genuine good person and I've been through a lot to understand what pain is like for somebody else and what struggle and what adversity is. I guess the one good thing that I could say that I would give to somebody is I would always be his motivator. I'd be their cheerleader. I'd be the person in the back or the front, whatever they want to help build them into the man that I know they could be. If you're asking if I have a whole bunch of money or a whole bunch of emotions and affections and all that to give, it's just something I don't see right now. I just don't honestly believe that I'm capable of love or someone's capable of loving me.

100 Days of Dating

DAY TWENTY-ONE: LET GO?

LET GO AND LET GOD.

I've heard this before. I know to do this. I know I can only move if he guides me. Yet, I'm still stuck.

I'm still stuck because I beg for signs from Him, but I'm not sure I've received them.

If this isn't where I should be, move me Lord. If we are not meant to be, free me from this love spell Lord. I love him, but if this isn't right for me, show me Lord.

All I've heard is silence. Maybe that's the sign.

To You Again
By Mary Szybist

Again this morning my eyes woke up too close
to your eyes,

their almost green orbs
too heavy-lidded to really look back.

To wake up next to you
is ordinary. I do not even need to look at you

to see you.
But I do look. So when you come to me

in your opulent sadness, I see
you do not want me

to unbutton you
so I cannot do the one thing

I can do.
Now it is almost one a.m. I am still at my desk

Kiana St Louis

*and you are upstairs at your desk a staircase
away from me. Already it is years*

*of you a staircase
away from me. To be near you*

*and not near you
is ordinary.*

*You
are ordinary.*

*Still, how many afternoons have I spent
peeling blue paint from*

*our porch steps, peering above
hedgerows, the few parked cars for the first*

*glimpse of you. How many hours under
the overgrown, pink Camillas, thinking*

*the color was wrong for you, thinking
you'd appear*

*after my next
blink.*

*Soon you'll come down the stairs
to tell me something. And I'll say,*

*okay. Okay. I'll say it
like that, say it just like*

*that, I'll go on being
your never-enough.*

*It's not the best in you
I long for. It's when you're note less,*

*numb at the ends of my fingers, all is
all. I say it is.*

DAY TWENTY-TWO: DON'T GIVE UP ON LOVE

DESPITE IT ALL, I STILL BELIEVE

I believe that love is attainable despite heartbreak. I believe being single can be a sign of strength for both women *and* men. I believe time and love work together in harmony to create an authentic sound that we dance to in this life thing. I still believe in love.

Rachel Junes, 41, brought me to this realization. She reminded me that love comes with struggle, and that struggle isn't always rooted to being with someone. You have to get to a point of being completely comfortable with where you are in life, with who are you are, and understand that every situation we're in, regardless of how long, is only temporary. We won't hurt forever. We won't be sad forever. We won't be single forever (unless you're into that sort of thing). The point is, the show must and will always go on, we just have to remember to keep playing our part. This is Rachel's story.

Tell me about your love life. Are you single, in a relationship? Married? Divorced? It's complicated?

I am single. And I've been single for quite some time. But I think I'm okay with it. Before, I wasn't but since I've been single, it's been beneficial to me. I needed to get out of this bad relationship that I was in and the drama that came with it. Plus, I just wanted to cut all ties with men and focus on myself, focus on bettering my life and just taking time to get to know me and not have to worry about anybody else.

You said you've been single for a long time. How long?

About eight years. A long time.

Do you want to be in a relationship?

I do, I think that now since I've accomplished so much in my life, I think I'm ready for one but I'm hesitant because I'm very scared. I haven't been with someone in a long time. I'm very independent, I don't know if I'm able to share my time with someone else. I still have a lot of stuff going on in my life, but I think I am ready. But it's just the fear factor of dealing with someone else.

Tell me about your greatest heartbreak. Does that have something to do with your fear?

Yeah, that was the last guy. I felt like I was the side chick. We'd meet and spend time together and I thought we hit it off really well. But on Valentine's Day, we were supposed to have an all-day hangout and I didn't hear from him for hours.

He was saying, "I'm gonna come, I'm gonna be right there." And nothing. Then towards the end of the time, he told me he was doing one thing, but he was doing something totally different, and I found out he was with someone else on that day. When I broke it off, he kept trying to stalk me, trying to talk me, and saying I'm overreacting. I found out a lot of lies about him after the fact so that was a window that opened up to show me that someone that I gave my all to could really do that to me.

It was very heartbreaking. And on Valentine's Day! So, I was just like, "That's it, I can't deal with this. I cut you off." I cut everyone off. I needed to regroup.

What would your ideal guy would look/be like?

I'd still like someone who's tall, I'd like someone who's warm, who's so funny that I could just laugh myself to sleep. Someone who's caring, someone who's family-oriented. Someone who's a go-getter. Someone who is about his business. Someone that cares for me to the point where they would do anything to make sure that I am happy, I'm satisfied, but also knows how to love and take care of himself so that he doesn't seem like someone who has issues. Someone who likes to travel, have fun, see the brighter things in life, instead of being a Debbie Downer all the time. He has to be a sharp dresser. And just loves the Lord, that's the number one. That's someone that I'm looking for.

Do you think that if you remain afraid you'll meet this person?

It's hard for me to trust anyone. There's all these psychos out here right now. You can put your trust in someone but the next minute, they do something totally different and it's like, "That's not the same person I met," it's scary. You watch the news, you see things that go on in the news with people that meet online and they just do something dramatic, like kill you or something sick. I don't know there are so many factors that make me scared to date.

I want to date, but there comes a point where I have to let God direct my path, because if I choose someone, I feel like I'm going to make the biggest mistake, like the last person I had. So with all these factors, I'm just trying to play it by ear, I want to make sure that whoever I'm with, I need to take my time, get to know them, to make sure that this is something that I want to get into.

I feel like when it comes to love, there are two types of people. You have the ones that are like, "No, I need to be in love right now because I'm at a certain age." Then you have the ones who are seemingly carefree, "Whatever happens, happens." Where do you fall?

I used to be that type. I'm getting older. I'm at a certain age right now. But I think that at this point, I rather not rush it. I'd rather take my time. I don't want to jump into something that I'm going to regret just for love, just to get married at a certain time, just to get a baby at a certain time. All that doesn't matter to me.

I could be 50-years-old and if I don't find someone at that time, I would wait for love because I know that the time will come. I don't want to feel like I'm pressuring myself just because time is running out. I've accepted the fact that maybe … I may not have children, or I may not be married at a certain age, and I'm okay with it. I'd rather have someone that loves me and I love them and it's genuine, and I'll wait. Because I don't want to rush into something and then it's suddenly I'm back to square one again, not trusting anybody. I don't want that, I feel like I have a lot of love to give, and I definitely want to be in a relationship, but I'm willing to take my time to wait for it. I've waited this long and I'll wait a little longer.

What are some of the steps that you take to put yourself out there? While trust is a big thing for you, seems like you do have a goal of wanting to be with somebody.

My co-worker was just saying, "What are you doing to put yourself out there? You've been single for a long time. Have you done Internet dating? Have you done the dating app?" I said, "No!" He goes, "Well, how you gonna knock it until you try it?" I said, "I want to try it, but you know, it's just a different type of dating for me." I'm used to meeting somewhere on the street, going out to a lounge or a club or a restaurant. Or maybe happenstance, like, waiting at a bus stop and someone pulls up and says, "Hey, I think you're cute, can I drive you to a bus stop?"

That happened to me, seriously.

You got in the car?

I did!

What!?

Because at first, I was like, "Okay, who are you? I'm not getting in the car with you." And I was so late, the bus was not coming. He goes, "Please. I have a Coca-Cola uniform on and my partner's in the other car over there. We just did a delivery. I just think you're cute and I want to give you a ride to wherever you need me to go." So I look, I didn't see a bus. I said, "Okay, let me go in the car." He was like, "That could work out." This guy and I could have still been together 'til this day, but that's a long story in itself.

But I like stuff like that, so I could tell our story like, "Yeah, your father hit me up at a bus stop." I love stories like that. I don't want to say, "Oh yeah, I met him on a dating app." I mean it sounds so crazy, but my co-worker said, "Don't knock it 'til you try it." So I promised myself that within the next two months, I'm going to try to do a dating app or online dating for like a thirty-day period just to see what's out there. I'm going to try to go outside, even if I'm by myself, to dinner ... or just put myself out there. I love being around my friends, I love to go out with my friends, but I need to do this for myself, just to see if it works.

100 Days of Dating

Do you remember what it felt like to be in love?

It was such a long time ago. But if I think about it, I do remember. It was fun, it was warm, and it was cool to snuggle up with someone and watch your favorite movie or have dinner and to have good conversation, go out on a date, stuff like that.

Showing love for someone that's not a family member. I miss that. I think there were periods in my life, experiences that I wish I had someone that loved me, to be there with me during the worst times. But I think that it was okay for me to be by myself, because at that time, I don't think being in a relationship would have helped. But now that I've been past that storm, I think I'm ready to fall back in love again, so I could know what it would feel like this time around.

Now that I'm much older, I'll be a little more mature in how I love someone, so that it won't feel like, it's something that's happening right now. It's something that I want to be long-term. Longevity. A long-time love like my parents. They've been together 52 years and I want that kind of love. I think once I prepare myself mentally to be there, I could definitely fall in love and get back to that place.

Are you happy?

I am. I am. I am a little bit.

It's like in movies, your voice was indecisively fluctuating like, "I am. I am?"

I'm thinking about, and it's like, "Question mark? Question mark? Period. Exclamation."

But that's the thing, happiness I'm not sure is something that you can think of or dictate. It's something you feel.

Yeah. I think I have my happy moments and I also have my sad moments. But at this moment, I think I'm happy. I feel like I'm happy. I could be happier. But I'm happy.

What advice would you give to somebody who is in your situation?

I would tell them, "Don't give up on love." Even when you take a little break, love can happen again. Love is out there. Once you have faith and know that God is going to put that person in your path, I know that it can happen. Don't feel like you will never fall in love again. Love happens to the best and worst of us.

You have to make sure that you are ready for it, though. Because you've been alone, don't act like you can't be a loving person anymore. You still have it in you. Just love yourself and you'll find that person to share the love with. But don't give up. It's still out there.

DAY TWENTY-THREE: NEVER BEEN IN LOVE

LOVE?

Russian playwright and story writer Anton Chekov once said *"I've never been in love. I've dreamt of it day and night, but my heart is like a fine piano, no one can play because a key is lost."*

I thought that was so bazar. What does he mean he's *never* been in love? Surely, everyone has experienced love in some form at least once in their life. I understand love is not the same everywhere to everyone, and loving someone and being in love with someone are two different things – but to have *never* loved just seemed unbelievable.

Until I sat with Apiyo Osanya, 54, who too is a stranger to being in love. The idea of love is foreign to her. Unlike many of the women I've spoken to or have come to know, while she is aware of love's wizardry, she's never once been under its spell. However, this doesn't stop her from wanting to find it. It hasn't slowed down any part of her life, yet, there is still something seemingly missing.

Apiyo exudes strength and beauty always, her energy belongs in a class of its own, and she needs nothing from no one. She craves a freedom and connection so rare that it should trump the traditional standards of love, despite what society says she should be doing in your fifties. But I do believe love is ageless. While she might not know what love is today, I believe there's always tomorrow. This is her story.

Tell me about your love life. Are you single? Married? Dating? It's complicated?

It might get complicated at times but I consider myself single and I'm dating. I have two options.

Spicy. How's that working out for you?

There's a guy I met on *OKCupid*, Terry. He's 51, which is annoying because he still manages to be younger than me, but he's over 50 so that's good. That one has been a bit interesting because he's in a weird place. He is a present parent and he's been divorced for four years. I think he is still working a lot of shit out. In terms of the aftermath of the marriage, he has to deal with the ex because of the children. I don't know where he wants to be in terms of relationships. He clearly wants to date, but he doesn't want to be in anything serious, so there's all of that.

We really click, we enjoy each other's company, but he tends to not really communicate it in a way that I would prefer. He doesn't directly talk about things. I feel it's kind of this on again, off again thing. So, we recently reconnected after being off for a couple of months. I have no idea where that is going to go.

And then the other guy, I reconnected with him. He is someone I met a while ago, but he is younger. Considerably younger, but I really like this guy. He is also divorced, two kids. Doesn't really want to get back into anything, it's a May-December thing that just works for us. There's just this connection there. I think we both have gone through some changes because we have just reconnected after not seeing each other for a couple of years. It feels good.

I know it's not going to be anything, but I've learned with him that that's okay. And it's okay with me, because relationships are difficult and they are time consuming. And I am at that stage in my life where I need space. I need my own space. I need time to myself. So it works out that way.

So, you don't want to be in a relationship?

The kind of relationship that I would prefer or that would work for me, I use Oprah and Stedman as an example. They have their individual lives and they have been together for a very long time. They have their separate abodes, which is very important.

I don't want to be married, and I don't want to live with anybody. But I do want to be in a relationship that is monogamous. Where the two of you are a couple, but it doesn't have to be that weird living together, we're doing everything together, always hang out with each other's friends. It doesn't have to be that. But that connection is what is important to me.

Why don't you want to get married?

I've lived with someone for ten and half years, and it was very difficult. So, I've been exposed to marriage or *what marriage could be*. But I think I just like the idea of freedom. Marriage is nice because you are one with a person, you become a unit, the world sees you as one, and that can be nice and that can work. Maybe it makes me feel constricted. I don't know, but I don't feel the need to be married. I do like being in a relationship, a monogamous relationship. An emotionally committed relationship.

I guess, another part of the reason I don't want to be married is because I feel you don't have to be married to be in a loving relationship with someone. That doesn't require marriage. The relationship just requires mutual respect, friendship, and love.

Have you ever been in a committed relationship?

No.

Did you love the person that you lived with for 10 years?

I didn't get the chance to because things went downhill very fast. It was very sad. He's a difficult person and there were a lot of things going into it that I wasn't aware of that I learned about the hard way, and it was hard. I found out that there's some people you just cannot help. He was just too far gone. He's the way he is and it's just never going to get better. I did my best, but I ended up enabling him because in trying to help and change and work with him, I was out of my depth. I just had enough with him.

Do you think that experience jaded the way that you now live and view love?

Definitely. Even though I understand that is not what all marriage will be like. Relationships are so difficult and then in this day in age nobody wants to *try* in relationships. Everybody wants no strings attached. Friends with benefits, right? They want the benefits of a relationship without putting the effort in. So, I don't know if it can ever be achieved. I don't know what that is. I don't know if that's the new millennium, or the way things are going. Is it really because so many men are being raised by single women? That's what a lot of men are trying to say.

They don't have male examples. So, I don't know what the reason is. I've been thinking about that a lot and trying to figure out why that is. That's what I was saying with this young guy. I think we understand each other better because he's matured and he's doing well. His life is going the way he needs it to be. He's happy and he's doing well.

I've accepted certain things, but we keep coming back to each other, so I know that there's something there. There's this bond, so now we have this affection for each other. I wouldn't say he's in love with me, but the most I'll say is there's this affection.

Have you ever been in love?

I don't know. I don't think so. I think I've wanted to be. I don't think I really have been. Because I think of all of the men I've dated, and it really hasn't been that many, because when I date someone, I tend to be with them for a while. It's just how I am. I just know that in love feeling, whatever that is, I don't think I've ever experienced it. I don't even know if I would be able to recognize it, if I did. I just don't know what that would feel like.

Like, do you know what it feels like to be in love?

Yeah.

Yeah? And how did you feel when you were in love?

Elated. It's a constant high. It's like you're floating. You're high in the air but you're not afraid because you turn around and you're with someone. Then you realize you're floating because of that person. You know you're taking a risk, you both are, but you're not afraid. If anything, that fear is replaced with comfort. To be in love is a terrifying comfort.

No I can definitely say it now, no I have not had that kind of feeling with anyone. But I do know what it's like for someone to make you feel good about the fact that they're part of your life when you're with them. And it goes back to this young guy. You know he's 22 years younger than I am. He was 26 when we met and I didn't know that.

Oh shit.

He went after me to be honest. I saw him and was like "oh he's cute." But he's young, I was 48 at the time.

Dude, you're a MILF.

I know! (laughs) I hate that term.

Being that you've never been in love, have you ever experienced heartbreak?

Oh, I've had heartbreak. The person who broke my heart, I mean truly broke my heart was my best friend in high school.

How would you describe being happy?

I think being happy is when you feel everything is right in your world, for the people that you care about, and yourself. You know, when things are going well. Your job is going well, you don't have to worry about paying rent, or paying the next bill. You don't have to worry that somebody is ill, and you can't help them in any way. Everything is going well and especially with the people what you care about. That's all, you're happy. There is nothing to be unhappy about.

So as long as you're satisfied with yourself and you feel that you're doing what you're supposed to be doing for yourself, then yeah you're happy.

DAY TWENTY-FOUR: YOUNG LOVE

COLLEGE SWEETHEARTS.

Young love: A bond between two youthful kindred spirits, seemingly unafraid of the unknown, instead they welcome it. This kind of love is hopeful, pure, exciting, can often be complicated, but worth the work. It is the reminder of love being ageless, a reminder that love is often in the place unexpected with a person you might not have thought. This kind of love requires an endurance to swat away temptation, a level of unique trust in a world of external influences, faith, teamwork, communication, and an openness to maturity.

I've seen a love like this. I've felt a love like this, temporarily. I want a love like this now. But even in its youth, love needs boundaries. Love needs honesty. A lasting love needs to be matured on both ends, something I've once overlooked.

Dominic Rivera, 23, stands body deep in his youthful love. It was in his freshman year of college that love swept him off his feet, pushed his plans aside, and demanded maturity. It demanded a level of growth necessary to admit his faults. A level of vulnerability to change his behaviors if it meant doing right by his woman. A level of strength to realize this love can and should attribute to his growth as a man. Truth is, this love thing doesn't have to be half as hard as we make it. If you want something, you work to keep it. Period. Dominic is working overtime, so what's our excuse? This is his story.

Tell me about your love life. Are you married? Are you single? Are you in a relationship?

I'm in a relationship. We've been together going on five and half, six years. We don't know when we first started dating, but we met at college orientation, the rest is history.

I feel like this is such a unique situation for the simple fact that most young men get to college with a mentality that says, "Every girl is going to be mine." How did you manage to have an opposite mindset?

I guess that was my mindset when I was first going to school, because I went to an all-boys private high school. But when my girl and I first met, we had to talk about that. We basically said, "I'm not ready for a relationship right now." I admit that I said that in the beginning and then it completely changed. Once you meet a person that you feel you can really connect with, everything goes out the window. Your plans go out the window when the right person comes around. I think that's your change.

Would you classify this as your greatest love?

Yeah because I feel like when you're younger you don't really know much. All you know is shit from TV, and not even my parents really talk about that. But when you're older you start to understand relationships. Now that I'm able to make my own decisions, able to make my own moves, this love is definitely the greatest honor because I'm fully in control.

Have you been in love before?

Nah, not really, not like this. You have love for certain people, but when you look back at it, you realize the difference. This is my first time.

What do you think makes your girlfriend "the one"?

Mentally, we both want the same things in life. Meeting someone at college is a big thing. People can meet each other anywhere – at a party or whatever, but when your place is at college, you both know that you are elevated to a certain point in your life, and the goal is to be somewhat successful. That's a major part of knowing that was the person for me; her personality, really being able to talk about anything. It's really weird because it's hard to explain. Sometimes you know in your heart, you just bond with a person, you just know this is the move right here.

You just know, you really connect with a person or you feel comfortable around them, their family, everything. There's different stages of relationships. First, you get to know each other. Then you get to see how it is to stay around this person. So, you check off different things, you get around their family. There's always something that people think is going to be a deal breaker in a relationship. If everything is still going forward, I know for a fact this is definitely it. Six years later, everything is still fun.

I know what that feels like. But I've found when it comes to men, even when they believe strongly that they've found the one, they'll still think it's greener on the other side. Have you ever had those thoughts?

I think as a man you will always be able to have those thoughts. But you always have to bring yourself to the reality that if you have somebody you know is down for you 100%, loyal to you, it's just really not worth it. Not every thought needs to be acted upon. I think that comes with maturity.

Even back to the earlier question about this being your greatest love. My greatest love is definitely this just, because of the fact that I'm much more mature and I know down the line what's important as far as somebody that you see yourself with, having children with, and stuff like that.

Leaving to be with somebody else? That's corny, because at the end of the day, you got to think about, was this the wrong one? Even if you do get to a day where you had a crazy ass argument, you're tired of each other, shit like that, you have to just hold it down. I think it just comes with a level of maturity for a lot of guys. I think all guys in general are going to have those thoughts. There's Instagram, the internet, you see pretty girls everywhere. It is what is. We know everybody looks good, but at the same time, you have to know, I got this person I met. Out of the billions and trillions of people in the world, I found the person I connect with on every level imaginable. It's not worth it to have a sexual experience with somebody if you connected with your person, like Sam, so to speak.

Did you have prior qualities that you wanted your girlfriend to have before meeting Sam? If so, did those preferences change at all?

Yeah. I guess in a weird way I wanted to be the breadwinner and wanted my girl to be laid back, chill, fly, take trips, etc. But then I meet somebody like Sam, that's really bossed up, it was just the way she let me take control. Even though I like nice things and can be materialistic, she reminded me to make sure I have all my shit together before I focus on the materials and unimportant shit.

Sam is hardworking, she's smart, and she definitely motivates me. At first I just wanted to spoil my girl, she'd just be living her life, and I'm making a little money. But I know Sam would never just be that type of person. So it's like, damn, I found somebody who's whole style is different. I needed somebody that definitely was independent on her own, she doesn't need me for nothing. Now it's a team. If I look out for her, she could look out for me too.

So what do you think the secret is to you and Sam? How do you two keep it going?

There's really no secret. As two adults, you have to be able to have a conversation with each other when things get heated. You have to be able to sit down and just listen to what each other says after an argument, and let one another speak and explain their gripe with the situation or what they're upset about. You have to listen to each other, that's a major key.

Giving each other space when it's necessary. A lot of people, when stuff goes wrong, they feel they have to check on each other all the time. I think what works is being able to give each other space, clear your mind, and then being able to go back after. Even if it's a day later and have that conversation with each other. Not that it's always that easy every time, because obviously arguments have happened.

But when you listen to a person, and you really take time to affirm what they say, you learn more about yourself and how to grow. When I was in school, I used to be wild, drinking all the time, acting crazy, Sam would tell me I look crazy and that she hated that. I mean I still go out, you know I always go out, but it's just a thing of she didn't like that about me. I was able to take that, and say, 'Yo, I'm not trying to get drunk, blacking or falling out or all that shit no more. I'm not going to do that. I'm going to have one or two drinks and keep it chill."

You have to grow up and mature. So, if a person comes to you with an issue in your relationship, instead of finding a way to make an excuse for it, really take a moment to listen to that and try to change that about yourself and see how you feel about it.

What advice would you would give to young men who are still playing with women that could possibly be the one, yet they're just not ready or mature enough to realize it?

If you know for a fact that this person is not the one, don't string somebody along. Don't do shit like that, that's the worst thing to do. If you're just trying to talk or mess with someone, you need to let them know that from the jump. If, for a fact you know, you got a person that's down for you, but you really are taking that for granted, you need to really mature up, do what you need to do. Be the person you know you can be for that person, because based on how they treat you, everything could really work out for you.

At the end of the day, we all live to grow old, to see the future, so you need to always be thinking about the future. Don't live for the moment, live for the future.

DAY TWENTY-FIVE:
IT'S TIME TO KNOW YOUR WORTH

POETRY SOOTHES THE SOUL.

I found this poem the other day and thought it would be a perfect addition to this journey I'm sharing with you all. I hope this touches you the way it's touched me.

It's Time to Know Your Worth

By: Diedre Dixon

Like a 2-carat diamond set in platinum cut in the princess shape
The value of it really began while it was in its original state
Like fine wine that has matured for years and developed exquisite taste
The value of it really started in the vineyard when it was only grapes
Like caviar that is served at affairs that are the most prestigious
The value of it is determined while it is just an egg inside of a fish
Like a dozen red roses brilliantly arranged and presented in a crystal vase with Baby's Breath all around
The value of them really began in Spring when they were just planted seed in the ground
Like fine art displayed in an intricately carved frame and placed in a mansion for all to admire

The value of it really started as a canvas, a variety of colorful paints and an artist who was inspired
Though all of these things have great qualities, are expensive and, in some cases, are priceless
Only someone with the knowledge of their worth will go beyond the desire of these things to possess

They will care for these things no matter what the expense because they are the desires of their heart
Surely, your life is worth much more than diamonds, wine, caviar, roses or a frame that displays fine art
Like a diamond you have endured the test of time and have resisted the hardest of things
Like fine wine you have matured with time and joy to all who know you your smile brings
Like the delicacy of caviar you deserve to be treated like a woman of prestige and grace
Like a dozen long-stemmed red roses you are cherished, loved and embraced
Like fine art you should be adorned like a queen in her court and royally respected
You should realize your value as a woman, mother, grandmother and great grandmother who won't be neglected
Forget about mistakes made in the past that only come back to lie about what you deserve
God has forgiven you for the apologies of your heart; He was listening and He has heard
There is so much for you to gain in life, if you would allow life to give you these pleasures
You must believe that nothing is too good for you to possess; even the desires your heart treasures
There is a plan and a purpose with you in mind; it's the reason your mother gave birth
I said all of this to say to you, "It's time you know your worth."

100 Days of Dating

DAY TWENTY-SIX: FOUNDATION FOR LOVE

GOD MUST BE AT THE ROOT OF IT ALL.

We know that God must be the center of whatever it is that we do, are doing, and have done in order to succeed. We pray for guidance for exams, jobs, and huge life decisions, but how many of us take the time to acknowledge the guidance we need in our relationships? Or more importantly, the guidance we need for ourselves before even getting into a relationship?

Brianna Daley, 25, reminded me of the foundation of God which is necessary to create anything long lasting with someone. Loving someone doesn't mean losing yourself in that person, or even allowing them to make you *whole*. You should be whole already, you should be certain of yourself before entering a relationship, you should be strong in your character before falling in love. Easier said of course, but getting it done is where faith comes in. There is no rush to this love thing. There is no competition, no right or wrong answers to any of this. But we do have time, we should appreciate our lessons, and then remain open to the willingness of learning to implement those lessons to what we do and who we're with. We need a foundation in our lives. We need foundation in our love, for without it, how will it grow? God is love, something Brianna not only remembers but lives by. This is her story.

Tell me about your love life. Are you single? Are you married? In a relationship?

I'm in a relationship and we've been together for three and a half years.

That's awesome. You sound really happy to say that, which is great. How would you describe the dynamic of your relationship?

I feel like Mo and I are just two peas in a pod. We just get each other. Of course we obviously have similarities. That's why we get along and stuff, but I appreciate the differences. I guess we do have a good dynamic; we can talk to each other and we're very open. I feel like we're very like-minded, so it just makes it easy to communicate.

We've always heard that opposites attract. Is it ever complicated sometimes being too like-minded in the relationship?

In the beginning, I would think, "Oh, we're not going to work," or, "We're not even going to be anything" because I thought he was way too hype for me. I'm calmer compared to him. I felt like he always needed excitement. I think as he grew up, he chilled out. I don't think it works against us. If we do differ on something, it's okay. It just makes me appreciate that person more because we're so alike in so many ways, but we are different in certain things.

Being that your partner has chilled out a bit, have you gotten more hype at all to compromise in a way?

I feel like I'm not a pumped person up in public, but I can definitely be that way with my friends. I can get crazy. I can just be myself. I'm able to reveal that side to him because I'm not like that with everyone.

Would you classify this as your greatest love?

Yes, for sure. He's the best, DJ Khaled voice.

Have you been in love prior to him?

I thought so, but nope.

Which begs the question, what is love to you? How would you define it?

Well for sure, God is love. So to me, if He is not the foundation you are sure to fold. It's written in the Bible, love is patient and love is kind. I'm a bad Christian; I don't know the whole verse, but love is just all things good. But just because love is all things good, that doesn't mean it's always good. I can love him, but I don't always like him and I think it's vice versa too. You don't even have to like me, but you should always respect me. That's love.

Do you feel in the past, that you never quite got that kind of love? Referring back to you saying you thought it was love that you were in before.

Yeah, for sure. I feel like if you love someone, you respect him or her even if you're mad at them, and even if you do disrespect, you catch yourself real quick and are apologetic. If I love someone, you're obviously a reflection of myself. I feel like we're all a reflection of each other, like humanity is, so if I'm not treating you well apparently I'm not really treating myself well. Before? No way. Then in the end of that past relationship that person told me, "Oh before I said I loved you, but I didn't really love you, love you." What's funny is he never even had to reveal it to me because his actions did, but God would have them say it because I needed to hear that.

I used to tell you I loved you, but never did. **Somebody actually said that to you?**

Yeah. And it's so funny because his actions totally revealed it to me, but I guess you have to confess it.

Tell me about your greatest heartbreak. Do you remember what that felt like?

Oh, do I. The person was just not the right match for me. The thing that was most confusing of all was me and this person were like, "We have so many things in common" but it was stupid stuff like "We both like white cheddar Cheese-It; we have so much in common." Uh, no. Where is the depth? I guess there was none and that's why it didn't last.

I love myself. I feel like I outpour love, but I just don't think that person loved himself. Or maybe he did love himself too much. Conceited or whatever. He just wasn't nice to me. He wasn't good to me all the time. He was just mean, comparing me to other girls, just everything bad in a relationship. Of course, then you question *Oh, so then why stay?* Because it wasn't always all bad all the time, but that bad definitely outweighed the good.

Do you think that relationship tarnished your character at all? After being treated so poorly?

Oh, definitely not. In life, you can look at a situation as a horrible thing or you can take the lesson away from it. So, at first, I did question why I stayed in that relationship for so long. I was so dumb. But I learned, and will never ever be so dumb again. Never ever will I waste that precious time like that again. God didn't create me to be an unhappy being, so why should I allow this other person to influence my happiness?

You spark a point in mind for me. I had a conversation with a friend and she is so against the fact that I still have a good relationship with an ex that has literally dragged me through the dirt. My response to her is that I just feel that I am always better than that person. The reality is that I could stop talking to him and just cut him out of my life or I can literally repay his acts of pain with kindness. What are your thoughts? Would you ever see yourself becoming friends with that ex again?

No, I don't think we should be friends because we didn't start off as friends to begin with. About the friend thing, I think often times in a relationship, there is friend in the word "boyfriend" "girlfriend" and you would never even treat your friend that way, so why you would you treat someone you lay with, someone you so called love, that way? I don't think we were ever really friends to being with. I think we could be *friend-ly* but he's not going to be my friend. I don't use that word loosely. I don't have that many friends to begin with, so I'm definitely not likely to bring my third wheel back in. I'm quite alright.

How would you define happiness with and without someone?

Definitely God. And I hate that phrase that people say, and my Momma says it too; don't ever be flattered when someone says, "you complete me." Uh-uh. I'm a whole being. You should be a whole being, but you're going on now, what, incomplete? That's whack. What next, I should just wait around for somebody else to come back in and complete me? I'm always going to be searching? No. God is always enough. I am a whole being. He created me as a whole being, so God is the source of my happiness. It's just whether you believe or not. I choose to believe in God and it's all about if I choose to have faith in him, if so then my life is going to be lit. It doesn't mean I'm not going to have challenges or obstacles. I just know that whatever I'm going through, God will always be my happy place.

You sound very much rooted in God and in your belief. How much of that spills into your relationship?

I think a good amount. I feel comfortable talking to Mo about God and we have open discussions. At first, I thought it would be different since he grew up Muslim, but if anything it just goes back to what I was saying. We're alike in so many other things so if we're different in that area, it's okay. You opened up my eyes to a new world and hopefully I opened up your eyes to something that's true. But as long as we're both willing to grow spiritually, and I can speak to him about it and I don't feel weird I think we'd have a great future.

DAY TWENTY-SEVEN: BLISS

LOVE IS HAPPINESS.

"Peace. It does not mean to be in a place where there is no noise, trouble, or hard work. It means to be in the midst of things and still be calm in your heart." – Unknown.

Love should be a condition in which the happiness of another person is essential to your own. Love should ignite a balance of serenity and peace. I think we often forget this balance; we forget that while relationships require hard work and dedication, at its core, there should be bliss. Do you remember why you fell in love? Do you remember how? It was probably the easiest thing you did. It probably caught you by surprise and swept you off your feet. That initial feeling, that understanding, that freedom you gave yourself to fall into someone was a risk indeed, but a risk worth taking.

Amber Danner, 21, has allowed this peace to consume her and her happiness looks gorgeous. As I've watched my friend glow over the last few months, she's given me a glimpse of what pure bliss looks like. How being confidently lost in her relationship has uplifted her spirits and ignited growth beyond measure, beyond what she's expected. The path to this purity wasn't easy to find, but I can't think of a journey worth taking that doesn't have its bumps on the road. Love is the key to open the gate of happiness, and Amber has most certainly opened hers. She's given me hope that there's a set of keys waiting for me too. This is her story.

Tell me about your love life. Are you single? Are you in a relationship? Are you married? It's complicated?

Currently I'm in a relationship and we've been together for about a year and a half. We will make two years in December.

How do you feel everything is going?

Everything's actually going, really, really well. I'm in a space where I'm so happy that I legit didn't think this was possible. I'm really happy in the space that I'm at right now.

That sounds amazing! What do you think ignites that happiness in you?

I feel like I'm in a relationship where Franklin and I, we balance out each other. He's such a successful person; he does what he has to do, he's honest, he's caring, and he's never shown me a side of him that I disliked. And I know that might sound really crazy or you've never heard that before but it's true. I've never seen a side of my boyfriend that I dislike. Everything about him I like, he's enjoyable and he's fun to be around.

So there's not one thing that you dislike about this person?

There are things, of course, he'll do that will annoy me but it's not something I could look back on. You know how you used to make a list of pros and cons of someone? The cons would be very minimal. One thing he does that I dislike is the noise he makes when he chews his food. That's so minimal that's not even something you'll message to someone else, like "Oh, he chews his food too loud." That's the love of mine.

You're fairly young so it could be hard to say this but would you say that he's your greatest love?

Yes. I'm only 21 but I've been in three serious relationships where each relationship was more than a year. And I can honestly say that being with him made me realize that the previous two were not love at all. So, I can definitely say that this is my greatest.

How would you describe love?

Being able to communicate without having arguments. When you see that person you care so deeply about, and automatically get excited over nothing. You think of them whenever you're upset, and become happy at just the thought of your person - I think that's love right there.

What do you think is the secret to keeping your love going?

It's honesty. Everyone in life makes mistakes, but if you can sit down and be honest about what you've done, and admit that you're wrong without someone telling you that you're wrong, that's a plus. That right there is exactly what is keeping us together, the fact that we can both be so honest with each other and not always feel like we have to hide everything or anything at all.

How did you and your boyfriend get together?

We were both RA's in college. But I can say if felt like we weren't meant to be because he had problems with someone I used to deal with. I was even told "don't talk to him," "he's not a good person, he's mean" blah blah. I ignored what everyone else thought of him and I still befriended him and I guess that openness ignited our relationship.

Did you feel any kind of hesitancy at first knowing that he was somebody your ex didn't care too much for?

Absolutely not. It started off as me being friendly to him because he was my co-worker. I'm not going to be a mean person to somebody I work with. We clicked automatically and were cool. I can't wait to go by what everyone else says, I had to figure this out for myself.

What advice would you give someone who was hesitant of what the next steps could be for them in a new relationship?

Put your old situation in the past and make sure you're completely over it. When you're moving forward you can't really think about what happened already. Just remember to always be positive and keep everything to yourselves.

Would you say that you're completely over your past?

Yes. Absolutely. Yes.

What were some of the steps you took to get there?

When he and I first broke up I was the one who decided to end the relationship, because I felt like it wasn't going anywhere. So, I didn't take any steps, I just realized my worth and walked away, and from then on, I didn't look back at all. I know it's hard to hear that, but it's true. Once I ended the relationship I didn't shed one tear, I didn't think about the person, I was just over it. He and I went through so much that when I finally broke it off, I knew there was no going back, so it was easy for me to move on.

I look at you and I've seen such a change in almost everything you're about. You just look elated. How would you describe being happy in a relationship?

It's just a natural feeling inside, whenever I see my man, I'm smiling and there's no stopping it. I always want to belong to him, it's almost impossible to describe. People have said they've noticed a difference in me and have asked, "Is it your new relationship?" "What is it?" "You're glowing," -- that's happiness right there. When other people can realize that you're happy in comparison to your previous situation, without even knowing the details. That's how you know it's real.

Kiana St Louis

DAY TWENTY-EIGHT: THE LITTLE THINGS

DO SMALL THINGS WITH GREAT LOVE.

Nothing is ever perfect, nor are any of us. However, what I seek is far from perfection. I want love. I want commitment. I want consistency and effort. I want to know despite everything that's going on in our lives, there's room for me. I want to be an exception to the rule. I like nice things, but I don't need them. I can get them myself. I crave a love so deep the oceans are jealous. I want to be what someone has always wanted.

What I Have Always Wanted

(By: Unknown)

When you came into my world, you invaded it with your lovely smile and your understanding heart,
And I quietly thought to myself about how different you were from the start.
You listened to my every word and never judged what I had to say,
And even after I was turning away from it all, you didn't get up and run away.
We developed a relationship filled with trust, with no walls to have to guard.
We both left the past behind us and stepped into the future that was bright, no matter how hard.
You have taught me how to love and I know you have no hidden agenda – you are in love with the real me.

I am writing this so that you can understand that spending time with you is the best thing in my life and I never want to let go of your hand.

100 Days of Dating

When we are apart, I can't describe just how much I miss you
But when you're here, I don't think you realize just how much better I am.
When we have time apart, I am able to see just what I have always wanted.
I've always wanted you in my life.
To hold you.
To kiss you.
To show you the world.
To pick you up when you're down.
To love you.
It's you that I have always wanted.
During all of my moments of despair, it's you I needed to turn to.
A woman that is as beautiful as you,
And kind, and understand, and loving
My only regret is that I didn't meet you sooner
But as we always say, the past is the past and there's no use in going back.
The future is what we need to turn to and focus on with each moment
Let's start today and make each moment we share together overshadow the past
For we have to realize that today, there is no turning back.
I love you.

DAY TWENTY-NINE: DUST SETTLES, WE SHOULDN'T

ARE YOU REALLY HAPPY OR JUST COMFORTABLE?

Often times I think we confuse the two. We get caught up our in routine, we allow our expectations to wither down, and we accept comfort ability as a means to avoid confrontation. But I believe Nelson Mandela said it best, "there is no passion to be found in settling for a life that is less than the one you are capable of living." There is no passion to be found in settling for love.

Steven Harewood, 23, chose happiness. Passion fuels all of his endeavors. Temporary comfort, uncertainty, games; they should all be a thing of the past. At some point you have to want better for yourself. Games end and you rarely have two winners. Unless it's mad, passionate, extraordinary love, it's a waste of your time. There are too many mediocre things in life; love shouldn't be one of them. This is his story.

Tell me about your love life. Are you single? Married? In a relationship?

I am currently single and I'm kind of just hanging out. Personally, I feel like I'm not into just dating and all that, but nobody has appealed to me in the manner that I'm expecting. So, I'm just like chilling until that happens, again. Until I get knocked off my feet.

What is the manner that you're expecting?

I would say the last time I got into a relationship, it kind of surprised me how much I liked the person. I haven't really met anybody that interests me like that since. So I'm not saying that I know how I want to be talked to or how I want them to approach. But I know what I want when I see it and I haven't really seen anything that made me wake up to a relationship or wake up to being open to that.

Have you ever been in love before?

Yeah. Way too deeply actually. I feel like I kind of got lost in the sauce, if you know what I mean. It got pretty crazy, pretty fast. I wasn't really in control of the situation like I wanted to be, but it was fun. You know how they say the best of times and the worst of times? It was one of those kinds of things. I definitely enjoyed myself when it was good, but when it was bad, it was like, shit, why does it have to be like this?

You mentioned control. The aspect of love is something that I feel is uncontrollable sometimes, from the way you feel to how you act. Do you feel like you need to be in control to love?

No, I don't feel like I need to be in control of it. But I definitely feel like I had no control of *myself* in the situation. I was just at the person's whim. I didn't really have a say in how I felt about things. Whatever circumstances hit us literally just zoned me out. I wasn't really grounded, I would act differently than I would normally in any other situation because of how deep it got. So, I feel like it was a little too wild for me in terms of what happened. But I don't regret it. It showed me a lot, I learned a lot. I'm happy with where I am now. I had to go through that still.

Do you hope to be in love again soon?

Soon? I don't know. Right now the way my life is going, there are a lot of things I'm hoping to change. There are a lot of things that are already changing. So, I don't know if I would be able to keep up with a total love relationship at this point in my life and my career progression. As things change, I don't know if I would be able to adapt to those changes while maintaining that relationship and keeping it healthy. I don't want to be in love if I can't keep it.

I appreciate you saying that. I feel like some guys almost can't be heavily into their career and be in love at the same time. They make it seem like it is so much extra work.

I don't think that's what it is. I wouldn't say that's what it is for me. I feel like, if love hit me, I would do my best to maintain it. I would obviously try to keep it. But knowing the changes my life is going to go through is why I feel like it would be different.

Kiana St Louis

I'm trying to become a public figure in terms of my work, not necessarily a celebrity like Tom Cruise or Jay-Z or whoever, but just my name. So, I know how that lifestyle gets when it comes to women and I wouldn't want to get tied up too early and feel like I'm regretting things when I'm there. I want to just manage that so I don't hurt anybody with the stupid decisions that I might make given what my life is going to be.

What happens if somebody happens to sweep you off your feet? Will you push it aside because it might not fit in with your life changes?

Nah. I wouldn't do that. I feel like that's stupid personally. I would respect the timing of it all because I feel like everything happens for a reason and if I do feel that strongly about somebody, then who am I to duck that because I had a different plan, you know?

I would try to maintain it but I wouldn't really love it. Maybe I do want somebody to talk to me now so when I do get to where I'm going, I already have somebody that I know is down for me and not necessarily all the other things. So, I don't know, that's where I'm leaning.

What would an ideal relationship or person look like to you?

I actually don't know how I can classify that at this point. Looking at how I am, I know I'm pretty picky. I already have an idea in mind but I don't necessarily want to say that. But it kind of would end up to be a situation where something that I approve of just happens. It's hard to explain without sounding like an asshole.

Forget what you'd sound like. Just keep it real.

Okay. I don't feel like I can settle at all. Because I feel like I don't want to wake up at 45 and be like, "Damn, I should have picked somebody else." I feel like if I'm not fully committed to what it is, meaning if it doesn't hit me when I see it, then I can't go through with it, or even push that forward. And I feel like I have felt like that before, at least in terms of what it was, so I wouldn't want to get into something if I don't think I felt as strongly about it.

I feel like I have two kinds of ways that I act around people. I just want somebody that I can be completely open with because a lot of times I have to close off certain parts of who I am to get along with certain people or be with others. So, I need somebody that I can be completely open with. I just have to really have to be 100% comfortable. Even with the last person I was with, I wasn't that. I wasn't there, and it kind of bothered me at times but I was already in too deep.

What have you learned from that relationship that has helped you grow?

I think one thing I learned is that you can't force things. You have to know when to let go, because if you hold on too long, you might make things worse than they really should be. In the last case, I don't know if it was something she did or I did, but we definitely ruined it by holding on too long. Like ruined any type of friendship at all, so that's something. You have to let go when it's time to let go. Things happen as they're supposed to. You can't force things. And I think the last thing that I would say that I learned, is to just try to be good to the person and do the best by them.

That's just my whole thing now, being good. Sometimes people will do their own thing and take care of themselves and completely forget about you. You just have to do the best that you can for a person. Up until you can't anymore, and then you have to let them know what it is.

DAY THIRTY: DECEIVED

YOU CAN'T KEEP LETTING THE SAME PEOPLE HURT YOU.

At some point, you have to draw the line. It doesn't matter how much you love someone, how pure your heart is, or how badly you may want a relationship to work; when it's time to move on, you have to pack your bags.

Day 30 is for me. I've been a ghost this past week for a couple of reasons. One: The weather is the devil. I've been stuck at home sick trying to figure out if I should be wearing shorts or a North Face. Two: I made a poor decision to let my past into my present and the only thing that did was mess me up. Completely messed me up.

I got too excited, too caught up, for nothing. I opened the door to let this person in and they used me, lied to me, and disappeared on me. It was almost like a really bad dream. I've been open with my readers throughout this journey. Taking you all through my series of emotions, my lessons, and my failures, so I needed this to be the same. I want to be honest with you, not every day is easy. I am not happy all the time. I often get upset with myself for not being done with this process. Today is one of those days. I thought this project would help me believe in love again or at least gain a better understanding through our shared experiences, however, I'm convinced love is selective. It sounds so good. It looks so appealing from afar. But it might not be for everybody.

Yes, I'm allowing this recent experience to jade me, but I'm trying to get over it. Can't you tell? I'm just tired of putting 100% into people that pretend to give me 50%. I'm over it.

But the absolute saddest part about all of this is I'm not over any of it at all.

Blind Sided

By: Paul Curtis

Love confuses the senses
It tricks us into seeing what's not there
We see what we want to see
Someone you love, who loves you back
In equal measure
Someone as happy, content, faithful
As you are
But love blinds us
It blinds us to the truth
It fails to register
All the telltale signs
Of sadness, discontent and infidelity
Until it's too late

DAY THIRTY-ONE: STILL GROWING

GROWTH IS EMBRACING THE UNCOMFORTABLE

I didn't want to continue this project after writing the previous chapter. Day 30 revealed my truth. The truth that this 100-day experience is the result of my love encounters, the truth that I am being completely honest not only with those who read along, but also with myself. The truth that the love I have for this man really takes me through a whirlwind of emotions on a daily.

But I realize where I currently am in life; this place where I feel a loss of control is associated with my growth. Sometimes growing is uncomfortable. When our new teeth grow in, teething seems unbearable. When it's time to grow out of our clothes, that temporary feeling of frustration is real. I think it's all related. The moment you realize you may have outgrown someone you thought you would love forever brings about that same unbearable frustration.

But I can't let those feelings triumph. I can't let temporary feelings dictate my permanent happiness. I have to keep going.

So, #100DaysofDating isn't dead, but after these last few interviews, I'd like to revamp the way I take this journey. Maybe more intimate posts? Maybe a vlog? Podcast? I don't know just yet, but I think I'm on to something. My initial goal was to hopefully connect with one or two people, but I've seemed to gain the attention of 2,000+ readers globally. This is bigger than me. This is now our story. Moving forward, a direction I will only be going in, I am removing myself, my decision making and simply being still. I've tried to take a lot of things into my own hands even after God has tried to take them from me. I think this situation was one of them. But, no more fighting. I will be still and listen and continue to grow until I meet the man who's been praying for me.

100 Days of Dating

As we continue, I'd like to introduce you to Keisha Williams, 22, another fearless lover. Things don't always work out the way we want them to, and often love throws us for a loop, almost testing our strengths to determine true weakness, or sometimes to give us a sign. But, some love stories require the back and forth and sometimes even the uncertainty, to help us realize if this is a person we need to be with or if this is just another lesson to learn. This is her story.

Tell me about your love life. Are you single? Married? In a relationship? It's complicated?

I am in a relationship. I've been with my boyfriend for almost 3 years.

That's bomb. How do you feel everything is going so far?

It's been rough in the beginning. We always say that we have chapters for our relationship. The beginning chapter was *trust* because he cheated on me very early in our relationship. He didn't make it better after he cheated either. I'm the type of person that doesn't take bullshit. But with him, I was all in love and all that, so I wanted to be with him. So I worked through everything even though it was hard.

And the chapter after that, I say was probably *communication*, because I'm not a good communicator, he is. The next chapter was *tolerance*, because it came to the point where we were just tolerating each other, meaning we were arguing and bickering over little things. And I think now we're at the point of *growth* because we both want to get into our careers. We've talked about taking the next step as far as what we're going to do in terms of marriage and kids. Questioning, are we really going to be together? Are we doing this for real?

How was it for you being in the beginning of the relationship and having to undergo cheating? What was that healing process like for you?

He didn't make it easy for me because he was still wilding out, cheating sexually. And after that, I used to go through his phone and I'll see him talking to females, flirting. He just made me feel like I wasn't enough. So, it took a long time for him to build that trust with me because when he saw that I was threatening to leave, he was like 'You know what I have to get my shit together if I'm going to keep my girl'. And when he put in that effort it made it easier for me to forgive him and move on. I wouldn't say I got over what he did, but I moved past it and I forgave him. So, he had to help me get over it by acting right.

What was the effort that he put in to make you stay?

He kept his phone unlocked and didn't have a passcode. So, if I ever wanted to go through it, even though I shouldn't have to, it was open for me. When he did put a lock on it, up to now I know the code. He would spend more time with me. He tried to be more honest with me about things that he knew I would get mad at to show that he's really trying. He showed me more honesty and openness.

You mentioned before that communicating wasn't exactly a strong point for you. Do you feel as if you're reaching that point now and getting better at it?

Yes, I do. He's definitely helping me with that part because he's an open person. He's an open book. He'll say, "Listen, we're going to talk about this. We're going to get through it because how else are we going to move forward." Me? I'm the type of person to shut down when I'm upset. He'll be yelling at me and I'd be looking at him with a stank face like *'boy, bye.'* So, he had to break me out of that shell because you cannot be together, you cannot be with anyone if you don't communicate. How is that going to work? You have to see where each person is coming from, what each other's issues are. You have to listen. Not just listen to talk, but listen to understand.

So, would you say that this is your greatest love?

Yeah. I would say that the only person I think I ever loved before him was in high school. I was really young. I was 14 going on 15 and we were together for like a year. I thought it was serious because I was young trying to be grown. Now that I can think back and compare it to this relationship, it wasn't nearly as serious.

We still sort of communicate up to this day, but not too much because my boyfriend's not comfortable with it. But, yeah I would say that was my first love. But this is my real, adult, first mature relationship, first love.

Do you think you see yourself in this relationship being married, being a mom, and truly moving forward with this person?

For the most part I do, sometimes I have my doubts, but more times than not I see myself with him permanently.

Doubts?

There are certain things about him that I feel like I can't deal with sometimes. It gets kind of overwhelming as far as my relationship with his mother, which is not good. He can be ambitious sometimes, but then he let's go of himself a lot of the time. For me, that's not a trait that I need as the head of a household. You need to be on your shit at all times because that's how I am. No matter how much I don't want to get up and go to work I'm going to do it because I have to. You know, it's not a choice. It's not an option. It's something that I have to do.

Sometimes he feels like regular work is not for him. He thinks he deserves more in life. I'm like 'I understand that'. I think a lot of people do. But you have to level up. You don't just become great; there are levels to it. You have to start somewhere and sometimes he doesn't feel the need to start somewhere. He wants to just be great, make a whole bunch of money, and be this supportive person. Sometimes I have to give a lot of pep talks when it comes to his ambition and his mindset and everything. I don't always want to deal with that. He's also kind of insecure in a lot of ways, and sometime that's a turn off.

Women love potential. You can easily love somebody so much because you feel like they have what it takes to be this great person. But what happens when they turn out to be someone else? Do you feel like it's a level of potential that you have for him, that also drives your reason for staying?

Yeah, but I think that it's more than just potential. I often weigh out the pros and cons because if the cons outweigh the pros, then there's no reason why I'm with you. If I have everything to complain about and nothing good to say about you, then I shouldn't be with you. So, when I do that whole list, his pros definitely outweigh the cons, *all the way*. The way he loves me, the way he cares about me, the way he puts me before anything, even himself and his family. We've been through a lot as far as him and his struggles when it comes to work. If he'd lose his job or something like that, I held us down a lot.

But regardless of who you get with, you're going to have to deal with something. Everybody comes with something. I come with something. You come with something. Everybody does. So it's all about what you can and can't deal with. I think what he comes with I can deal with, that's why I've been dealing with it, you know?

What advice would you give someone who's also in this stage? The stage of figuring out what next steps look like and dealing with the reality that everybody isn't perfect, but there can be a somewhat-perfect love.

Yeah that's exactly how I feel. Nobody's perfect. Like I said before, no matter who you get with, they're going to come with something. So, you have to know that the grass is not always greener on the other side. There have been many times that different guys have either come into my life where I've thought *if I wasn't with my man I could possibly talk to this person*. But you really don't know somebody until you really know somebody.

So, I look at the way I'm treated, the way that my man feels with me, and the way he loves me, and that's something that I'm cherishing because there's not a lot of that out there. I know that for a fact because I hear females complain about them on a regular basis. Think about your relationship fully (pros and cons) and ask: Is this something that you can deal with long term? And if you can't then it makes no sense dealing with them, but if you can then do so.

Kiana St Louis

DAY THIRTY-TWO: WILD THOUGHTS

SOMETIMES OUR THOUGHTS GET THE BEST OF US.

There has been many times where my head, heart, and body have disagreed. I've wanted to be in love so badly, I've settled for being convenient. I've craved the attention of the one I loved so much so that I ignored all internal signs. I've made poor decisions based on my body's need for instant gratification. In sum, I'm not perfect and I'm a victim of not only having wild, wild thoughts but also bringing them to life.

Hearing DJ Khalid's recent collaboration with Rihanna and Bryson Tiller, instantly reminded of my own thoughts. I thought about this project and how impulsive love makes me. Love making falls right alongside those impulsive moments. I'm sure we all have them - actually, I know we do. But the thoughts themselves aren't the "issue" but instead how we act on them. Whether you're in a relationship, single, or mingling, we are no strangers to temptation, our minds always run wild.

Even now, I'm reminded of Terri Wood's short poem, "The Dream," a poetry piece she included in Gina and Quadir's love story in *True to the Game*. Maybe you've read it before, maybe you never have, maybe you can't even relate to this chapter at all. All points are cool with me, but to those reading and truly feel me, wild thoughts are always a little spicy. But I wouldn't it have it any other way.

The Dream

By: Terri Woods

My eyes are closed, but I see you so clear

I stare in your eyes and the world disappears

Leaving us together so no one can see

Your body moves closer so you're next to me

100 Days of Dating

Your fingers unbutton and take off my clothes
Your hands moving all over from my head to my toes
Without delay, you start to play
Your brown warm fingers will find their own way
It's feeling so good and when I touch you back
Your long and your hard and it makes me wet
I kiss your chest in a rapture sublime
As your fingers play music in three quarter time
We're caught in rapture without a doubt
You push my head lower, I open my mouth
Hours pass by, you pick up my face
And the look in your eye states so simply your case
This body is yours and you're gonna take it
If I said no, you know you would have raped it
You flip it and turn it and throw it around
Until you have my face down on the ground
You've found your position, ass up in the air
You get behind me and force it in there
Pushing whatever is stopping your stroke
You fu*k me for hours like you're going broke
You've totally flipped and you're out of control
Your love is insane and I'm your goal
You're ready to nut not a minute too soon

Kiana St Louis

I hear the alarm and I'm back in my room

I open my eyes and hear the door shut

I thought I was dreaming, but we really did fu*k.

DAY THIRTY-THREE: WE COME FIRST

YOU DON'T HAVE TO BE IN LOVE TO KNOW LOVE

I sat with a good friend of mine, Justin Brantley, a little while ago and we talked about love. We also talked about his truth - the fact that at 23 years old, he's never actually been in love. In fact, because of this he admitted to being hesitant about participating in this project. He felt he didn't have much to offer on a topic he knew so little about, but he couldn't have been more wrong.

Love has no blueprint, no guidelines, no list of do's and don'ts, just feelings - just actions. We show our love in different ways to different people in different situations. Whether romantic, platonic, or just out of kindness, that form of expression is valued regardless because I believe we all just want to be loved in some way. While Justin might not have experienced the commitment of being in love, he has had moments of passion and affection, he's been confused, he's been hurt, and he's both needed and wanted a person to confide in just like the rest of us. If you ask me, he's lucky to not have been caught up in all the fiasco love brings. We're so young. There's still so much to do, to see, to live for and people to live with. There's no rush Brantley, but you know that. You know more than you think. This is his story.

Tell me about your love life. Are you single, married, in a relationship?

Right now, I'd say I'm very much single. This is my first summer having an income, though I had my "grad summer" last summer '16. Now, I finally have the ability to go places and do things and really enjoy my time. I'm keeping it single right now.

That's awesome, congrats on the income! Do you feel as if you couldn't have fun or as much fun if you weren't single?

Thank you, Ki. I think right now, I would definitely be able to have as much fun, but I'd have to allocate my time differently. As it is now, I'm going to be away from home for a week and I know when you have a significant other, they expect and appreciate having that time to spend with you because that's a foundation of a relationship, in my opinion.

I respect that. I often feel like sometimes people get into relationships just because, and sometimes forget the work that needs to be put in afterwards. Have you been in a relationship before?

Yeah. Believe it or not during all of my years at SUNY Oswego, I didn't have a labeled relationship. So, my last "girlfriend" was in high school. And I've just been keeping it single for about six years now.

Why?

It's a mixture of things. I haven't been ready to commit, but there have been people in my life who I've felt deserved that title. But at the time, I wasn't ready or I was trying to juggle too many things or I was trying to reach a goal. And that didn't work out. Or there were times where I just felt like the people who I needed in my life weren't there and I would be wasting my time, essentially.

Have you ever expressed this to the people you've dated?

The latter, not so much, but the original mindset of me not wanting to settle down, I expressed to two different individuals over the past six years. While they understood, it definitely began a rift in our relationship.

Yeah, I can see that. After a certain amount of time in this life, whether you two are dating or not, the person eventually wants more. You know?

Yeah. Definitely.

Did you ever want more?

It's funny; I always wanted more after the fact. So, that saying of "you don't know what you have until it's gone," I definitely realized my appreciation or feelings for certain people over the past five years after we had already gone our separate ways. I think back like, *Oh, wow. If I would have done this one thing differently, that whole situation could have changed.* But in the moments when I'm talking to people, I can't say I wanted more. It's really an interesting paradigm.

Have you ever been in love, Justin?

I really haven't. So, similar to what I was just saying on that idea of wanting more at the wrong time, I can definitely say I love a lot of people and I have a lot of love for a lot of people, but I've never actively been in love in my 23 years. It's funny because when you asked me to do an interview, I was hesitant. I understood the major concept and not being in love is a story as well. But I'm thinking to myself, *what am I going to talk about?* Because I've never been in love. *I've never actually been in love.* And I think about that from time to time. Towards your original point when we started the conversation, I can feel myself learning something through this conversation already.

While I know you haven't been in love before, do you have thoughts on an ideal woman or characteristics of what an ideal woman for you would be like?

I definitely go back and forth. And when I talk to people they laugh, "Oh, you have a type." Or, "You're looking for someone who doesn't exist." I like to break it down and just think of what are the main things that I know, no matter what, not even just appearance, which I can stand behind. I want someone that's going to be able to push me and help me grow because though I do have a drive on my own, it's always nice to have someone who's always building and helping you. I want someone who I'll be able to take home to mom and dad. I know that's very cliché and it's easier said than done, but I want to have someone who I won't have to hear 21 questions about. Questions from momma dukes about why someone did this, this and this. But she will.

An ideal woman to me, she has to be able to smile. She has to love life. I know opposites attract, so that's probably not something I'm going to be able to find all the time, but I definitely appreciate someone who likes to smile. Because for me, that's the first thing I look at, above all else.

Have you ever had your heart broken?

Yeah. I've had a couple heartbreaks. My junior year, there was someone who I trusted with a lot of my secrets and while we were just talking at the time - we didn't have a label on it. She was special. She was my support system. She was my friend. She was my girl without the title. And very soon after things got crazy in school, she left me. It wasn't immediate, but things changed rapidly. For me, that was very hard to get over because I had already lost so much in a short amount of time. I lost network, connections, and even family members.

So, to have lost this young lady who I was very interested in at the time, it hurt. It hurt more than all the other outside factors. I think what made it even worse on my end, was that after everything was said and done, I think I saw her once or twice in public and the way I acted pushed us even further away each other rather than trying to make things work.

I haven't really had too many relationships where someone actually pushed me. She was someone I felt like I could bring home to mom, and also someone who I trusted. Junior year to me was our most important year. That's when you're on the verge of going to that next level and you just finished learning the layout of school; it's your prime year. But yeah, that kind of turned me into who I am now.

Do you think that lack of labeling the situations with these people has hindered building that relationship aspect for you?

Yes, I do. I definitely do. It's unfortunate that we live in times where it's a race to see who cares the least. We try our hardest not to show that emotion and to not "show feelings" and I think the label is a pinnacle of that. So, for instance, when you give someone a label publicly or privately, it kind of sets in, now there's lots of responsibility attached to this name. If you're my girlfriend, that means if you say, "Hey, let's stay home and not go to the party." We're going to stay home and not go to the party. But if we just talk, I'll text you at two o'clock in the morning and we'll see what goes on from there. You see what I'm saying?

I think if I, going back to personal standpoint, most of the people I've talked to, if I put a label on it, I think that would have really changed how that person felt about me or would have changed how we interacted with each other. I think that is what I was scared of. That's what kind of prevented me from taking it to that next step.

I agree with you 100%. I feel like everybody glorifies being petty these days. But isn't the dating stage supposed to be leading up to the relationship point? Why do you feel like we separate it so much? Why can't a person you talk to be treated like the person that you want to be in a relationship? If not, then why would you even be talking to them at all?

I think sex as a motivator is what kind of changes people's aspirations from what they are actually trying to do. I don't want to blame society because it's kind of a scapegoat, however, we always have this thing in the back of our mind where if I'm talking to someone, they're probably talking to two other people at the same time. That has been the case in most scenarios where we're talking to one person, but we're still single so we're playing the field. With that in mind, you don't want to get yourself caught up, you don't want to make yourself vulnerable by moving it from the talking stage. But if you actually want to be with them, it erases. It makes you kind of hold off on everything else that you're entertaining.

But, like you said, we should be working towards a common ground, not just seeing where this goes and then two weeks later, I'm going mean mug you when I pass by you in the streets. I think we also know that time is always short, so in college it was, okay after this semester are we still going to talk over the summer? I'm not going to see you as much. After we graduate, am I going to even see you anymore? Now moving into the "real world" I think that does change a little bit. I'm actually excited to see how that goes in the coming months and years.

With all of the experiences you've been through, label, no label, heartbreak, what were some of the key things you learned about relationships that you feel like you can implement now that you are in the "real world"?

I think that I tend to answer this for everything, but being intentional with what you want, with what you say, I learned that you have to frame things how you expect it to go. So, if you truly want a relationship, you're going to have to put the time and the effort. You're going to have to show compassion. You're going to have to learn about that person. And if you want talk to someone, don't lead people on. You don't put them in this place where they have to question what you are. And they know, "Okay. This is your intention coming into this. This is my intention coming into it. We can go our separate ways or we can decide to keep going with this and see where it takes us."

I think with my experiences I know not to give my all until I feel it being reciprocated. I learned that no matter what, at the end of the day, I still come first in my own life. I have to put myself first because being a 'yes' man and bending backwards may very well only get both parties hurt. But when it hits you and when that time comes, it's out of your control. Don't force anything, because you might still be trying to find yourself and you might distract that progression and that momentum trying to chase someone emotionally and sexually.

DAY THIRTY-FOUR: DON'T LOOK BACK

"It takes huge effort to free yourself from memory."
– Paulo Coelho

The past is an awful place to get stuck in. It's even more toxic when you're stuck there with someone you love. It's like you both want to move forward and you'd like to do it collectively, however, the only memories that seem to keep you going are the ones you've made years ago. But after some time, those memories aren't strong enough to sustain the character changes, character changes you've both been through.

Because we grow by our experiences, we are constantly changing. I am not the same person I was all those years ago; I'm not even the same person I was yesterday. And most times that's where the discrepancy lies. We want to make situations work even when we know they can't because we hold on to the love we once knew, instead of accepting the reality of what love has become because of what we know now.

Takira Nedd, 24, and I have this in common. We've been trying to make the past work since high school. But after a while, time started to show our hearts what our eyes couldn't see. I don't know if this means it's over forever, but for right now it's best we don't look back. This is her story.

Tell me about your love life. Are you single, married, dating, in a relationship?

I have a boyfriend, but he's not really my boyfriend, but he's kind of my boyfriend.

Kind of?

We talk and I spend the night, but we don't have a title.

But if anybody asks you'd say that was your boyfriend?

Yeah, I guess. But that's still my scapegoat. If something happens with us, I can say, "Well we're not in a relationship. Bye."

Do you not want to be in a relationship?

I do, but I'm kind of scared; Kyrie traumatized me. I just broke up with him in March. Of course we've broken up and got back together, there was even a time where we stopped speaking for about a year and change, but we ended up back together. But I feel like he traumatized me right now. It was just a lot and he definitely played a major part in why I am the way I am with all relationships right now. I was with him at such a young age, but that was my first everything you know.

At 15, he hindered me from a lot in my growing years. So, yeah it's great I'm new to the dating scene, I talk to someone, and I really like him. But you know when you date multiple people, you get to know what you want to like? For me, I can't talk to multiple people at one time; I'm still stuck on relationship molds. So, if I talk to you, you can't talk to anyone else, I don't care.

Can you describe how you feel about relationships now?

I still love, *love*. I'm happy to see people in healthy relationships, but I've been in a relationship where I was in denial that it was abusive. I had to come to terms with it as I've gotten older and realize that yeah, I was in a really controlling and abusive relationship.

But that didn't stop me from still wanting something real and healthy. The person I talk to now, I feel like I'm less picky with – before, you had to do this, this, this, and that, now I'm more open minded, but not settling per say. I realize people are different, and I want to be in a relationship where we're both happy, I don't want to have to compromise my social life to fit into the relationship, whereas the last relationship I was in I couldn't do a lot, there were a lot of boundaries. You can't wear this, you can't do this, you can't speak to this person, I don't have that right now with the person I talk to because we have more trust with each other. Overall, I feel I still want love and I deserve the love that I was giving to the person that didn't deserve to have it.

After realizing you were in an unhealthy situation, what made you stay, or let alone go back?

I think it's because even though there were times we'd break up, and I would get the courage to say *all right, I'm not talking to him anymore*, the new people I would choose to talk to just didn't seem better than the situation I was in.

It was like, 'well he does this to me, but you still don't treat me better than he treats me, so I'm just going to go back,' and it was like that for a long time. Then I had to realize that people are different. Stupid things would turn me off; I'd think to myself, *this guy doesn't call me to say good night every night, why not? Kyrie does that, let me just go back to him, I'm bugging*. Then I also had to realize there is better out there and you can't really look for it, it just has to come when it is time.

I had to face the fact that I was settling by being in a relationship with him, and I was only staying because this is what I knew and what I was used to, and I thought there wasn't better, and was scared. I just had to get that and stay by myself for a little bit. I was still speaking to him, but we weren't in a relationship, but I decided to sever old ties, I had to say no, we can't even be friends, because even though we were friends he still tried to pick what I could do and I still felt like I had some type of obligation to him and tried to respect his feelings.

Would you say that Kyrie was your greatest heartbreak?

Hell yeah girl, I cried a lot at night. I was very sad, depressed, didn't want to eat, didn't want to talk to anybody. I was just depressed. You know me, one time I googled: "Can you die from a heartbreak?"

What came up when you put that in?

You can, it happens to older people when their significant other passes away. There are people that have passed away because their significant other has passed away, and they're lonely. They've been together for so many years that they don't know how to live without the other.

Wow, that's deep. What were some of the steps you took to get back to the old you?

Kiana St Louis

Well, when I first started realizing that the relationship wasn't for me, I started doing things that I wanted to do that he wouldn't allow me to do. He didn't want me to drive, so a couple of years ago when we first broke up I went and I got my permit now I have my license, and I officially started driving. Before he would say, "No, I don't want you to drive because then you're going to get a car, and I'm not going to be able to know where you are at all times."

I just started doing stuff for me. He didn't want me to work, like why can't I work? We were living together at one point, and he didn't want me to leave the house. I would go hang out with my best friend, go to her house, and he would follow me there. He'd wait outside, like 'okay, it's time to go.' It was just a lot, so you just have to start doing that you want to do.

That's a lot at a young age too, you're right.

Yes. You know being young, I thought some of the things that I was doing was a part of how you're supposed to be an adult - you're supposed to listen to your man, do whatever he say… no fuck that, nope.

Tell me a little bit more about the person that you're with now. What is it about him that attracted you?

Honestly, at first, I didn't like him. I knew him for a couple of years, we had mutual friends and we'd always hang out together in group settings. He always tried to talk to me, but I just wasn't with it at first. Then one day he asked, "Do you want to go on a date?" And I said okay. I went on the date, we had a nice conversation, and I just was like wow, I really did not know he was the type of person he is. Sometimes you should give people a chance. We've been kicking it ever since.

And it feels healthy to you now?

Yeah, it definitely does. I hardly get annoyed and nothing affects me. We have communication, everything is just open, and honest. You can tell the difference when you're genuinely happy and you look forward to being happy because of the situation that you're in.

After everything that has happened so far, do you think you're happier without your ex?

Yeah, definitely I'm finna get this twisted off my shoulders! I feel more carefree, I'm doing things that I want to do with my life. I'm just able to do stuff without feeling like, am I going hurt this person's feelings by doing this, or is this going to affect this person, you know? And then it feels great to know you're being supported with what you want to do, by the person that you're with.

What advice would you give to somebody who was also going through the same situation?

You have to know what you want; you have to think about the first sacrifice to your happiness. I really had to lay out my wants and investments for myself, and once you lay it out, you realize you should always put yourself and your happiness first. You have to think: *If I sacrificed that much inventory, just to be here, am I putting more into this than he is?* If so, then do you want to really be with him?

You just have to do things that make you happy. It could start small, like with me, at first, he didn't want me to drive, but I went to the DMV, I took my permit test, and I was so lit. I came home, and he was just like "Why would you do that?" I didn't even study, I passed on the first try, 100, and he was just like "Why would you do that?" It was a killjoy, like was he dead ass? I was just like, wow, I can't even share something that I'm happy about with somebody I'm supposed to be in love with. But, is this where I want to be, or no?

How would you describe love?

I feel like love and happiness, they're one and the same. But you should really be in a happy place, I mean, not always. Things aren't always going to be sweet but, it should never hurt. A lot of people say love is pain. No, it's not, it's really not, it's not pain at all. When you look at the bigger picture, you should always want to be like, at least this is then, that small issue we had, at the end of the day I still love him, I'm happy. I wouldn't want to be anywhere else.

Kiana St Louis

DAY THIRTY-FIVE: FROM THE SIDELINES

Contributed poetry by: Rita Dove

*It seems I have always sat here watching men like you —
who turn heads, whose gaze is always either a kiss
or a slap or the whiplash of pure disregard. Why fret? All
you're doing is walking. You're this year's It, the
one righteous integer of cool cruising down a great-lipped
channel of hushed adoration, women turned girls
again, brightening in spite of themselves. That
brave, wilting smile — you don't see it, do you?
How she tells herself to move on; blinks until she can.*

DAY THRITY-SIX: MASTERY OF LOVE

THANK YOU AUNTIE ROE.

"Happiness can only come from inside of you and is the result of your love. When you are aware that no one else can make you happy, and that happiness is the result of your love, this becomes the greatest mastery of the Toltec: The Mastery of Love." - don Miguel Ruiz

She doesn't know it, but my aunt just gave me one of the best gifts of the year when she handed me the book: *The Mastery of Love*. In the fold, she wrote that she wished she followed the advice but it's never too late to start again. Even those words left a mark on my heart.

I'm only 12 pages in and I've learned that in order to be confident in who I am, or rather simply know who I am, I must be the master of my **awareness, transformation,** and **love**. All words we've heard before but probably haven't dissected or put in conjunction with defining who we truly are.

I've started this healing process about four months ago and have seen growth not only in my writing but also in who I am. I see the woman I'm becoming. I see the woman I want to be. As I look forward, as I continue to read these words I'm learning that my lessons are constant. I am my strength. I am the master of my life. I control my happiness and when I think about the woman I want to be in 5 years or even a few days from now, I just want her to be genuinely happy. Not simply happy at the moment, but happy doing what she loves, happily living on her own in the city she adores, happy with her friends and family, and dangerously happy with or without someone by her side.

Kiana St Louis

DAY THIRTY-SEVEN: THE EMPTY CUP

Poetry heals. Words have become my medicine.
Contributed Poetry by: Erin Hanson

Did you hope I wouldn't notice,

You gave me empty words to drink?

Well my tongue's tasted more lies,

Than you would ever dare to think,

You're not the only one,

With truth like poison in their veins,

Whose ribs are shaped like cages,

Holding tightly to the pain,

I knew the bitter flavor,

Of a heart that's given up,

Before my lying lips,

Had even touched that wretched cup,

And when you pour a glass,

Of words to cover what you hide,

Perhaps don't leave your secrets,

Clinging tightly to the side.

100 Days of Dating

DAY THIRTY-EIGHT: HAPPILY SINGLE

Singing to myself: "This time next year I'll be livin' so good, Won't remember your name, I swear. Livin' so good, livin' so good, livin' so good. This time next year I'll be livin' so good, Won't remember no pain, I swear..."

SZA wrote *Ctrl* about me. I'm convinced. I say that only half-jokingly because every song is a like a chapter from my life. You could even piece together a few of these interviews and put them in the footnotes if you wanted! She, along with her lyrical blessings, are at the top of mind this afternoon not only because I've binge listened to her album twice this morning, but because the above lyrics specifically resonate with me.

In the midst of conducting these interviews, I'm comforted by the fact of knowing that I'm not alone in the way I've felt and sometimes still feel. We've come nearly to the half way point on this journey of identifying ourselves through love, and I find myself excited about what the future holds. Today, I can say I'm truly happy being single.

Yes, there are nights I feel alone. But those nights don't outweigh my days. Thinking back to the beginning months when I first started this project, at the peak of my break up, I thought I was going to be sad and angry forever. No joke. Even as I allowed my words to dance across the screen, often times I'd have to fight myself to believe them. But I can't even find that Kiana anymore. I don't know her.

I'm in this limbo right now. Everything about my life is seemingly up in the air, but I'm rooted only by my faith in God. Some people get to this place and start to panic. If you're like me and reading this, you're probably a person who's always somewhat sure of your next moves, whether that be in love, work, home life etc. But right now the only thing you're sure of is what you'll have for lunch. Don't worry, I'm there too. It's different, it can be scary, but it doesn't have to be. I view this as period of opportunity. We can literally do and be anything right now. Our only risk is being too afraid to take the new chance.

So, as I patiently wait for my 24th year of life, decide on what's next in my career, and pour myself into words, happiness is at my core. I'm falling madly in love with myself and I don't regret a single thing.

100 Days of Dating

DAY THIRTY-NINE and DAY FORTY: THE GREAT LOVE DEBATE

THE CONFERENCE CALL.

I tried something a little different this time around. Because I've had such detailed one-on-one conversations with both men and women from various age groups on the topic of love, I was curious to see what it would be like to conduct a group interview. I wanted to see in real time just how alike our experiences are. I wanted to see just what could happen when both men and women join in to share the stories of their lovers, their pasts, their mistakes, their secrets.

It's hard to fake it when you're put on the spot. Luckily, that's never a problem for my interviewees. My humble experiment was far less than a group interview and was more so a bunch of friends quizzing each other, challenging each other, and connecting in ways we hadn't expected.

My first love debate was joined by returning interviewee, Ebony Lewis and new to the series, Marcus J, 23. In a series of candid talks, the three of us caught up, laughed, and talked about crafting the perfect relationship, only to realize there is just no such thing. This is our story.

Kiana: Guys, let's talk about love. Are you guys single? Dating? It's complicated? Married? Divorced? What's happening?

Marcus: I was divorced.

Ebony: He's hilarious. But hmm, I guess I'm dating, now.

Marcus: I want to know whom.

Ebony: The old friend, remember? We've got to catch up.

Marcus: So, it's an official thing?

Ebony: It's not like it's an official thing, dating is just so ironic. I was just having this conversation with my dad. I feel like dating is when you guys are single, you might meet someone else that you find cool, but you know you still got your bond. You're vibing, it's progressing. Eventually, if I feel like I want to bring it up like, "Oh, yeah, I think we should make it exclusive," I'll say it. But I am enjoying taking my time, and I am having fun getting to know him. I want to understand him and want him to understand me.

It's really fun. I feel like with Jim [my ex], I rushed into that shit. Even the guys before him I rushed into that shit too and it's just like, "Yo, it's been a world of problems." There is beauty in taking your time. There is no need to rush. It's all about having fun, that's all I am saying.

Kiana: That's so dope to hear Eb, especially in thinking back to your previous interview when you were still heavily in your exploration phase. It's nice that in a matter of months, there's been growth.

Marcus, what about you?

Marcus: I'm in a relationship and we're exclusive. I am taking my time still, but not really because I do like to do things. If I want to have a regular relationship, I try to make things interesting. So it could be seen as rushing sometimes, but I do take my time and have a girlfriend. That's who I take my time with.

But when people ask, I say we're just dating.

Ebony: What?

Kiana: Why?

Marcus: Not in a disrespectful way but I'm like, "Why am I dating *this* one?" You know what I mean? I guess its two different feelings. Sometimes I do want to do that type of free form dating because I never did it before, but then it's like...

Ebony: But, why? You know you're going to be the type of person to want more. I know I'm the type of person, if I see a guy's main girl text him, I won't even take him seriously. So, why even put yourself in that position?

Marcus: That's why I don't go through with it.

Kiana: Do you love your girl?

Marcus: Yeah, I definitely do love her. I couldn't say no to that.

Kiana: So why even refer to dating? Are you still open to meeting other people while being in your relationship?

Marcus: I don't know, but it's crazy because I do meet females often. I just met some lady today that was a florist and we exchanged Instagram info, but I would never pursue that right now. That's not what I'm looking for, I'm not looking for another girl. But if a girl just came to me like, "Yo." I might be curious, but I probably still wouldn't do anything with it, I am trying not to.

Kiana: Have you ever cheated before, Ebony?

Ebony: No, but I thought about it.

Marcus: Why she came at you with that crazy question? (laughs)

Kiana: The connection just happened (laughs). I thought about you and what you said, Marcus. If you were to ever take that florist up on anything, or anyone else rather, you'd certainly be cheating on your girl.

Ebony: I thought about it and I don't know. I knew I was going to try not to cheat. I just don't want that karma, number one. That definitely does exist, and I would just hate to feel that way, that sucks, right?

Marcus: Host, have you ever cheated?

Ebony: Spicy.

Kiana: Yikes, this went left.

Kiana St Louis

Marcus: The people want to know.

Kiana: Unfortunately, I have.

Marcus: Was it worth it? Sounds like a yes.

Kiana: It's like...

Ebony: Because it's not no.

Kiana: Yes and no. Can it be mixed? I don't know.

Yes, because when you are in the moment with somebody- and this wasn't just *somebody*, this was a person, but he wasn't just a random person to me, we had history, which also made things complicated. It was seemingly bound to happen and in the moment everything felt worth it because I care about that person, simply being able to be with them felt worth it.

But the down side is, I'm not that kind of person. So it was hard to look at someone I chose to be committed to like, "Hey what's up," knowing what I had just did. I felt heavy.

Marcus: That's a good way to describe that. Put that in the notes, *heavy* because you're going to be carrying a lot of weight out here. That's probably why you're so free, people know when women carry baggage, and it's obvious. Not just because you're trying to be with them or anything, but when you hear them talking, you can work with them and just hear and be like, "Damn, they thinking about a lot and everything's all right." I feel you guys walk around like pretty clear minded.

Kiana: No more questions for the people, straight dictatorship. (laughs) Have you guys ever had your heartbroken?

Ebony: No, but I had my feelings hurt and it really sucked.

Marcus: On the record, I had my heart broken. I have to say that just feels crazy. It's like a physical pain feeling in your stomach. And you can't do anything but feel like, "Damn."

Ebony: No, I haven't felt anything like that but it really deeply hurt my feelings, but I didn't even cry. I know when I feel deeply about things, I cry a lot.

Marcus: So you never cried over a guy before?

Ebony: I don't think I cried *over* him ... But there was this guy in high school and basically people knew we were messing around. There was even some boy calling me by his last name, like people just knew but we would deny it, you know what I mean?

It was never official but this girl, that was my friend, ended up having a thing with him and she would talk to my best friend about it, everybody but me. So it was like, you all know what you're doing is wrong, not to mention it was around the time of my birthday. So I was like, "You all hurt my feelings," and I cried but I wasn't heartbroken because I wasn't in love with him.

Marcus: Yeah, you were just like "wow"

Ebony: That wasn't even the "hurt feelings" I was talking about. There was this other guy I dated for four years and he really just played me for no reason for this other girl. We spoke about it, I'm like, "Yo, if that's what you want to do I'll bounce. I won't ask you to choose. If that's what you want to do we could be friends that's all I care about." He still lied anyway and that really hurt my feelings. He had no reason.

So, I've never been heart broken, but how can you honestly not care about a person that's just genuine with you? That's crazy.

Kiana: That's a fact. It's like people just don't care I guess.

Ebony: They only care about themselves. That's really it. People just do what they want. They might say, "damn" for a second. They might even feel bad but they don't feel bad enough to not do it for their own benefit.

Kiana: Which is sad because it's that selfishness that makes love hard. But I guess that's what makes the hunt for love so much more worth it. When you find somebody worth it, someone who's as *selfless* as you are then nothing else matters, right? Or so we can only hope.

To be continued...

100 Days of Dating

DAY FORTY-ONE:
ALL IS FAIR IN LOVE AND SACRIFICE

"I guess that's just part of loving people: You have to give things up. Sometimes you even have to give them up." - Lauren Oliver

We are no strangers to sacrifice. In fact, I believe a lot of our common ground is founded on the simple act of giving things up. Sometimes, we have to be real with ourselves to know when time is truly up for situations in our lives, or even when the time is up for certain people. It's a reality with love, sometimes we can't have it all.

But then, in the same breath I believe we often mistake sacrifice and compromise. Everything we do in the name of love shouldn't feel like a loss. We should be willing to set some things free or be okay with not doing something to appease the one we love, right? Loving someone is a shared experience, one where choosing to love and choosing to be in a relationship already opts you out of selfishness. It's removing the "I" for "we."

Orville, 22, and I battled with this one. We tried to figure out what makes sacrificing hard, why it needs to happen, and how making tough decisions impacts our love lives. We didn't have all the answers but we did come to a pretty solid conclusion: All is fair in love and sacrifice. This is his story.

Tell me about your love life. Are you single? Are you married? Are you dating? What's going on?

I want to say dating, but what does "dating" mean? Every time I ask my mom she'd say, dating is just seeing people. So, I guess it's not like you're exclusive but it's trying people out.

Yeah, in this day and age terminology is so different. But I'd say dating is our equivalent to "talking" to someone or people.

So, I'm dating ... Okay.

Are you talking to more than one person?

I feel like "talking" can be broken down too (laughs)

Is there anybody in your life right now that you're trying to pursue a relationship with?

No. I'm not ready for a relationship. I'm not on that type of time right now. I don't want to say I'm being selfish, because selfish sounds bad. But it's like selfish in a good way.

I can understand that. When was the last time you've been in a relationship or have you been in one at all?

I have been in one. The last time I was in one was probably around last year. Yeah, last year.

How long did it last?

It lasted probably like two years I think.

Did you love her?

I did.

How did you know?

I knew because that's where a lot of my time and energy went. I was invested in her, and put more time and energy again. So, that's how I knew, I just wouldn't do that with anybody, you know? What's the point?

And so after putting in that amount of energy before, you know right now that's not something you want to do?

Yeah, exactly.

Have you ever had your heart broken?

I have not actually, thank God. I know that probably sucks. But no, I think that's because I haven't really given 100%. Meaning, when it came to relationships, I've always put in less than.

You don't give 100% in relationships? That sounds crazy.

Not the entire time, but it's different. I can't keep it at 100% forever because in the back of my head, I'm aware that heartbreak is possible. Opening myself up like that could give her the power to actually break my heart. So, I don't.

Have you ever let anyone get close enough to you to show you different?

People have been close enough. They've definitely been close enough, but as far as me truly whole-heartedly being able to be say, "yes, I want this," -- no. No one has been that close. I know this sounds bad (laughs)

It does and doesn't at the same time. We're so young, you haven't met her yet, and that's okay too. But why don't you let people in?

I mean, yeah, there's definitely time for it. Not to say that a relationship will hinder you, but it kind of does. And to be honest, I don't know why I haven't. But when it comes to relationships, I have to question, *do I have time for all of this?* Most times I'm usually the busy one.

What is one of the biggest lessons you've learned after having been in a relationship for those two years?

I would say sacrifice. That's definitely if not the biggest, it's certainly up there. Sacrifice. I've learned what it means to take the time to truly understand what someone is saying, reversing roles, it's simple but it's so crazy. If you actually think about how the person will feel before you do or say things, it really changes how you move; it changes everything. I've learned you really should think before you do shit, and choose after your thoughts, that's sacrifice.

How would you describe love?

I kind of want to say sacrifice again.

Love is sacrifice?

Kiana St Louis

Yeah, like it might be cliché but I think sacrifice is really big, I'm big on that now. Everything you do is a sacrifice. If it's not one thing it's the other thing, so you are sacrificing something, but definitely for love.

Why do you feel that way?

It's based on the decisions you make. With sacrifice, you've got to choose one thing over choosing another; especially in a relationship and in love. If you love somebody you could choose to spend time with him or her or you could sacrifice that and do something else.

But it doesn't have to be a *sacrifice* though. Why can't it be, you're choosing to do this because you want to do this? Choosing to be with your girl over anything else shouldn't feel like a loss.

I mean, but you're choosing something over something else though in a sense. Again, if it's not one thing it's going to be the other thing. I could either be spending my time with you or I could be spending my time with my bros, chilling, I could be at work, or anything.

So would you rather do those things over being in a relationship?

I'm not saying I would rather do those things, I'm just saying it's a choice. You have to sacrifice, sacrifice doesn't have to be negative.

Do you have so many things to do a day that you have daily sacrifices? Do you understand what I'm saying? That's where I'm coming from with this, it's not even so much that it's a negative connotation, I'm just questioning why you seem to have so many options that in turn make you feel like you're sacrificing what you're doing to be with your girl?

Sometimes I feel like everybody wants a piece of my time. Shit is crazy. It's like I'll tell people I'm busy and they'd just be like "Yo, he's not really busy. He's lying." But I'm so serious! I thought I was busy before, now I'm super busy. I've got a 9 to 5, it's slow for so many things.

I come home and I'm tired. Things need to be planed, you know? So in a sense I'm sacrificing if I'm coming to see you because I could be sleeping. If I love you, I'm going to come see you instead of sleeping, so I'm sacrificing sleep time to go hang out with you because I love you that much.

(laughs) These sound like personal dilemmas. It's a sacrifice, you're right. I think you might need to re-evaluate what you do during the day.

That's true (laughs). Matter of fact, maybe I should reposition this: A big part of love is compromise. You can't half step that.

Kiana St Louis

DAY FORTY-TWO:
20 SOMETHING & SELFISHLY IN LOVE

"The sad thing is most people have to check with someone before they do the things that make them happy. We're all passing through; the least we can do is be happy, and the only way to do that is by being selfish." - Gene Simmons

Cuban Activist Jose Marti once said that a selfish man is a thief. I completely disagree.

I think a selfish man or woman is one that is not a thief but instead a leader. You have to be confident enough to make the decision to choose you and your needs before that of others. Yet, being selfish is considered a taboo. They want us to be great, thrive in all that we do, be #relationshipgoals and anything else you could imagine, all while also giving our time and energy to different things and people constantly.

But how can we take care of others if we don't first take care of ourselves?

On an airplane, we're advised to put on our safety masks first and *then* assist others. This is so we can be our best selves, so we are able to save our life and maybe someone else's. What about that is wrong? I think we need to reevaluate the idea of "selfishness" when it comes to love. In being selfish, you should recognize your standards, know what and whom you'll accept in your life, and precede with caution. We shouldn't always be selfish in love, but in the beginning of new endeavors and *then* exercise being unselfish when you believe you've found your match. To be selfish is to understand balance – balance between you and your counterpart(s).

100 Days of Dating

Shannell Hayes, 24, and I are in an understanding of this. Being young and figuring out this love thing requires self-awareness first and foremost. It's so easy to get caught up doing the wrong thing with the wrong person for too long. Creating time to understand yourself and your wants doesn't make you a thief of time, it makes you a compassionate lover, and something I think many of us forget is essential to any healthy relationship. As we go through our 20's, Shannell reminded me of how important it is to figure out exactly who we are. This is a decade to be bold, to be risky, and to be our most selfish. This is her story.

So, tell me about your love life. Are you single, are you dating, are you in a relationship, you're married?

I'm currently in a relationship, on my way to marriage.

Oh, really, that's amazing! I have to admit this is a first for the series.

(laughs) I'm on my way there.

So, when you say, "On your way there," what do you mean?

I mean this is a person that I chat with, we're together all the time and, we've discussed marriage. So, we're in that state where he's asking, "What kind of rings do you like?" "Do you like this?" We're talking about moving out, getting our own place, and making it official.

That's so exciting! It's funny that you bring that up. I was having a conversation with some friends, and we were asking ourselves, are we there yet? Us, 20-somethings, is it time for marriage and babies?

I think so, definitely.

So you say that we should be at that stage of marriage and children?

Absolutely. But don't get me wrong; I don't think that because you're in your 20's you absolutely have to get married. But I do think in our 20s we should be getting to that point where you have to stop just dating for fun. At a certain point, you have to stop being immature, and you have to grow up. It's not saying, be Mr. or Mrs. whoever tomorrow, but you should be leading towards those steps and finding the mentality or the mind space to want to find the person that you're going to marry.

I agree with you on the points of maturity. So, you don't think we're too young for this, or that *you're* too young?

Who dictates who's "too young" anyway? There are people getting married at 18, as soon as they're allowed to. I think there's a risk of if you marry at a certain age, you might feel like you haven't accomplished all that you wanted to. Maybe you didn't have enough sex with other people. But, are you mentally ready? I don't think there's really an age for it. I just think that when you get into your mid-20s, you have to stop playing. You don't have to get married, but you should be ready to be married.

Do you feel as if you've had enough different experiences and sex, to say you're ready to fully commit to this person?

I never pictured that I would be the marrying type. So, the thought of committing to just that one person makes me feel- not like I'm trapped but, I realize that thought in a sense, and it's kind of like my immature side. It's not like I'm not really ready to commit, I think that I'm ready for it. For me, there's no such thing as "I didn't get to have sex with this person, I'm not ready to get married." No.

You have to get to a point in life where you have to change the way you think, it's not about "this is the last person I'm going to have sex with." It's about *is this my best friend? Can I wake up next to you every morning? Can I spend every day with you? When I get tired of you, am I going to pick up and never see you again or are we going to work through it?*

I understand the person you're dating is also your baby's father. Do you think this is your greatest love?

To give you an honest answer, when we first started dating, he absolutely wasn't. But my mind and my heart were so caught up on somebody from my past. So, I don't know if it's a matter of he wasn't that person or that I wasn't letting him be that person. But that's definitely not what it was for a long time in the beginning.

But being that we do have a child together, at some point I did have to tell myself, *you need to be a little bit more open to allowing this man to be his full potential so he could be in your life.* Once I did that, he did become that person. It took time for me to love him the way I do now. It definitely wasn't like "boom! We're in love." I had to really get over somebody else to realize that they were just temporary and he was more of the forever.

How did you get over that other person?

It was a battle. We had a really deep relationship. So, we tried to get it together but it was a lot of back and forth, sometimes we wouldn't talk. Then we kept drawing back to each other. So, it wasn't an overnight thing at all. But, I had to stay away from them and try to talk to them less. After that I met someone new- of course, you know, meeting someone new always makes it like a little bit easier.

But in meeting that new person and not wanting to hurt them because of this old person, it made me realize, I had to make a choice. I was either going to be stuck on this person, who I'm just clearly not going to work out with - because if things were going to work out, I would've been with them. Or, I have to let them go, and try to start something with this new person who, obviously loves me. I had to give them a real chance to be loved back. So, it was just like a lot of drawing myself away from that person and not wanting to hurt the new person.

And again, I just had to realize, I didn't want to be stupid anymore, you know? That's a big part of it. You just have to wake up one day and say, "Do I really want to keep being dumb for this one person?" If they really loved me, would they want me looking stupid?

Would you say you're happier without your ex now?

Kiana St Louis

I wouldn't say I'm happier without them. In my perfect world, I'd be with the person that I'm with now and my ex and I would still be friends. But I realize that a friendship, a genuine friendship, with my ex is something that's never going to happen because, whether it's on my side or their side, there are just too many feelings involved. Now it's mainly on their side. I'm over it, but because of those feelings that have yet to go away we can never have a real friendship.

So, would I say happier? No. But, I'm- content sounds so settling- I don't want to say so content. I'm at peace with it. I know that I made the right decision and that makes me feel peaceful with how it is now.

What advice would you give to someone who's in a similar situation, someone who had been battling with their past, and almost blocking their future?

Think about yourself. It's not always going to be a female, but I do know that in general, when women love somebody we think about their feelings a lot and it makes us feel stuck with them. We think, *they want us back, let's go for it*, or *I don't want to hurt them, let's go for it*. But you have to think about you.

Do **you** want to keep going back to this person? Do **you** want to keep getting hurt by this person? Do **you** want to keep going through the stress that the back and forth causes? Either you guys are going to be together or you're not. Are you happier when you're with them? Or are you happier when you're without them? The decision isn't always to leave. You just have to take the time to think about yourself and truly see what works best for you. Some things are as simple as that.

100 Days of Dating

DAY FORTY-THREE: SECOND CHANCES

"Because this is what I believe - that second chances are stronger than secrets. You can let secrets go. But a second chance? You don't let that pass you by." - Daisy Whitney

Time after time we give the people we love the opportunity to make countless mistakes. We prepare ourselves for the hurt, create the mold we need for thicker layers of skin, accept the sappy apologies and promises to "never do it again," all in the name of a second chance. A second chance, which most times probably means the third or fourth time around.

However, Cheng Tessier, 25, has run his well dry. At some point, we have to grow up and sometimes that means dropping the playboy hat. It doesn't mean he's going to trade the hat in for a ring, but he did realize that he couldn't half-ass playing the game if wanted to really win. In fact, Cheng knows now the only way to make his second chance his last chance, is to go big or go home for the one he loves. This is his story.

Tell me about your love life. Are you single, married, or engaged? What's going on with you?

I would say that I was single. But, I've been dealing with the same person, for about 5-6 years now.

But you guys aren't in a relationship?

No.

Why not?

Well, we have our differences. She thinks that I'm not going to love her and care for her and that I'll probably be a player, which I'm known for with my past. I guess she doesn't think we'll actually get to the finish line.

But you don't think that?

Nah, I don't think that. I think right now where I am in life at my age, I'm actually ready to settle down and commit to one person. I've decided to go all in and try committing to this one person.

That's awesome. But I'm curious, why have you been going back and forth with this person? Why haven't you just tried to meet somebody new or try it with somebody else?

Well, I have tried with other people but usually when I try to talk to other people, I end up comparing them to this one person. They're always lacking the characteristics or maybe the personality that this person has. She's just different. She's like my best friend. She's somebody that I know I could be 100% comfortable with. Somebody that I know I can bring around my family and my friends. I can take her anywhere; she's like a chameleon, she can fit in any position and play any part.

Yeah, I get that completely. And that's why you keep going back?

Yeah. You know, when you're comfortable with someone and you know someone so much and so well, there's no point in trying to meet a new person and attempt to get to know them when there's someone in front of you that you can build something with.

Do you love her?

I just think... yeah.

Yeah? You sound kind of sure but also not so sure.

I'm 100% sure. I don't want to say, "Yeah, I love this person" because I have love for her, but I've never been in that position where I could say, "Hey, look, I love you" and the person tells me I love you back. I know that I have love for this person. I care for this person more than I care for anybody else. It's got to be some kind of love there.

How do you define love?

Love is a commitment between two people. People always say that they love each other, but I think love is more than just saying the word. I think love is when you and that person are allowed to fight, and you give to that person. If you have your last dollar and that person needs that dollar, you give that person the dollar, it's half of what you have.

You have to be committed to that person. You have to actually know this person, know what makes them upset and know what makes them happy. These things matter when it comes to saying that you love someone. You have to know that if this person is in a different country for six months, are you going to still love them and not cheat on him or her or try to be with someone else. That's what I think love is.

Have you ever had your heart broken?

Yeah, I have had my heart broken.

What happened?

I was dating this girl while I still liked someone else that I'd been talking to for six years. I was into this girl. I finally decided, okay, let me be serious and be in a relationship. I was dating her for about a year. I realized that we just weren't on the same page, mentally, maybe physically we were on the same page - but mentally we weren't on the same page.

I ended up going through this completely different phase because I realized that if I was to keep having unprotected sex with this person, I would never be able to lose feelings for her, and so I went to a different state. She ended up giving up and moving away. It took me a long time to get over her, but it was just more of a rebuilding process for me. I had to rebuild myself. I had to get strength and come back to where I wanted to be in life. I was so down. I would be depressed, not wanting to get out of my blanket. I was really sad, but I was able to actually fight through all that and I'm here today. I'm as happy as I ever could be.

How did you get over it? What were some steps you took to mend your broken heart?

I hung out with my friends a lot. I spoke to a lot of people that went through similar situations. I'm not going to lie, I did have a couple nights where I found myself drinking and trying to numb the pain that I couldn't feel. At the end of the day, what really helped me get over the situation was the support of my family, friends, and just talking to people about the experience and learning from it. I just learned from that and everybody else's experiences. Talking to family and friends helped me realize that that person just wasn't for me. If she was for me, she'd still be in my life.

That's so true. I don't think people realize that enough. Sometimes, we want love so bad from a certain person that we're willing to go through everything and every option except letting go. Have you ever experienced the situation of "the girl that got away?"

Yeah, I can say that.

Is the girl that "got away" the one that you're kind of dating but not really?

Yeah.

So, in trying to get her back, what are some of the steps you're taking?

I try to send her messages, "good morning" every morning, "good night" every night. I try to contact her as much as possible. I try to take her out, I try to make her dinners, you know, buy her flowers. Any little thing that I can possibly do, to show her that I'm 100% interested, I do.

Do you think it's working?

(laughs) I hope so!

What is the biggest lesson you've learned in terms of love?

100 Days of Dating

The biggest lesson I've learned is to actually get to know a person. A lot of times people just have sex and think, *I'm in love* based off the fact of having sex. There's more to just having sex. There's more to just saying "I love you." There's a lot that comes with being in love with somebody.

This whole situation with us made me grow up because she wanted me to be something that I wasn't before. I like where I am in life, I wish I had done this sooner.

Kiana St Louis

DAY FORTY-FOUR: WHY I CHOSE YOU

"Never be ashamed of how much you love, or how quickly you fall. Love fully, love completely, but most importantly, love naturally - and don't ever apologize for it. Don't ever be sorry for loving the way your heart knows."

Contributed poetry by: Mina Milad

I've always underestimated myself,
Always tried to humble myself,
But when it came to true affection.
Settling was out of the question

I used to settle for the ones in my league,
Continually thinking that my game was weak.
So what if she's just alright?
It's just a girl, am I not right?

But this is love we're talking about,
A force larger than all doubts.
This girl could be my wife.
She could reflect my entire life.

And so when I saw the perfect one,
I thought, it's her or none.
Might as well give it a shot.
For once I'll be the man I'm not.

I chose her because she was the best.
I fell in love with her; God knows the rest.
Convincing myself I'm more than a mess,
God gave me perfection and nothing less.

DAY FORTY-FIVE: EX-BOYFRIEND, THE FUCK BOY

"Somebody asked me if I knew you. A million memories flashed through my mind, but I just smiled and said I used to."

Spoken Word from an ex. Contributed by: Shaine Fraz:

You like to say love disappeared.
And I swear it never left, but she talk like Kanye "Ima let you finish"
shrug her shoulders; cut me off, Swift.
Drinks on the table it was no one else's business, Henny in my system there was no one else who witnessed how she never took a breath like a run on sentence so I'm in the club flexing working on my fitness; arms out stretched on my chest crucifixion.
I'm forgiven but could never get a word in not even one syllable I'm talking in synonyms I,

Never
ever
nevermore, words with friends. Triple word how absurd you be trippin shit, on my Instagram insecurity I'm tired of it I'm with my boys chillin rarely smoked but might burn a spliff; ease the pain so insane Major Payne fatigue is in.
I got a glimpse of future, I use to, try to hit you up reconnect, Bluetooth, I'm in her ear lying for the sex, I miss you, she on top giving me the truth: this all you. But fuck it though I'm not tryna be your man, but when she leaving out for work I be sleepin in and when she home I tax that ass like I'm Uncle Sam nothing ever change so after head she be at my neck
next

Kiana St Louis

Flashback to the present
--and--
she still telling me how I don't get it
stressed
unproductive in her presence, you not even in front of me I'm still tasting lemons; Yo, my star player wants a trade should I let her go? Cut too deep for bandaids should I let it flow.
Throwback to the past vampire clothes but the blood different I'm a sucker for that red though: she was floating 6 inches from the earth floor, you's a victim baby true blood, spoil us! Show Me What You Got lil mama let your "Kingdom Come" dressed in all black spending money black republican? Awesome and some; I was sliding home she was catching, clamping; say I turn her on like a touch screen, Samsung; with a touch of color you would disobey your mother as I slid under your covers
mid-day massages
"Midnight Maunders"
at least that's how it use to be, now Award Tour got her trippin almost frequently
we use to fight for love she said now she a causality!
"and how you gonna make this bout you it's about me, phone ringing since 1am it's about 3
thought you was slick huh,
thought I was sleep, you damn right love disappeared"
but she never leaves.
She's still waiting to exhale, but she never breaths.

100 Days of Dating

DAY FORTY-SIX: WHEN THE TIME IS RIGHT

"The right thing at the wrong time is the wrong thing." - Joshua Harris

We fight that reality sometimes, or maybe I should speak for myself. However, I do believe Joshua Harris is on to something: The right *person* at the wrong time is the wrong person. But often times, even though the heart knows there's something off, I've fought for that wrong person anyway. Most times much harder than I ought to.

Dealing with rebound situations can fall under this category as well. Like the time you needed to get over your ex and found solace in someone new. The rebound could be such a great person, but you're clearly not all the way invested because your heart still lies where it probably shouldn't, somewhere with your ex wrapped up in hope. So, what does that mean for the rebound? Right person, wrong time? I'd say wrong person altogether.

The fact is, love and time need to dance together. It's a waltz, made for two. I realize that anytime I tried to interject, I'd knock them both off balance. The two dance to the beat of patience, which is where we should be. Lavon Johnson and I figured this out together. We've both challenged time at the expense of love before but realize the most cliché thing, what's meant to be will be. We can't fight what we can't control and that's probably the most important thing I've ever said, simply because one cannot control love. We can't make the ones we love act right or love us back. We can't make rebounds work if that person truly isn't for us. But we can make sure that every other part of our lives are moving even if our relationships aren't. There's so much more to do with ourselves than be hung up on one person, than be stuck trying to figure things out, or home crying.

Shannon Alder said it best, "the most confused you will ever get is when you try to convince your heart and spirit of something your mind knows is a lie." It took us some time, but I believe Lavon and I get this now. This is her story.

So, tell me about your love life. Are you single? Married? In a relationship?

I'm single, currently dating. Not in a relationship.

How long have you been single?

This would be three years now. Three years single.

How's that time span been for you? Do you feel like you've learned a lot about yourself within those three years?

Yes. I think you do learn a lot about yourself being single and you truly see yourself outside of a relationship. These three years, I think if I were in a relationship I would've never known myself the way I do now.

What do you know about yourself now that you hadn't known before?

I know now that I can be on my own. I think when I was in a relationship, I always felt like I needed someone to be happy. I learned that I can be happy by myself. I learned things I like outside of a man. So, much more so what I learned by being single.

Definitely. Have you been in love before?

Of course, twice. I loved one more than the other, my first love was everything.

Do you remember what it felt like being in love with him?

It was probably the best feeling in the world at the time. I just felt free. I just felt really good.

Why did it end?

Differences. We didn't see eye to eye on certain things. I think we both were growing and were at a stage in our lives where we were just trying to see what was next. We had just graduated college and I think that he had a vision for himself, and I had one for myself as well. I think we weren't able to work out because we couldn't get those visions to line up.

When you broke up, did you feel like that was one of your greatest heartbreaks?

It was my greatest heartbreak.

So he was your greatest love and your greatest heartbreak. How did you get through it?

Time. Time is really important, and you can't fight it, unfortunately. But you can start trying to focus more toward yourself and not toward the heartbreak, if that makes sense. It's a hard process, it is, I'm not going to lie and say it's easy. But you take each day at a time. Each day, that's what I did.

Having been single these past three years, what are your personal thoughts on the role technology plays in our love lives?

A lot. Technology keeps growing and now plays a big part. People idolize the relationships they see online and think this is how their relationship is supposed to be, and that's not always what it seems. People seem to be so happy online but, oh my God, they give you relationship goals and they're not. Deep down inside, they're not. I think people look at these relationships and think this is what they want. They think that what they see is real life. That every day, a couple's happy, a couple doesn't go through anything, it's not like that. Nobody can say it's ever like that. So, I think technology now, plays even more of a big part on relationships than before.

Do you think because people have these unrealistic goals that there can be a negative outlook on relationships?

No, I think it just puts too much pressure on relationships. People can lose sight of themselves wanting a relationship they see broadcasted online. So I don't think it's a negative, I think it's more so pressure.

Can you say that you've been completely happy these past three years as single?

Yes. I would say that. For me personally, I just enjoy being single. When I was in a relationship, I thought *oh my God, if I'm ever single it's going to be the saddest thing ever, I'm not going to have someone to call*, etc. But no, I can say that I'm happy, I'm enjoying it. I'm actually enjoying it. I don't have to go through the shit that I went through in a relationship and I'm more focused on myself. I'm actually happy.

That's good! That makes me hopeful. So, when you are ready for your next adventure with someone, what are three qualities that you feel you'll definitely want from your next partner?

Someone who likes to communicate, someone who likes to listen, and someone that's trustworthy.

Have you had issues with those things in the past?

Yes, because guys don't really like to communicate, I think it's usually the female constantly communicating. Some guys don't like to show emotion, so it's really hard to communicate with someone who's guarded or thinks that every time you're trying to explain something that's going on, you're arguing with them. So, communication is number one for me.

Do you think women should communicate less? Or stop initiating it so much? Then, maybe guys will get the point.

No. Why? I think if there's something that you want to say, you should communicate it. That's why you're with that person, right? Communicate! It doesn't always have to be an argument, that's how guys view it, "Oh she just wants to argue, she just wants to nag", but it's really not. *Most of the time*, anyway... Most of the time it's late at night, and you just want to talk. And if you can't communicate with your partner, who else are you going to communicate with? You don't want to keep telling your friends, your friends aren't in a relationship with you. So, you should be able to communicate to the person you're with, that's your source. But guys don't look at it that way. Most guys don't look at it that way.

What advice would you give to somebody who has been in a similar situation as you?

I say take your time. I'd say use your friendships to fill up more of your time. You don't always have to go into a situation thinking "Okay, this is the guy I'm going to be with, this is the guy I want." No, because it doesn't work like that. I'd say friendships are so important. Use them and take your time. Don't be in a rush for relationships. Things that happen fast, end fast too. So, just take your time on everything and the rest will work itself out.

Kiana St Louis

DAY FORTY-SEVEN: LOVE IS...

"Love and peace are not just words, they are a way of life. And in an honest living, love will always conquer." - Ahmad Ardalan

Love is patient. Love is kind. Love does not envy, it does not boast, it is not proud, it is not rude, it is not self-seeking, it is not easily angered. Love keeps no record of wrongs and does not delight in evil. Love rejoices with the truth. Love always protects, always trusts, always hopes, and always preserves. Love never fails.

Love is letting go of fear. I've known this a long time, I've read the bible verses, but I've also had to be reminded of this recently by Noel Hayes, 23. In our talk, Noel gave insight into his thoughts on the world of love & today's technology, why patience is a virtue *especially with love*, and how being a good friend almost cost him a potential relationship. This is his story.

Tell me about your love life. Are you single? Dating? In a relationship? Married? It's complicated?

I am single right now, but I do speak to a few people. No one seriously currently, but yeah, that's my status as of right now.

When you say speak to different people, is it like you're dating? What does that mean?

This generation's definition of dating is a little different. As far as my research, I've been seeing that dating is not just having a title, it's more so even in the "speaking process," which could be considered dating. Everybody has their own definition.

How do you define it?

I would define it as getting to know somebody. You're dedicating your time to that one person. It's not different people at the same time. There's no title like, "That's my girlfriend" or anything of that sort.

Of the people that you are talking to now, do you see a future with any of them?

I would say there's definitely a possibility, but I like to take things slow. That's the type of person I am. If it's supposed to happen, it will happen. That's how I go about things.

That's a safe way to go for sure. Have you ever been in love?

Let's see, I would say slightly, but not fully. I don't know if that's possible, but yeah. I was young, like high school time. So, I would say partially been in love. Yeah, put it like that. I'm saying that because I was young. Being more mature now, I feel like love has a different definition.

Thinking back to how you've loved a girl before and how you plan to in the future, what are some of those differences? What does that future love look like?

I would say future love would look like spending time with that person even though we're busy, time is definitely something of the essence. I feel like if you really love somebody, you dedicate love to them, you would dedicate your time to them as much as possible.

Definitely time, getting to know them. You can't fully know somebody, so you should get to know them on a daily basis whenever you can, and of course show it. Action speaks louder than words as well. You could plan something that's spontaneous. Go out somewhere that's not eating or the movies. Do something that's not the day-to-day, ordinary thing.

Do you want to be in a relationship or have the kind of love you're describing with somebody any time soon?

Yeah, but I'm a busy guy. When women see that, they don't really try to go further, I guess. I'm really trying to make time for more people now because I'm getting older. I'm not scared of not getting married or having a relationship. I just pray about it and that's how I move. I pray about it and if somebody comes my way and we have a mutual feeling, then yeah, I'll try to make it work. If it doesn't work, then it wasn't meant to be. I'm definitely hopeful for something of that sort.

Do you think you're too busy to love or to fall in love?

No, I wouldn't say that by far. Love is in stages. That could happen two years down the line or a year. Depending on those two individuals. I would say as time goes by, of course when I'm well in it, I'm going to try to be less busy. I'm not *that* busy, but I feel like I could allocate more time to somebody else.

You actually mentioned something that I wanted to break into a little bit more. You were saying before that in this generation, it's so different these days, especially when it comes to "talking," "dating," or just the lingo. What are your thoughts on the role technology plays in our love lives?

I'd say social media plays a big role in the love life. I have this conversation with my brothers and family all the time about social media and relationships. I feel that social media definitely damages most relationships. I've been looking and even on Facebook, this is just my opinion, but some people don't really know how social media can damage a relationship because there are people out there preying on you like, "Oh, I hope this fails."

They're waiting to be the next option, things of that sort. That's with technology and texting, of course. Texting, that's another thing as well. I just wanted to focus on social media because that's the main thing that's connected to relationships especially in 2017. Everybody wanted to have that Hollywood relationship, not knowing what's going on in their lives behind the camera.

I think a lot of people would probably agree with you on that. I generalized it a little bit and said technology because I think about not just what happens on social media, but the simple fact that we've completely changed the way we talk to people now. Online dating is a huge thing.

Oh, yeah. That's another aspect.

It's the apps we use; it's the way we talk to people. It's less about talking to people for real or face to face, but more so connecting because it seems so much easier to do that.

Right. That's definitely true with things like Tinder, especially Tinder. That's another online dating thing that some people just play around with it. But I do think technology has its positives as well. I'm focused on the negative, but there's also a positive in it. Some people find somebody who's definitely worth their time through online dating and that's probably how it was meant to be for them, so yeah. It definitely has its pros and cons.

So true, that's a good way to put it. Have you ever had your heart broken?

I would say no because it was *almost* kind of like that. My heart just fell. It was with somebody I really wanted to get serious with but due to certain circumstances, I couldn't continue that. We were only in the "talking stage." That's what I would say the feeling would be connected to, but I wouldn't say I've officially got my heart broken or anything of that sort.

What happened? Why didn't you guys make it to the next level?

Oh, because I'm a loyal person. I feel that especially in a circle of close friends, if one of your friends had history with someone you're interested in it wouldn't be fair knowing that it could probably break the friendship if you continue pursuing that person. That was the case. The female had history with one of my friends. As I was talking to that person, I was seeing the friendship almost changing.

Okay, so you sacrificed a potential relationship to keep your friendship going. You decided to skip out on it altogether.

Yeah. I made that decision. She and I are still cordial, we check on each other here and there, but yeah. That wasn't meant to be, so that's a prime example. Even though it was a great experience, it just wasn't meant to be, I guess.

But to counter that thinking, how do we know if it wasn't meant to be if you stopped it?

That's true. It's just the morals that I have, my morals of loyalty and respect. I'm not going to pursue something like that because that's just not me. Even though I'm in it and I'm thinking I like it, I'm not going to feel fully connected. That thought is always going to be in the back of my mind. I don't want anything of that sort.

You played it really safe. I guess that makes you a good friend.

Yeah. I'm too nice sometimes. That's just me. I try to change it, but it's not in my nature. Girls come and go. If it's going to happen, it will happen as I said before.

Very true.

There's no rush.

After you've dated and talked to and partially loved and almost had your heart broken, what are one of the biggest lessons you learned about love?

One of the biggest lessons I learned? Love is definitely patient. Love is kind. So you have to take your time. Don't rush into anything. Try to feel that person out first. Even though it takes a long time to feel somebody out versus other people, but I think that's one of the important things. Physical appearance sidetracks a lot of people and they don't try to learn about people. Try to know a person first instead of jumping the gun.

100 Days of Dating

DAY FORTY-EIGHT: INVEST IN YOURSELF

"Happiness is when what you think, what you say, and what you do are in harmony." - Mahatma Gandhi

Good investments are usually hard to find. There are often so many things to consider: the longevity, overcoming any skepticism, trusting your investor(s), the list can go on. But there are far fewer risks when investing in yourself, your dreams, and/or your happiness. You will already have the upper hand when investing in yourself because you'll have the most important thing needed for business - *control*.

We know this. Yet, we allow romantic love for others to cloud our best judgment. We invest all of ourselves, all of our time, all of our thoughts and sometimes even our dreams into our relationships. We give up so much of ourselves selflessly, most times because of the person we want to be with, but because of how they make us feel. Love is a high and some of us give up anything to have it. Even our best selves.

While we can't control love, what it does, or sometimes who we share it with, we can control the depth of our happiness. We can control how far we're willing to take things and people. Love doesn't have to be a choice between loving someone and loving yourself. You must simply love yourself first, foremost, and always. That *is* the investment.

Tiffany Francis, 24, is a prime example of the benefits of a self-investment. Over the years, as our friendship has grown, I've had the humble opportunity to watch her grow, to watch her exude radiance when faced with life's battles, and have seen her blossom even after love worked out differently than she planned. But through it all, Tiffany has remained in harmony with herself, her goals, her dreams, and secured the place for her happiness. This is her story.

Tell me about your love life. Are you single, dating, in a relationship, it's complicated?

I am single. Happily single, actually.

I feel like I haven't heard someone say it like that in a while. What makes you happily single?

I feel like it's been a different space for me. And it took me some time to get to this point because I feel like I love, and I love hard, so it takes a long time to allow my heart to let go of people. Being single, and newly single, I think it opened my eyes up to many things about myself and who I will allow in my life in the romantic sense.

But in being single, I've learned that sometimes you have to just love people from a distance, period. It's okay to no longer talk to people every day and be socially forward in their life. You can still love someone even though they hurt you, but it's really about understanding the pain they caused you and understanding that they're probably not the best choice in your growth and your confidence level and for you just being the best woman you can be. When you do finish things in a relationship, it strips you. It takes a lot from you. And when you feel that imbalance within yourself and that you're no longer growing and being your best self, you have to put things in perspective.

I shall always be my number one priority. Friendship or not, a person should always be your cheerleader and pushing for you to be the best. And when that's no longer happening you need to reevaluate things between you and the person.

You mentioned that you were newly single. How long ago did you break up or cut off whatever it was that was happening before?

Seriously, it was like we dated, but he wasn't going to make it to the next step, kind of thing.

How did you know that was the situation? I sometimes feel like women almost play themselves when they know that someone isn't long-term but keep fighting for it.

100 Days of Dating

With the person I dated, I just fucking knew he wasn't long-term. Even with the way I allowed the relationship to grow, I allowed certain things to happen, because in the back of my mind he wasn't the guy I wanted to be married to. It never seemed like he was the guy I wanted to have kids with. Which also made me question myself, because I'm like, "Why am I feeling him, why am I doing all these things if I know this feels temporary?"

That's why I'm saying; being single put so many things in retrospect, because you don't realize the bullshit that you're doing. It brought up a lot of red flags in me. I'm like, "That is not okay. What were you doing it for? Were you bored? Were you lonely?" I don't see why we entertain people who we know we aren't to trust. You can just be friends! It's okay to be friends with someone.

We set ourselves up to be hurt sometimes, by not paying attention when they show you all the damn signs don't align with what you see to be a good partner for yourself. When we're still there fighting for it, you have to ask yourself why. Why are you loyal to people who aren't loyal to your well-being?

I think a lot of that stems from the fact that sometimes loneliness creeps in and ... I don't want to say confuses us, but blocks what happiness could look like because you're too busy being lonely. So, the minute somebody else comes in, it's just like, even though I know this isn't for real, it's for real right now.

I do think that plays a part, but sometimes I don't know if it's necessarily loneliness. Sometimes I feel like it's the high that comes with being in a relationship, that feeling of being wanted, possibly? People love that shit. I think that's why people love: People want to feel wanted; people want to feel appreciated, as if they mean something to someone. That feeling is unmatched, especially when it's true. I think people chase that feeling and we negate anything else, even if it's right in front of our face, screaming, "No, don't go any further! Hazard!"

Very true. Have you ever been in love?

I have, yeah.

Why do you say it like that? Was it something or someone that you can reflect happily upon?

Yeah. When I first met him, I was like, "He's gonna be mine." I wasn't playing any games! You can ask my friends, I said it, "He is going to be mine." I claimed it. Nobody else was getting in the way of him being my man.

I finally got him, and he made me really happy, he really did. But he was also a fucking liar and a cheater. With things like that, it bugs me that you can be so in love and you can remember those moments. I got happy remembering certain moments with him. I do still have those feelings, but ultimately I got to the time where I had to question, *how could you be so perfect but yet such a horrible person?* That shit boggles me. I can't put my finger on it, because it's like, "How can you be so great and do everything right but then fuck up so much and make me feel like shit?"

How did you cope when everything hit the fan and you realized that the person you loved wasn't exactly who he said he was?

I realized that I hold things in. I don't exactly like to deal with my feelings. I keep busy. I'd start doing more work, or I feel like that's when I excel most. I'd take that hurt and I'd do something else with myself. For example, every time I was going through a major heartbreak or something like that, girl, my grades were looking the best. I get tired; I'd start killing shit at work. It just makes me excel.

But also, how else do I cope? Girlfriends. I honestly cope because they know me. They know that I'm not the most open person about certain feelings, but you can sense when my energy is off. Them being that constant reminder of, "Man, you're amazing, and he's a fool," still making me understand my role in what happened, but continuously reminding me of my magic at all times is the key.

Everybody needs somebody. You need people like that.

I honestly think that I have the most amazing support system. In situations like that, I can truly be vulnerable and be myself, cry my fucking eyes out, then party it up after because we not going to be depressed over some guy.

But they allow me to just be myself and go through the motions for Tiffany. Everyone's healing process is very different. They allow me to be myself, but give me sound advice in every phase that I go through.

Definitely. You mentioned earlier that being single taught you a lot about yourself and things are now in perspective. If you could, give us three lessons you've learned while being single what would they be?

I literally wrote it this week; it's a short list. Mind if I run through it? Maybe it can help someone.

Let's do it.

1. Speak your mind; stop waiting for the perfect opportunity.

2. When you recognize someone can't offer you the love and commitment needed to sustain a healthy relationship in your eyes, just walk away, and there's nothing to talk about at that point.

3. People treat you the way you allow them to treat you. So, if you make them believe you're okay with something, you're encouraging that behavior.

4. Don't be afraid to express what you need or want. Your happiness should always be your number one priority.

5. Don't let the fear of losing someone you deeply care about hinder you from receiving what life has to offer.

6. If it's real and true, action and words will always be parallel.

7. You can't change a person. State your issue; if he does not want to work on tackling that, you know where you stand. If the issues you stated are a deal-breaker for you, then he has to make the effort to change, or walk away. It's realizing what your hard-core values are, versus what you're more willing to compromise on. Which goes into what I'm about to say:

8. Stay true to your unwavering standards. Compromise knowing what standards are malleable and those that are set in stone.

9. Finally, always stay true to yourself. Value yourself, not just a good time.

100 Days of Dating

DAY FORTY-NINE: DREAMS

Last weekend I had the humble opportunity to be the keynote speaker at the first annual Cap'n Crowns graduation ceremony. This event was a chance for young black educated women to network, gain insights, and simply learn from each other. My favorite part about all of this, besides the fact that it was organized and founded by two of my great friends Sheneya Wilson and Bilikiz Adebayo, was that this was a call to welcome all graduates from across the spectrum. Whether you were graduating junior high school or college, the goal was to honor success while ensuring the steps for the future.

What I really wanted people to know is that there is no straight path, no secrets to success, no perfect plan, or correct way to do anything. We are all motivated by different things and people in our lives, so our journeys will always differ. What success may look like to you could very well be failure to me, but I do not define my course by the wind of others. I cannot compare my successes. I cannot think that other people's pictures, posts, or social updates are stepping stones for my own process. I can't move forward if I continue to stop and compare, or worst keep looking back. None of us can.

I shared my story, but not before sharing this poem entitled *Dreams*. I wrote this because I wanted people to not only hear me but also feel me as I undergo my own journey to success. Just like this project of love, I'm constantly learning how alike we all are, how afraid we are of the same things, how a lack of direction can be stifling to us all. This poem was written in hopes to inspire those reading to continue dream chasing. Regardless of how big or small, we can and will reach our goals to secure our cap's and invest in our crowns.

Dreams

Dreams bigger than China's Great Wall, I have them

Dreams so real even my thoughts can't fathom

I sit alone at night, pen and paper in hand drawing my future

Kiana St Louis

allowing the ink to draw blood on this sheet as a cold sweat sweeps over me, I find peace in defining the skill set I know.

Let the lines be cementing, tempting my thoughts, altering my reality,

creating anxiety, but I have little doubt in me.

I am real life goals.

If one door closes, let it be so

Instead, I'll find another entrance, maybe a window that will allow me to grow

Because quitting is a disease. It spreads slowly, it eats up your confidence and weakens you steadily

Giving up on your favorite things, is like cutting off a bird's wings

For if you really want to achieve your goals

You will never find an excuse

If you really want to live your dream

Petty reassurance you will never use

So, don't give up because you can't do something

Don't give up because you haven't achieved anything

You have it in you to do everything

Don't give up because you can't reach somewhere

Don't give up because you can get anywhere

You have it in you to attain success everywhere

My dreams are my reality.

I am Charlie, this world is my factory

100 Days of Dating

By faith I walk, Grind is my talk

I wear my future on my wrist so I look down only to admire it

My dreams keep me grounded.

I am fearful of little but hopeful for all

I can do anything through Christ who strengthens me big dreams or small,

I have them. I am them. I am my dreams.

Kiana St Louis

DAY FIFTY: FOOL'S GOLD

When Travis Linton, 26, told me he was in a relationship, I couldn't believe it. Not because he's a horrible person of any kind, but because when you're good friends with someone and have learned their traits, few things tend to surprise you. Until this.

His new love venture impacted me much more than I expected it would, or at all to be honest. The impact came not from the surprise of the relationship, but I was taken aback by his willingness to change his mentality and actions. I was in awe of the strength it took and is still taking to put his sole needs to the side to uphold that of his woman's. I absolutely love the fact that as a man, he has learned to admit his faults and is still willing to learn the rules of love. His love inspired me.

Travis and I would argue all the time about the differences between men and women, why women think the way they do, why men act the way they do, and a common argument for me is lack of commitment. I never understood why men could pour their hearts out into basketball with tunnel vision goals on the NBA, spend weeks in the studio making tracks they only pray the right person will hear, or working countless jobs to finance equipment or a trip, yet seem to have the most troubling time putting in work to be in a relationship. Is real love just not as tangible as fame or money? The debate would get heated, but Travis changed the game.

He reminded me that love and relationships are a choice. You choose to put the work in for your future career just as much as you choose to make your relationships work. Only a fool would choose the wrong answer twice, but I guess we're all a bit foolish when it comes to love. This is his story.

Tell me about your love life. Are you single, dating, in a relationship?

I'm in a relationship with a beautiful young woman.

Oh! Congrats. To be honest, I'm very proud of you, from a non-interviewer perspective.

(laughs) Thank you, Ki.

Tell me about her. How did it happen? How did you guys meet?

Well, we met at a party. We didn't say a word to each other all night. We just sat next to each other and vibed. It was incredible. Her energy was outstanding. I felt it. I really did. And she was beautiful. It was a win-win for me.

Would you say that you're happy right now?

What do you mean by happy? Because with work and other shit in life, I'm not really too happy with that, but with her, I'm happy. She makes me happy. She eases my mind off of all the other shit, so she is my happiness.

Do you love her?

I believe so.

You believe so?

I'd say that. I'm not an expert on love, but the way I feel, the way I feel for her, the things that she gets, I've never felt this way. You know? People that know me know that. I feel like I love her.

Why do you think it's hard for men to talk about love in this capacity?

Some people don't know it. Some men don't know it. Some men have never really felt what love is, and love means different things to different people. Some people in love do some crazy ass shit. You'd probably look and go, 'that ain't love.' Well, for them that shit is love. Right? That's what they know love to be, so, you've got to kind of take it with a grain of salt and just understand that some people are just not really that open.

For me, if I don't give her the respect that's due, if I don't speak about my feelings for her, it discredits her. I've got to let it be known. I can't give any bullshit with that.

Yeah, I get that. Do you think it's problematic if single people hang out with people who are in relationships? Is it influential to bad habits?

Kiana St Louis

I think it's about self-control. I think it's a lot of understanding what you're there for. Once you analyze that, if you're going out on your own trying to get lit and have fun, it's like, what's lit to you? In this moment, you know what I mean?

So, when I go out, and I know I'm drinking, it's either she's coming with me or I'm asking, "where you gonna be at," so when I leave I'll come find you, 'cause I'm on tonight! (laughs) So, it depends on where we are going. If we are going to dinner or something like that hopefully whatever it is she will be invited. Friends know about her, my friends are going to respect my situation ... real friends.

True. Would you say this is your greatest love?

I think every love is different. Every love is different at different levels of life. When I was in high school I thought I was in love but I look back at that now, it's different.

So, what level is this?

At the age I'm going into now, this is the rest of my lifetime love, pregnancies can possibly be involved -- this is next step type stuff. It's like 'what are we doing this for' type stuff.

Are we at that age?

Yeah, getting there but, that's with different people. For some people, it's different. I want a history with somebody. I want to know you, I want to have some 'we going through some shit' experience with you, you know what I mean? Everybody's different.

Have you ever had your heart broken?

I don't believe so. There was always a level of understanding and communication, and everything. So, there were times I felt a certain way but was my heart broken? Nah! Not broken I've been very disappointed though.

If you could lend any advice to the lovers in the world, men and/or women, what would it be?

You can't come to me for no advice! I'll tell you I'm learning every step of the way with this shit. With me, it was like her vibe was so incredible and I thought to myself, *I'm just going to give her a shot.* I love her and if she doesn't want to be with me tomorrow or if something goes wrong I'm still going to love her. It's deeper than that. With us, it's just an added benefit of me being with her. I would love her friendship if that were all it was.

But, I can't give you any advice. Not from me! Nope, I am not a veteran with this!

Why do you say that?

Advice to everybody is different, everybody you talk to is going to be different, and everybody has a different aspect and view on life. You just have to know what you want. Don't settle, for nothing, and communicate. If you're not communicating, man ... you should walk. You have to communicate through the good, bad, and the ugly, that's what we share. I look at her and I'm like "Yo, what's up?" Don't be mad and do some dumb shit, just talk. Communication.

Kiana St Louis

DAY FIFTY-ONE: AS I BEGAN TO LOVE MYSELF

A self-love reminder.

Contributed words by: Gabriel Gonsalves

As I began to love myself I found that anguish and emotional suffering are only warning signs that I was living against my own truth. Today, I know, this is AUTHENTICITY.

As I began to love myself I understood how much it can offend somebody if I try to force my desires on this person, even though I knew the time was not right and the person was not ready for it, and even though this person was me. Today I call it RESPECT.

As I began to love myself I stopped craving for a different life, and I could see that everything that surrounded me was inviting me to grow. Today I call it MATURITY.

As I began to love myself I understood that at any circumstance, I am in the right place at the right time, and everything happens at the exactly right moment. So I could be calm. Today I call it SELF-CONFIDENCE.

As I began to love myself I quit stealing my own time, and I stopped designing huge projects for the future. Today, I only do what brings me joy and happiness, things I love to do and that make my heart cheer, and I do them in my own way and in my own rhythm. Today I call it SIMPLICITY.

As I began to love myself I freed myself of anything that is no good for my health – food, people, things, situations, and everything that drew me down and away from myself. At first I called this attitude a healthy egoism. Today I know it is LOVE OF ONESELF.

As I began to love myself I quit trying to always be right, and ever since I was wrong less of the time. Today I discovered that is MODESTY.

100 Days of Dating

As I began to love myself I refused to go on living in the past and worrying about the future. Now, I only live for the moment, where everything is happening. Today I live each day, day by day, and I call it FULFILLMENT.

As I began to love myself I recognized that my mind can disturb me and it can make me sick. But as I connected it to my heart, my mind became a valuable ally. Today I call this connection WISDOM OF THE HEART.

We no longer need to fear arguments, confrontations or any kind of problems with ourselves or others. Even stars collide, and out of their crashing new worlds are born. Today I know THAT IS LIFE!

DAY FIFTY-TWO: LOVE DOESN'T CHANGE, PEOPLE DO

"All love shifts and changes. I don't know if you can be wholeheartedly in love all the time." - Julie Andrews

At first, I didn't quite understand what Julie Andrews meant in her above quote. To me, if I'm declaring my love for you - it's real, it's honest, it's true, and it's constant. That is what makes it love. So, how could she admit to believing love changes so often that it wouldn't be the same all the time?

Well, that's because people shift and change. Andrews is right. The way we feel about a person whether we are in love or not, has the ability to shift and alter due to how they act, respond, and treat us. Some people become *complacent* in love after some time and forget how to love. Some people *misunderstand* the concept of love and never truly learn how to love you. Some people *think* that they're in love and don't realize they need to be taught.

Kary Jolivert, 24, has experienced the shifts and changes people make in response to love first hand. She's heard the lies and inconsistent stories, she's seen someone she's cared for change right before her eyes. Therefore, she's been weary of love ever since. But is love truly to blame when it's people who take advantage of its effect? I think that's a question we're all still trying to figure out. This is her story.

Tell me about your love life. Are you single, dating, in a relationship?

Yeah, I'm fucking single.

Why do you say it like that?

I think the reason why I say it like that is just... I don't know. It's something that I've always been. It's like, at this point it's a part of me. It's part of my identity. I think it's kind of frustrating at this point because it's still a part of my identity, which is very weird.

What? Being single?

Yeah. I think a lot of it has to do with a lot of different things. I think a lot of it has to do with social pressures.

What do you mean by social pressures?

I think that as a woman, as I got older, I realized the biggest goal for you is to get married, I don't really want to go into that, but it's really fucking annoying. It's like Oprah. People bring up Oprah, and she's like the most accomplished person in this fucking world. They'll say, "Yeah, she's not married to Stedman." Because of that, there's a lot of questions of who she is and her sexuality. You know what I mean? Now, is she with Gale?

I feel like if she were a man, it would just be like, "Oh, he didn't want a wife," or, "That's it, he could get anybody he wants." But why can't that be the same for Oprah? She's out here chilling. She has billions of dollars. She's not trying to write any type of pre-nup, and she's just living her life. Why isn't it like that? I feel like as women, I always see that. That's one of our, if not the ultimate goal in life.

Regardless of what your social status is, people are going to have an opinion about you, your love life, or whatever it is. But I'm sure Oprah kisses her Benjamin's before she goes to bed and she's pretty okay regardless of what people think.

Yeah, and I think that's one of the things for me. We have this expectation for women, but there's no questioning of why a man is not married. That's when it's a problem for me. I think it's that we never teach young men and boys that the highlight of your life should be to be a husband, to be a father, right? Men can be individuals outside of that, right? Their identity doesn't mean that they're single. Their identity is their own. But for a woman, your identity is somehow marked by your status of being single, married, fiancé, or girlfriend.

Even all these shows are coming out. It's like WAGS, wives and girlfriends of a sports athlete, Love and Hip Hop. It's like you are secondary to everything. That's what I'm saying when I say I'm fucking single. That's who I am, but I know that's not part of my identity. I try to separate who I am from that identity, but I know the world is going to always see that.

Kiana St Louis

Have you ever been in love?

Yeah. I have. I think for me, it was more about being comfortable with the person. I think I'm a person that can't really connect with everyone in general. I could be very friendly. I don't think I have a problem being friendly with people, but to connect with someone? I think it's just very difficult for me in general.

But I did connect with someone. I think that because I finally connected with them I was like, "Oh my god. You're the one. Blah, blah." I do think I was in love with them, but they did not love me. I think that I just have to come to that conclusion. People try to say things to comfort me like, "Oh, he definitely cared about you, but it didn't work out," Things like, "cared about you." It's as if it was somewhat reciprocated on some level. The truth is, it probably wasn't. He probably enjoyed my time, but it probably wasn't like that. I needed to just come to the reality of I loved someone and they didn't feel the same way. That's that.

When you found that, or realized, he didn't love you back, were you heartbroken?

Yeah, I think for me it's like growing up, I grew up in a single-parent household. Well, for the most part. My mom got remarried. She got a divorce when I was three. Her major thing at the time of the divorce was that she wanted to hold out getting one because I was so young. I think she wanted me to grow up with my dad and with her until a certain age, I think her plan was at 10 years old. Just to get the divorce or have it phase out, right? Caribbean people are little bit different, I don't know, when they think about things like that.

My mom said, "I could not deal with the disrespect." So, she had to get a divorce. For me, when you love someone, you have the utmost respect for them, right? You might not be perfect. You might be stuck in your ways, but you have a lot of respect for them. So, to bring it back to my situation, not to say that the person was disrespectful, but it's like when you bring things up, and they keep doing things that you don't like. I feel like that kind of broke me. I thought to myself, *he couldn't get over his pride just to make me kind of happy*...I don't know how to explain that. I really don't.

I think you're touching on a good point when it just comes to being with somebody in general. It's literally the removal of you and your sole thoughts, wants, and aspects for the picking up someone else's. Love cannot be selfish.

Right. I think that I was heartbroken on that idea. I was being so selfless in a situation where a person was being selfish. He didn't lose any sleep. He saw it his way, and he rationalized it. I think sometimes rationalizing it is an excuse to validate your actions, which are sometimes just downright disturbing or disgusting. I've always been that kind of person, to question how someone rationalized slavery, you know? Somebody rationalized wars that were ridiculous. Just because you can rationalize something, that doesn't make it right.

After realizing that you were in a situation of unrequited love, how did you cope? How did you move forward? How did you move on?

Delete, I guess. Deleting the person. I think I just had to delete the person. I want to thank God for the friends that I have, but my mourning process was definitely just sharing that kind of pain. But at one point, I had to have a real discussion with my friends and myself, and say it's okay to mourn a loss sometimes, because it feels like a death.

Especially when you're doing things, and you have a routine with that person. There's a difference between mourning and dwelling. None of my friends really said, "You were dwelling here." I've never been a very expressive person, so when they saw that I was being expressive, they were like, "Oh, this is a really thing. You're really hurt." But for me, it takes a lot of energy for me to even talk about this at this point. It's taken so much energy out of me, I feel like I'm dwelling.

I think there is a difference between patience and tolerance. You know, patience is a virtue. You have to be patient with yourself, but you also can't tolerate certain behaviors when you're trying to move on from someone. I had to kind of find that in between and be patient with myself, and understand, "Sometimes you're going to think about this person when something happens, but just also understand that you have to come to terms with what it is. You're not with that person. It was a good moment in time, and it's over."

If you could maybe give some advice to somebody who was in a similar situation, what would you say?

Know yourself, know your worth.

100 Days of Dating

DAY FIFTY-THREE: I LOVE YOU, BUT I'M NOT IN LOVE WITH YOU

"You can be in love and you can be in a relationship. But they're not always the same thing." - pleasefindthis, I Wrote This For You

I think there's a difference between loving someone and being in love with someone. To me, you can love anybody and you can love anything. Love is intimate yet general in the way you express it, or how you say it. Love is conveying kindness, being patient, acting selfless in light of someone else you care about.

Being in love is deep. It's selfish because you have no room in your heart to share this kind of love with anyone else; the person for whom you are in love with consumes all. Being in love is equivalent to the act of cutting yourself in half, getting rid of parts of you to make room for someone else. It is inviting someone into your being to make you whole, meshing parts of you with them.

But sometimes who you love and who you're in love with are not the same person. Sometimes, you can be in a relationship without being in love. Sometimes, you can love someone while they love someone else.

Davon Francis, 24, has loved, been in love, and been in a relationship, but the actions haven't always lined up with the same person. As we've come to learn throughout this project, we cannot control whom we love. Our feelings grow, change, and sharpen with different people for different reasons at various times. But for Davon, while love has proven to have no guarantee, he's certain it is still a risk worth taking. This is his story.

Tell me about your love life. Are you single, dating?

Yes. I am single.

Why do you say it so sternly?

Because I've been single for almost a year now, but it's actually been a minute since I've been single though.

Because you're usually in relationships?

No, because I've been in *a* relationship for the last few years.

How long?

About three years.

Were you in love with her?

No. Loved the girl. Definitely.

There's a difference?

There is a difference. I feel like there's a difference.

What's the difference to you?

For me, I genuinely love her for the person she is, how she carries herself, how she treats me, how she treats others. But being in love with her should have been like, I can't be away from her for more than ten minutes or I can't wait for her to get home, the husband and wife stuff ... it just wasn't there.

When you know, you know. Or when the energy is there, you know it. I think being in love is deeper. There's more depth than just love, or loving somebody.

So you were with her for three years, what was that like?

Different. Longest relationship I've ever been in with a woman. How was it? It was dope, but at the same time also stressful and at times, draining. I think there's a difference between stressful and draining.

Why draining?

100 Days of Dating

Well, all right, let's start from the beginning. Of course when you start dating somebody you have the butterflies, the jittery, all that extra 'oh God' shit. The newness, that's what we're going to call it, the newness. I love the newness, the newness is nice. You feel me? It's dope.

First year was a breeze. Everything was perfect; I didn't cheat on her or anything. Well, I mean to my standards I didn't cheat on her but there was a moment in the first year where she took it upon herself to go through my phone. I was drunk at the time though and she saw that I was texting a few females, but I wasn't trying to meet up with them or go on dates with them or anything like that. It was just females from junior high school or high school or whatever that I just recently caught up with at the time. I think you were one of them actually.

Probably.

We were always cool! We never did anything, but I was just friendly. I wasn't flirting or anything like that, but I guess she just didn't like the way I was talking. So, ever since then, the whole picture-perfect image just got stained, it wasn't perfect anymore. So, she felt like "I can't be all the way with him, I have to have my guard up," all this extra shit, but she didn't go all out cause I didn't really do anything.

But, it was there though, so she wasn't going to forget it.

Right.

So, the next year, throughout the whole year, I was getting the treatment like I was doing something - even though I wasn't doing anything. And of course, my take on that is, if I'm not doing anything and you're treating me like I'm doing something and you're not leaving, I might as well be doing something and get something out of it, because I'm getting nothing but stress from you. You feel me? Others might look down on that but I'm just saying. I'm not doing anything, you're with me 24/7, so I kind of have no time to do anything if I wanted to do something.

You'd be surprised.

I'll take that. I definitely agree. We can always find the time ... I'm reminded though that I did cheat on her. I told you no, and I said that thinking I was telling the truth.

Did you ever feel bad about that?

After realizing that I did it, I was like "Oh shit".

But of course while it was happening, no?

I don't remember how I felt when that happened, to tell you the truth. I really don't. I think around that time when it did happen, we were on a break but not really.

Did she ever find out?

No. And, to be honest with you, I don't think I'm going to tell her, unless she asks me. Then I have to tell her.

Do you two still speak today?

Technically yes, but as girlfriend and boyfriend, no. We just try to keep it cordial. Because towards our third year, it was okay but at the same time it was very toxic. Sometimes, shit is great, but then once one thing goes left it's just really bad. When things are good they're great, but the second it goes bad, it's like Bobby Brown-Whitney Houston bad. This is what I mean by is it's dope, but stressful and draining at the same time.

I guess that's also just how relationships are though, not everything that you want and you work for is going to be peachy all the time. In fact, I feel a lot of the things that you really work hard for will be somewhat stressful. You can expect things to get spicy because, I mean, isn't it supposed to be worth it?

True.

So, you said that you had a lot of love for her but you don't think that you were in love with her.

I know I wasn't.

Have you ever been *in love* with someone else?

Yeah.

Were you two ever in a relationship?

Nope. I was never with her, never dated her, never went on a date with her, I never even kissed her when I was in love with her. It was love at first sight.

Interesting, did you ever tell her?

Recently, yes.

So, you're still in love with her?

Definitely.

Spicy!

I can't control that. I just can't control what I feel. I haven't seen her in a couple of years though, but then when I saw her, I was 16 all over again. That's how I knew I was in love with her.

Okay, so what are you waiting for?

What am I waiting for? I'm single.

So you'd rather be single than be with the girl you love?

No, that's not what I'm saying. I'm saying right now, I'm single. I'm in a position in my life where I have to get my shit together. I have no business with a girlfriend right now.

Is that a cop out?

It's not a cop out because at the same time she's also been doing what she has to do for her life as well. And she really doesn't have the time anyway, so if I'm going to jump into that knowing that she really doesn't have the time I'm going to go crazy. If it happens, it happens, but right now I'm just focused on getting my shit together.

Kiana St Louis

DAY FIFTY-FOUR: SELF-LOVE SEPTEMBER

"If only our bodies would marry the beauty growing inside them, it wouldn't be so exhausting trying to love ourselves." - Christopher Poindexter

Self-love. Sometimes, I have to remind myself to not be so hard on me. I get so wrapped up in where I'm supposed to be in life, in my career, in my relationships and I suddenly feel pressured. Sometimes, I'll put all of my energy and time into someone or something that isn't exactly giving it back to me, or even meeting me halfway. Why? Because I rather be happy for a short time in a temporary situation with a temporary person before allowing myself to feel the one thing I'm afraid of: being alone.

I do love me. I love my skills, I love my smile, and I love that I'm able to make other people laugh unintentionally. There are parts of me I don't always love, but I'm working on it and I think that's okay. But, in the spirit of being honest and allowing these pages to tell my truth, I must admit I don't always love me all the time. I think it is because of that, that I'll fall short and look for reasons to love me within someone else. This is also known as wasting my time. I know this but sometimes it happens.

We *have* to require consistency, not only of others, but most importantly of *ourselves*. Many of my friends will read this and probably reach out to me like "Ki, you're bugging." But the reality is, I'm not. I'm just real about what's going on. I don't always have it together. I'm far from perfect. I need to love myself a little more. But as with all things, I think an important first step is realizing the problem. I've got to love me whole-heartedly - not some of the time, but *all* of the time. As Rudy Francisco once wrote, "Perhaps we should love ourselves so fiercely, so that when others see us they know exactly how it should be done." No one will ever have my back the way I do. My story continues.

Contributed poetry by: Erin Hanson

100 Days of Dating

If there's one thing that I may tell you

Let it be: **You are your home,**

Your body is the only house

That you will ever truly own,

Maybe it's got some broken windows

And there are tear-stains on the floors,

Maybe you lock the things you wish you weren't

Behind its many doors,

But there is wisdom on its bookshelves

And a laugh to light the rooms,

There's a case upon the table

Where the love you've grown all blooms,

Dreams sit on the mantelpiece

Next to kindness and your trust,

Where you use them all so often

They have no time to collect dust

So please don't look at mansions

With that envy in your eyes,

There's more that makes a home

Than it's appearance or size.

Your body is your shelter

So you deserve to love it all,

Don't let the world stand round outside

Kiana St Louis

And tell you how to paint your walls
How lucky that you have somewhere
To protect you from the night,
And if there's cracks left from the past?
Well then just let in more light.

DAY FIFTY-FIVE: MY ADDICTION

"Sometimes the hardest part isn't letting go but rather learning to start over." - Nicole Sobon, Program 13

Contributed poetry by: Shelly

This addiction, my worst enemy
Has gone from days, months, to years
It's taken over my life, haunted me
It's become my biggest fear.

The consumption is overwhelming
without it what would I be?
But with it, it leaves me emptiness
and many left years of misery.

Many times I've tried knowing,
That I have to let it go
But I continue to torture myself
and spend my life alone.

Why is it that we hang onto
the one who doesn't care,
I have to try and change it
I have my own life to spare.

So with this voice inside me
And all the strength I have left within
I'll push myself to move forward
My new life is waiting, ready to begin.

Kiana St Louis

DAY FIFTY-SIX and DAY FIFTY-SEVEN: THE GREAT LOVE DEBATE (pt2)

THE CONFERENCE CALL.

When I first decided to do a group interview for this passion project, it was definitely a learning experience. I didn't know what to expect when bringing two people into one room to talk about a really personal topic - *love*. I didn't know if my subjects would be afraid to open up, hesitant to speak at all, or judgmental on the stories of others. It was a risk for all of us.

A risk, however, we were all willing to take, which made this entire experience less of an interview and more of an open round table discussion. This segment revealed to me the reality of what men think, why women react, and what all of this could mean for the world of love.

Part two of my love debate was joined by two newcomers to my journey, Kevin and Ashley, some of the purest souls I've met in a long time. In a series of candid talks, the three of us caught up, laughed, and talked about the essence of growth in a relationship, and the importance of understanding that everyone grows differently and at different times. It is not up to us to rush, change, or tamper with the process of growth, but instead realize our worth as we grow with or without the one we love. This is our story.

Kiana: Tell me about your love lives. Are you two single? Or, dating?

Ashley: Single-ish

Kiana: Single-ish?

Ashley: No, I'm single.

Kevin: I'm completely single. You can't sugarcoat that. It's been a year and six months. It's been a little while. Shit. Damn, I'm lonely.

Kiana: Being single for that long means you're lonely?

Kevin: Not necessarily lonely. That was a joke. Honestly, damn. I don't even want to think about it.

Ashley: I've only been single for three months.

Kevin: Being single is fun though. Being single is risky. When you're an adult, you can actually enjoy your single life too.

Kiana: What was it like before?

Kevin: Well, sad. For me, I couldn't go outside. If you can't see your significant other, what the f*** were you really doing? Sitting by yourself in your room, not doing homework, because I didn't do homework. Now if I want to, I can get drunk. Outside, I get to enjoy people's faces. I don't have to sit in my house and be lonely by myself. I'm allowed to have fun. You don't necessarily have to have a significant other.

I'm not going to lie, I feel like everybody needs companionship because no matter what, if you're single or not, you can't just sit around and be alone. People need friendship. But at the same time, I still have someone I go on dates with. It's not a real date; I just need someone I can eat with.

Kiana: Ashley, do you agree?

Ashley: Yeah. For me before being single, I used to be sad. My mom would ask, "What's wrong with you?" I'd say, "Nothing." The air used to hit me and I would start crying. Anything would make me a sad little cancer and go back into my shell, and then I'd be really guarded. I wouldn't talk to anybody. Now, I'm more like, "Look, you're good. You're okay. The world is not ending." For me, I think if stuff is supposed to work out, it will eventually. It doesn't matter. People are growing all the time. People are growing every day.

Kevin: People grow apart every day.

Ashley: Yeah. People do grow apart every day too, and you can't penalize someone else for growing at a different rate or a different pace or in a different way than you are. That's how I used to be, I would say, "No. This is bad." I used to be the one apologizing all the time like, "No. I'm sorry. Blah, blah, blah. What can I do to fix it?" People used to be like, "No, you're dumb. I'm breaking up with you."

I used to be soft and then it got to the point of realizing you can't beg someone to be with you. Even in friendships, you can't beg someone to be friends with you, you just have to let it rock. Sometimes that time has come to an end. Sometimes you just need space.

Kevin: What the f*** is space?

Ashley: What's space?

Kevin: Don't give me any fucking space. You giving me space means I'm going to smash somebody else. Don't give me space. Don't tell me you need space from me.

Kiana: I define 'space' as a low-impact break up.

Kevin: If you're saying you need space, that means I don't want to deal with you right this second.

Kiana: Exactly.

Ashley: Oh, no. Yeah. I don't like when people say, "I need space." I'd rather you say, "Look, we should not be together right now because this is how I feel right now," and that's cool. We both do our own thing and if I feel like going back when you're ready or whatever happens with time, then cool. If not, then it was really nice while it lasted.

Kevin: Was it?

Ashley: Or it wasn't. It depends on the situation, like with most of my relationships, did they end bad? I don't really know. I feel like they all ended bad, but people always end up talking to me again, so I don't really know. It was never ending on my part.

Kiana: So, you've gotten broken up with more than you've done the breaking up?

Ashley: Yeah. Then, I turned into a savage and I didn't want to hurt people, but I used to love gassing people's head because it just ... I don't know. I just felt like people used to use me and step all over me because I was real nice and I never really said anything. Then as I got older, I was like, "It's not okay to be shut down. If you have feelings, you have to voice them," and that's where communication comes from.

You have to communicate your feelings. The other person is not a mind reader at all. You can't expect somebody, even if you've been with them for years, to get it - they're not a mind reader. They're not going to be like, "Oh, this is how you feel?" Unless it's something that you go over tons of times, that's different.

Kiana: Have you two ever had your heart broken?

Ashley: Have I? No. Better question, when have I not? (laughs)

Kevin: The sad part is, most guys would say 'no' to that question trying to be super tough. Honestly, hell yeah. I had someone look me in the face and say, "I'm not in love with you anymore." That shit hurt.

Ashley: Yeah.

Kevin: That's why I call women liars. Women will tell you something and then not feel the same way the next week.

Ashley: I feel like that's people in general.

Kevin: It's annoying.

Kiana: I'm sure more than a handful of women can say the same for men.

Kevin: Guys are just liars. Honestly, I feel like they never fully tell the truth in the first place, they just lie to you. That's not saying all guys are like that because to be quite honest, with you, I can't speak for all guys but I know most of them are dicks. Guys are really heartless. They will tell you anything you want to hear just to get in your pants, and to be honest with you, men don't even know what they really want. They thought they wanted pussy, so they lie to get some. At the end of the day, they tacked down.

That's why life's just stupid. Girls on the other hand, see, I guess that's a double standard though. Because I'm trying to say girls are not as bad or something like that, but at the same time, you are all different. I feel like your emotions are so obvious, but then so complex at the same time. You wear your emotions on your sleeve and you think you got it right, but you can be crying and I think, "Okay. It's just this simple," but it's never that simple. Never. Girls are not simple and that's what kills me because I don't know, I don't understand. I'm such a black and white person. It's so straightforward with me. I don't understand how certain situations end up so complicated.

Ashley: I feel like I'm very simple. I have my complications because I'm human, but I don't ask for anything.

Kevin: You're a girl. I don't believe that.

Ashley: No, I really don't ask for anything. Not even attention. I just ask for time, dead ass time, like quality time. That's what it is. It's quality time.

Kevin: What is quality time?

Ashley: It's honesty and trust. It's you with somebody else not plugged into the outside world type shit. It could be sitting in silence and that's quality time to me because we're spending time together. I'm not materialistic because that's not how I was raised. My mom always said, "You grew up to have your own things." Not to say you're not going to get married or whatever. She's like, "But just always make sure you have your own, do for yourself first before you can do for yourself and someone else."

Kevin: That sounds nice, but to be completely honest with you, how many girls have that mentality? How many females really have the mentality to go out and get it themselves? I'm not saying like in the career aspect because I see a lot of motivated females, career oriented females and that's cool or whatever. But when it comes to relationships, they still feel like the man needs to do the most and do everything for them and it's just like, "I thought you were independent?"

Ashley: I also feel like that has to do with how people see their relationships in their lives, for example growing up and stuff too, or what they set a standard for. My standard, I always saw my parents, they were best friends. I just want that. They always met each other half way. Well, for what it was worth at the time, but that's how they were. Their dynamic was just like, "Oh, you got this, and I got this." That's how I am.

Kiana: You both have touched on so many great topics. But I'm curious, what advice would each of you give to the world of love?

Ashley: Take your time.

Kevin: Communication.

Ashley: Yeah, and communication.

Kevin: Communication is really key. You can say that shit, and it sounds corny as many times as you say it, but it's the truth. If you're not talking it out and you're not literally willing to speak on your problems, you're never going to get anywhere no matter how much you love somebody.

Ashley: You have to listen. Oh, you really have to listen. Communicating is one thing, but listening… I always tell people this: "You hear me, but you're not really listening." Also, listen to understand instead of listening to respond. I don't argue. For me, I'll get my point across, I'll let you say your part and if we disagree, we disagree. I feel like we don't always have to agree. You can't expect someone to be the exact same as you. Accept someone's differences but without saying, "That's how they are, so they're always going to be that way." But you also can't try to change someone either. It's all about time; you have to really take your time. If you're single and you're like, "I can't find anybody." I always tell people, "Stop looking and be patient."

100 Days of Dating

DAY FIFTY-EIGHT: LOVE HATH NO GUARENTEE

THERAPY.

Sometimes, we really just need an ear to listen, a shoulder to cry on, or a body for an embrace. Sometimes, we allow our situations to take such priority in our lives that we are consumed by frustration, anger, sadness, and discomfort. Our relationships weigh on us. The people we choose to care for and love promise to reciprocate the same feelings and actions that we show but the hardest thing to realize and truly understand is: People will not always treat you or love you the way you love them.

Adriana Batista, 25, a very good friend of mine needed this interview more than we both planned for. We've been friends since my sophomore year of college. Then, I didn't think we could be more different. From our choice in music, to our choice of dress, we were walking opposites. But as she's poured into me and allowed me to be the ear she needs, and shoulder to lean on, I realize we are the same. Many of us are. Love can throw curveballs we could never see coming. Situations explode, things get messy, and your life can feel upside down, until you realize you're not alone. Even after the craziest break up, after feeling like you'd never love again, you're reminded of your support. Adri, while romantic love has no guarantee, I promise you can always count on me. This is her story.

Tell me about your love life. Are you single? Dating? In a relationship?

Very much single, unfortunately. I don't want to be at this time, but yeah.

Why don't you want to be single?

For a while I never really had a taste of what a long-term relationship could be like. But as I'm getting older I'm seeing my friends from high school and even friends from college, tying themselves together with their careers, and with their love lives, and some of them are even starting families. It's kind of freaking me out. And so, it's almost like I feel a little bit of pressure, and so I want to kind of be there already.

I'm tired of this. I'm tired of dating because it's just really difficult, especially working and stuff like that. It's really difficult to make the time out and date and have the energy to do that. For me, it's more of a mental energy to do it because it's a lot to put interest into the conversations, what we're doing, and sometimes I just don't want to do that.

I can definitely relate in terms of just the exhaustion with dating. When I first got out of my relationship and was just trying to figure out life, I'm like "yeah this is going to be great!" Until I realized that you eventually have to meet someone new and that's a lot of work, trust, and investment.

Yeah, exactly.

You mentioned that you look at what other people are doing. Do you compare yourself and feel less than because they seemingly have it "together"?

Here's the thing, I know that all of that stuff is very much surface level and very superficial. I also know that stuff doesn't accurately depict what's actually going on in their lives. Sometimes, you just can't help but feel a little bit like ... I don't want to say jealous, but just slightly envious. I'm seeing that what you and your significant other has created is seemingly perfect. You kind of project that, especially with things like Instagram and shit like that. You see it all over the place. You see all the likes. It just makes you feel some type of way a little bit.

I think it's natural. I don't think there's anything wrong with it. I think that to counter that, you try to be a bit more proactive, and take more charge in your romantic life. So, that's kind of how I'm trying to remedy that envy, I guess, with trying to just be like, 'all right, well, if this is what I want to achieve, I have to go for it. But, it's just really difficult.

When was the last time you've been in a relationship?

I just got out of one. I was dating this girl for a little bit back when I was in Florida, and it was really great. I was really happy.

Yeah, I remember that.

It kind of ended very abruptly. It was really weird. We went through a really weird transition and it ended up just crumbling apart, and it was really stressful. Towards the end, it was really stressful. It was really difficult to deal with. It's also what puts me off today, as well as I just don't really feel like dealing with that aftermath. Because when you date somebody, you take a risk. You can't calculate the risk because one minute, someone could be all about it, super lovey-dovey and everything.

The next minute, it can easily be 'Oh, I lost interest.' It could be abrupt, and you can't help it. It is what it is, but you can't predict it either. You're taking a risk and I don't know if I want to do all of that again. I don't know if I really feel like taking that uncalculated risk to be, essentially, led on to then feel like I'm being tossed away.

So you want to be in a relationship, but you don't want to do the work to get there because you're afraid of that risk?

I don't know if I don't want to do the work to get there. I think my problem is that I want something that will-- I'm a numbers person. I need something calculable to tell me that this is a good thing that I'm putting energy towards because otherwise, I can't. Honestly, just because of what I'm going through mentally, I can't really ... It took a lot. The last couple of months have been really intense, emotionally and mentally for me, and I don't know if I could ... I don't feel like doing that shit again, you know?

If I'm going to really invest my time, I want to make sure that it's worth investing my time, I want to know it's going to last, and there's no way to guarantee that. There's no way guarantee any of it.

I'm listening to you and I'm heavy hearted. If you're looking for these answers in love, you're not going to find them.

I'm not.

Love is not calculable.

It's not. And so, then what do you do? I'm kind of just... I don't know. I'm on a refresh - trying to restart and trying to re-figure out how to navigate again. It's a lot, it's a lot of thinking, and it's a lot of reevaluating. I lost work because of it. I couldn't focus. My mind didn't allow me to focus. I couldn't keep it together. Now that everything's kind of shifted, everything's over, and everything has passed, I'm kind of restarting again, and starting anew.

I'm in a new place, new job, new life, essentially. At this point, I have to pick and choose. Do I choose to keep my head down and really focus on work, chill and just keep cool for the next couple of months, or next year or two? Or do I kind of try to balance work and almost collapse because of the pressure, you know?

Yeah, it definitely sounds like you could use some time off. Not even just on a relationship level, but in general. Sometimes we need to really take second to ourselves and disappear to refocus.

Yeah, and that's what I've been doing. That's what the last couple months were about. That's why you didn't really see me on social media, well not that I post a whole ton anyway. But, that's why you don't really see me out there. But, I'm more isolated because I'm trying to restart everything.

Did you love your ex?

I did. I really did.

Would you classify this as your greatest heartbreak?

I think so. I really think so. I was all in. I think I was ready. Ki, you don't even know. I think what stressed me out and caused me to freak the fuck out was, you know how you can see something crumble before you? That's exactly what was happening! And then the more I tried to fix it, the more I fucked it up. I saw it happening and when I watched us break apart, it fucked me up. Then it freaked me out, then it freaked her out, and everything just imploded on itself, in literally the span of a couple days.

So, it's a lot, and I'm going through a lot, and so I'm trying to just map everything out. I'm trying to get my mental health together again. I'm trying to get my financial life together again. I'm getting my job life together again. I'm just trying a little bit harder every day.

I can completely understand. I feel like we try really hard to make sense of a lot of things. We try really hard to calculate things. We try to move forward and push ourselves because we feel like its time to be over something or someone. But the reality is that we don't have control over any of that, not over love, not over time, sometimes, not even of our own emotions. What we must realize though, is that we are not our heartbreak(s). We're not the struggle. As tough as this was, as tough as it's going to be for you, you literally just have to take it day by day, but you also have to understand it's not going be great every day, either.

The minute you almost sort of let go a little bit and remember who you were before all of this happened, I think you'll find peace.

That's exactly what that is. I'm kind of getting over the mourning period and on the way to figuring out my identity and my life, and trying to figure out who I am after this period. The crazy shit about it is that's the crazy thing about love. It was not a long period of time. We were together only for a couple of months, and I think that they kind of attest to the theory that love really doesn't really have a time. There's no timeframe. You could love someone in any timeframe.

Kiana St Louis

DAY FIFTY-NINE: NOT MY FAVORITE SONG

"Hearts are breakable," Isabelle said. "And I think even when you heal, you're never what you were before." — Cassandra Clare, *City of Fallen Angels*

Everyone heals differently. There is no designated time, process, or way to go about mending yourself after a broken heart. The one thing life guarantees is an ending. We are grounded in temporary. Everything about our lives and situations are built upon the premise of experience, while we may not know how something will turn out while we're in it, we do know that it will eventually end. I've learned to view my heartbreak in this reality as well.

I refuse to be bound by my temporary experience. While my heart yearns for the love we've once shared and is now consumed by the pain of our failed efforts to restore it, I speak on my process and declare *I am not my struggle*. Everything about us that made me smile will be replaced by new memories. You once were my favorite song, until I stopped hearing it and forgot the words.

Contributed poetry by: Erin Hanson

I remember when we realized

Our favorite songs were the same,

I felt like you had looked at me,

And seen straight into my brain,

You'd stroke my face while singing,

As I drifted off to sleep,

And I swore that those fond memories,

Were the kind I'd always keep,

But even good songs finish,

100 Days of Dating

And as the winter's silence grew,

My cheeks went from a rose pink,

To a molted black and blue,

So I grabbed the person I'd become,

And fled into the night,

You told me that I'd come back,

And you still think you'd be right,

But let me tell you something:

Our song was on the radio,

But it's been so long since I heard it,

I've forgotten how it goes,

And I've learned it takes just seven years,

For all your cells to be replaced,

So one day you will have never touched,

The skin upon my face.

Kiana St Louis

DAY SIXTY: LIES ON YOUR LIPS, BUT THERE'S LOVE IN YOUR EYES

"Love dies only when growth stops." – Pearl S. Buck

Ms. Pearl was definitely on to something. I think there's a bit of a misunderstanding with growth at times, especially in relationships. Growth is letting things go and being able to speak about how you truly feel. Growth is understanding the upkeep of a relationship is more than just the consistent "Good morning" text. Growth is knowing when you're wrong and being humble when you're right. Growth is doing something not because you want to, but because you know the one you love wants to. Growth is love, until it stops.

Michael Wade and I have been friends since elementary school. I've watched him run with the boys in the courtyard at lunch at P.S. 203. I've seen him win awards and try to fit in at Hudde Junior High. I missed him throughout high school but caught up with him in college at SUNY Oswego and realized, while he still may resemble the little boy I met all those years ago, he was a new man. Growth. But he and I aren't so different maneuvering love. We've both learned some tough lessons and are still trying to figure things out. But one thing is for sure-- the only way to find love and keep love is to grow. And sometimes, the most important part is knowing when it's time to grow alone. This is his story.

So, tell me about your love life.

That's the first question?

That's the first question. Are you single, are you dating, in a relationship?

Oh my goodness. This is such a loaded one. So, a couple of weeks ago, I had a conversation with a young lady who I considered to be my girlfriend. We were dating.

Did you officially ask her to be your girlfriend?

Yes, I did. My girlfriend had expressed to me, that we weren't in a relationship and we needed to work on our friendship. So we did. That blindsided me.

So, what does that mean?

I'm single. For the first time ever, I guess.

Okay. Do you like it?

I'm lonely. That's what anybody would be though, right?

Not everybody, but most of us for sure.

Well, you also have to get used to it. I'm not used to this. Or I'm not used to saying, "Dude you don't deserve to be with anybody right now."

Is that what you think?

Oh, you weren't expecting that. Yeah, I have work to do on me.

I can understand that. But I mean it's also fairly new, the whole breakup. You said it was just a few weeks ago, correct?

Imagine that our whole relationship was actually not a relationship to her. So there was a lot of me not getting what I thought I should've gotten in regard to affection, time, and conversation while we were together.

How long were you guys together?

We were together for two years. But then it turned into me wanting to be on and off at certain points in time. I understood why I was doing it, but I wouldn't expect her to fully understand.

But what that became was detrimental to the relationship, so I had to take accountability for that. It was to the point where we didn't even know what was next… we weren't on the same page, obviously. I thought she was distancing herself but the relationship was already nonexistent.

It's crazy how people could be in the same book but on two different pages.

For a fact. It happens a lot though.

So, did you love her?

Yes. I did. I was surprised. I was surprised because you think you can never love again, but I love a lot of people.

I'm curious, how do you define love?

I have to define love for myself, so I don't really know … I think definition comes with focus and focus comes with details. So, the more details somebody can tell you about love, the more they know love. It doesn't have one definition. So for me, love is the first person you like to tell news to. When you're a child, you get a grade and you want to tell your mom, you want to tell your dad. When you get older and the grades start to get not as, "Hey look what I did" you start not to tell mom, you start not telling dad. But you'll confide in somebody else. You'll confide in your friends. "Yo, what you got boy? Have you heard?" And then that's when different kinds of connections, relationships, and bonds begin.

You love your friends and you love your parents. Loving relationships come with experience. You get shown love that isn't the right love and that can come from your parents as well. My mom just admitted to me the other day that she showed me tough love because she didn't know how else to show me love. She never received love, so to me, I can't be mad at her for that. Not saying that's what I do to women, show them tough love, but me seeking that affection from women, I know that what my mom was showing me was something that I probably didn't receive as love. I wanted to be loved and I wanted affection, so I seek that in women. That's kind of what love became for me from women because we learn from experience always.

Would you say that she was your greatest love? Being that you had-

So many?

Well how many people have you loved?

That's the thing. I didn't separate love, I don't separate friends, I don't separate circles and I make blanket statements and that's kind of the thing that I'm learning. I'm learning in order to guard myself, I dub people and things easily because I don't trust, and that's something that's concrete in love. So, although you learn to keep people around because you understand relationships at the same time, I know who I fuck with. Sometimes I don't fuck with who I fuck with, but I always know who I fuck with. I don't fuck with people who would never see me, never hear from me, but at the same time (excuse my French) that's actually cold.

In all honesty, you learn well from experience. With the experience I had with my mom, I wanted to seek affection somewhere else. And me seeking affection from women added to me chasing women and everything, hence the reason why it feels weird to be single.

Being single doesn't have to mean chasing after women. You don't have to be in something when you're single.

Yeah that's a fact. But I don't know anything other than that.

Other than what?

Being in a relationship. So that's true. I definitely agree. But it's cool to be in this environment, but to what limit with this environment because relationships become drugs. Some people don't make it out because they fall in love. Uzi.

Why is everything connected to Uzi today?

Just saying. Love is rage. He raps about so many things in a certain way because he's an artist. He expresses his feelings on tracks based on his influences and he's had some different influences, so that's what you get. What is interesting is how everybody connects to it. Because everybody's been in a relationship, been from and pumped up out of relationships since we're young. That's why people are like, "Take your time. Don't bother with relationships. Who knows?" A father could be like, "My little daughter isn't going to be in a relationship," because he doesn't want to see her cry. They do not expect that. They're screaming at the top of their lungs because they don't know a better way to express. Re-culturing needs to happen when it comes to love. That's really all I can say on that. People define it for what it is. It feels a certain way.

Uzi isn't for everybody, I guess. Have you ever had your heart broken?

Yes. But you victimize yourself, you put yourself in a situation to be victimized. I victimized myself. I've been cheated on and I've stayed in that relationship and didn't get over a bunch of other stuff, which in turn made me worse.

I've learned you can't be with someone and not feel for them. That's dumb. Then how can you guide with that? Sometimes you need to sit your ass alone, which is what I've been doing, and then think. But it's like sometimes those thoughts are a lot because you've just stopped running. I've been running through relationships. I just stopped running. It's savage.

If you could give some advice to the world of love, what would it be?

It would be to understand that everything that is done is received. Communication is way more than speaking. It's nonverbal. So, if you speak to somebody or communicate with somebody or allow them to understand something in a certain way, they're going to remember that. So now, when it comes to them getting older and them expressing that to somebody else, they're going to express it in that same way. So we have to be really cautious about how we treat people and how we say that we love people because those are some scars that take long to heal.

Kiana St Louis

DAY SIXTY-ONE: CHOOSE HER EVERYDAY (OR LEAVE HER)

"Intimate relationships don't last because you love each other. They last because you make—and remake—a choice."

I had the most intense 4-way FaceTime call with my girls one night. The topic: **Why are men so lazy?** It seems like guys are prepared to climb over mountains, bust through walls, or stop fires - all in an effort to get a woman's number, time, or attention. Yet, the minute they get it, all of the consistency goes out the window. Coincidence?

I think it was fate when I found this article minutes after getting off the phone with them. Taken from The Good Men Project, Bryan Reeves has officially joined #100daysofdating. This is his story:

I spent 5 years hurting a good woman by staying with her but never fully choosing her.

I did want to be with this one. I really wanted to choose her. She was an exquisite woman, brilliant and funny and sexy and sensual. She could make my whole body laugh with her quick, dark wit, and short-circuit my brain with her exotic beauty. Waking up every morning with her snuggled in my arms was my happy place. I loved her wildly.

Unfortunately, as happens with many young couples, our ignorance of how to do love well quickly created stressful challenges in our relationship. Before long, once my early morning blissful reverie gave way to the strained, immature ways of our everyday life together, I would often wonder if there was another woman out there who was easier to love, and who could love me better.

As the months passed and that thought reverberated more and more through my head, I chose her less and less. Every day, for five years, I chose her a little less.

I stayed with her. I just stopped choosing her. We both suffered.

Choosing her would have meant focusing every day on the gifts she was bringing into my life that I could be grateful for: her laughter, beauty, sensuality, playfulness, companionship, and so ... much ... more.

Sadly, I often found it nearly impossible to embrace – or even see – what was so wildly wonderful about her.

I was too focused on the anger, insecurities, demands, and other aspects of her strong personality that grated on me. The more I focused on her worst, the more I saw of it, and the more I mirrored it back to her by offering my own worst behavior. Naturally, this only magnified the strain on our relationship, which still made me choose her even less.

Thus did our nasty death spiral play itself out over five years?

She fought hard to make me choose her. That's a fool's task. You can't make someone choose you, even when they might love you.

To be fair, she didn't fully choose me, either. The rage-fueled invective she often hurled at me was evidence enough of that.

I realize now, however, that she was often angry because she didn't feel safe with me. She felt me not choosing her every day, in my words and my actions, and she was afraid I would abandon her.

Actually, I did abandon her.

By not fully choosing her every day for five years, by focusing on what bothered me rather than what I adored about her, I deserted her. Like a precious fragrant flower I brought proudly into my home but then failed to water, I left her alone in countless ways to wither in the dry hot heat of our intimate relationship.

I'll never not choose another woman I love again.

It's torture for everyone.

Kiana St Louis

DAY SIXTY-TWO: SHALL I?

"To fail to love is not to exist at all." – Mark Van Doren

Contributed poetry by: 365greetings

Shall I forget the face of a bright sunshine?
Whose beauty is comparable to an angel so divine;
Shall I overlook your smiles that are so sweet?
Just a glimpse of you knocks me off my feet.

Shall I pass a day without seeing you?
Or miss a chance to prove my feelings are true;
Shall I think twice to win your heart?
Living without you will tear me apart.

Shall I not recall the way your hair dances in the summer air?
And how your laughter warms my cold winter;
your gentle breath swifts' right through the autumn's call,
Shall I confess this love or wait until the next fall?

Shall I hold your heart or will forever yearn for it?
I long for the day when our lips would meet;
shall I live another day without saying how much I love you?
Or shall I die as a friend veiling these feelings for you?

100 Days of Dating

DAY SIXTY-THREE:
TO GET OVER YOUR EX, GET UNDER YOUR NEXT?

"True love cannot be found where it does not exist, nor can it be denied where it does." - Torquato Tasso

I've heard this saying before, "In order to get over somebody, you have to get under somebody new." At first, like with most things, I automatically negated this thought. To me, this quote was clearly in favor of the rebound. It is glorifying the idea that it might be okay to use somebody in an effort to make yourself feel better about the situation you're currently in. Which to me just doesn't sit right. And I get it, sometimes you just want anything to numb the pain, but that's not what people are for. It's all good to talk about getting under someone new, until you are that someone and possibly put to the side.

Some relationships begin as seeds of friendship, are then watered with love, blossom, and flourish for its time, and then wither away. There's really no stopping the flow of the inevitable, and that's something we all should learn. You have to know when to let go and grow elsewhere. But that aspect of growing elsewhere shouldn't be forced and definitely shouldn't be at the expense of someone else.

I don't want my train of thought to be confused, however. I am in favor of getting over any ex anyway possible, believe that, however, I think we need to be a little bit more cognoscente of our actions, our intent, and of course with what we say. If you break up with someone, I think it's important to breathe single for a little while. To me, that means enjoying your vibe and allowing all things to flow. After a break up, you know fresh in your mind the kinds of feelings you never want to feel again, you know what you'll stand up for, you'll know what you'll tolerate, essentially, *you should know what you want and don't want.* Hone in on those things and refuse to settle. But never rush a broken heart. You're sure to do much more damage than you are repair.

Kiana St Louis

People aren't fillers, objects, or things to play with. If you know you just want somebody to make you feel a certain kind of way for a certain amount of time, be honest. They have just as much of a right to choose you as you do to choose them. Clarity and honesty, we could all use it. Maybe that's what this quote is missing too. Just a little bit of clarity: "In order to get over your ex, get under someone who's for sure down to be on top." Ha.

Peace & Love

100 Days of Dating

DAY SIXTY-FOUR: LEARNING TO LOVE

"A man is given the choice between loving women and understanding them." - Ninon de L'Enclos

Most times when finding the right words to piece together your love language, sentences seem so obsolete. So I always look to stanzas for clarity and always find them in poetry.

Contributed poem by: Erin Hanson

Why must it be so hard

For us to come to understand,

That there are things we cannot change

Hidden amongst the things we can?

For we can rearrange our hearts,

Dust out the corners of our minds,

We can teach our eyes to see

Only the things we wish to find.

Yet once we decorate our walls

And sweep our sorrows off the floor,

Why do we look to someone else

To show us how we can be more?

For here is where the line

Between our can and can't gets tough,

The point at which we all must learn

That we are already enough,

Kiana St Louis

That since we cannot choose the home
Our only soul was born into,
We should rearrange its rooms
But learn to love its window's view.

100 Days of Dating

DAY SIXTY-FIVE: LOVE LANGUAGE

"So the lover must struggle for words." – T.S. Eliot

I've always loved the way letters tend to dance together to the sweet melody of our vocabulary. The words we create, the meaning behind them, the power they have... language is a masterpiece. Words matter, so in turn what we say to each other matters.

Yet, many of us fall at the hands of word abuse- the act of simply saying things because you can, but not because you mean it.

Why do we feel the need to front so hard? Why can't we simply own our feelings, express them, and allow love to flow on its course? Both men and women put up such a strong exterior, an attempt to be so guarded that no one has the chance to come in. We may act a certain way but never motion our lips to release their truth, then wind up confused or disappointed when someone doesn't respond to something the way we'd hope. But how would they know?

Mikayla Joseph, 29, has too wondered why her lips could not say what her heart and body once screamed. After countless relationships, a failed engagement, and an almost wedding, she finds herself at a crossroads: The path between wanting love and struggling to truly believe in it. Yet, as much as she may want to fight it, the reality is she wants nothing more than that happy ending. This is her story.

Tell me about your love life. Are you single? Married? Dating? Over it all?

I'll take all of the above for $200, Ki. (laughs) No, but on a serious note I am single. Recently single, up until about three months ago actually.

What happened, why the change in status?

If I had it my way, my answers and status would be a lot different. But that's the thing about life; it's set up to go every way but yours until it's truly your time. To answer your question though, I was in what seemed like a beautiful, loving, and perfect relationship with my best friend for the past 4 years. I hate this saying, but the truth is, he really was my everything.

He made me laugh when I was crying. He made me feel beautiful when acne would attack my face at the most inconvenient times. He prayed with and for me. Sometimes it seemed he believed in me more than I believed in myself. He was my partner, my lover, my cheerleader, again, everything to me - until he wasn't anymore. I couldn't tell you when it happened, Ki. As much as I'd like to point it out, I don't know when he stopped loving me, but it happened. And he let me know that right after taking back the ring he gave me.

Wow. My heart just dropped. You were engaged?

I was. We were. Until he changed his mind.

Changed his mind? How do you ask somebody to marry you and then say forget it?

Girl, three months later and I'm still trying to figure it out! But that's why it was important for me to finally talk through this with someone. I wanted to see how I could connect the dots. Things started to make sense after I stepped out of my bubble. It wasn't until after I stopped being head over heels and really opened my eyes that the situation became clear. He had been telling me he was falling out of love with me for a long time, I just didn't hear him until it was too late.

Listening to your partner goes far beyond just hearing the words they say. If anything, it's truly understanding what they don't say, and knowing how and when to move accordingly. And that was the thing with him, he stopped saying a lot and started doing things that were odd or just unlike him. But instead of asking questions, trying to figure things out, or just doing anything about it, I didn't do anything at all. It was almost like I wanted things to be so perfect that I ignored the imperfections completely.

That's so true. We hear it all the time, "actions speak louder than words" but I think we especially need to adhere to that in the line of love. To understand someone and learn to love them, you have to hear them even when they're quiet.
You mentioned your ex was doing things differently, what were some of the signs you noticed after the fact?

His general love language changed. Oscar was a man of consistent affection, the rare type to not only pay attention to the little things you like but constantly remind you of them. That's exactly it, he showed his love for me by paying attention. Which is why it was easy for him to be my biggest support in the many endeavors I've pursued, because he knew me in and out, he knew the detail, he understood because he wanted to.

But he slowly stopped showing up. He slowly stopped answering. He slowly stopped paying attention. I didn't know it was because he didn't want this anymore, in fact that never even crossed my mind. I thought maybe he was just busy with work, or even the thought of the wedding was becoming too much, but I guess it was all of the above.

So, he proposed to you and then began to switch up?

The switch up probably happened before, but I didn't bring myself to notice until then. I just wanted to be happy, Ki. I'm about to be 30 and I thought I finally found something but I was wrong.

To play devil's advocate, I don't think you were "wrong" so much as you were just in love. It's hard to right and wrong a situation because 4 years of what you had wasn't a lie, it was real. It just didn't last.

Okay, I guess I can take that. I just wish he told me the minute he felt things were off or the minute he realized I wasn't it for him. It's because of that I'm not sure I'll ever forgive him. Real or not, right or wrong, I deserved the truth. Yes, okay, I should have paid more attention, but I shouldn't have had to *find out* something like that. That's some shit you don't guess. Either you want it or you don't.

He was a coward. He admitted that. Nice to hear him say it, hurts just the same.

So, where does this leave you now? Do you still believe in love?

I'm still figuring things out. My wounds are still so fresh. Sometimes, I wake up and still feel him next to me. Immediately after that feeling, I'm overwhelmed by my sadness and the reality that he isn't there anymore and will never be there again. I'm haunted by those feelings. But you know, it will get better. This pain in my chest won't be there forever. I believe I will love and laugh again and when that happens I'll take everything that I've been through and make a new story.

You can't make someone love you. You can only be genuine in your love, your spirit, and always be real with yourself. Do I still believe in love? Of course. My experiences mold me, I become parts of a newer me after the lessons I've learned...regardless of how hard those lessons are.

I'm hopeful. I'm bruised but not broken. And I think a huge part of that is because I knew who I was before Oscar, and I still know and love me after him. Some people are here to teach other people lessons, even if things don't always work out. What did Oscar teach me? He taught me that I am powerful beyond measure, with and without him.

100 Days of Dating

DAY SIXTY-SIX: HUMANS

"It's worth making time to find the things that really stir your soul. That's what makes you really feel alive. You have to say 'no' to other things you're used to, and do it with all your heart." - Roy T. Bennett

Contributed poetry by: Erin Hanson

Let me tell the tale

Of a girl who didn't stop

Who climbed up every mountain

Without a pause upon the top.

She'd dance until each blade of grass

Was clothed in drops of dew,

And the sun knew her by name

But the silver moon did too.

For a fear had settled in her bones;

A fear of sitting still,

That if you're not moving forward

It must mean you never will.

So in time her dance got slower

And she looked at all she'd seen,

But found gaps inside the places

That she'd never fully been,

For she was a human doing

Kiana St Louis

Human moving, human seeing,

But she'd never taken time

To simply be a human being.

This poem by Erin Hanson has spoken volumes to me. I'm from a generation driven by goals, success, and the actions of doing. My peers are creators, architects, teachers, trendsetters, and have become the example of true entrepreneurship, leadership, and the epitome of what hard work and vision can do.

However, my peers and I are so focused sometimes that we forget that there is beauty in the slowness of life. There is a joy in not knowing what is next. There is peace in the undefined. Sometimes, the beauty of life and love is not a plan; it is not wrapped up in your goals, but is instead found in just being who you are. Love is no mystery it just requires attention. Don't forget to give time to yourself, to your friends, to your family and most importantly to your heart's desire. For your life's biggest regret is not becoming who you were truly meant to be.

100 Days of Dating

DAY SIXTY-SEVEN: THE BENCH

"Love is what you've been through with somebody." - James Thurber

Whether you've lost love due to the death of a relationship or the passing of one's life, love is what you've shard with someone. Hurt, pain, loss, these are feelings we are all no strangers to, yet we try so hard to hold them in, to act like they are not there, or simply deny them at all. To know love is to know the good and bad parts that come with it. There is no shame in admitting pain or loss. In fact, admitting our pain makes us stronger than ever.

Contributed poem by: Emma Marie Etwell

Sitting alone,
On a bench that's made for two,
Only one side is empty,
For that place is meant for you.
As I look out
Onto the beautiful sea shore,
Memories overtake me,
And wishes of making more.
Do you remember this special place?
And the moments we had here?
You made my life that day,
And that I will always hold near.
I find myself walking,
Not knowing where to go,
But I always end up
In that special place that we know.
I sit down, can't move,
Waiting for you to show,
And when I feel your hand on mine,
That's when I will go.
Do you see, my darling,
That this bench was made for two,
And one day in the future,
It will be filled again by me and you.

Kiana St Louis

DAY SIXTY-EIGHT: WHEN A MAN FALLS IN LOVE

"The love that lasts longest is the love that is never returned."- W Somerset Maugham

Today's chapter is brought to you by the writings and reflection of author C. JoyBell C., a leading female thinker and writer in our world today. She is a mentor to many other modern-day leaders, as well as an inspirational figure to people from all walks of life, according to GoodReads.

As I continue to research and understand the differences of others and our thoughts on love, I was moved by JoyBell's thoroughness in deciphering the inner workings of men falling love. While of course there is no right or wrong answer to any of this, it is always humbling to gain a little more insight into the thoughts of our counterparts. To fall in love is to powerfully evolve as both a man and woman. This is JoyBell's story.

"I have met so many heartbroken men. It's a catastrophe. Women are easily overcome by the process that happens when a boy falls in love and becomes a man. Men's hearts are so often broken. Still, you have to leave your broken heart in a place where- when the woman who knows how to see what a gift is, sees it- your broken heart can be picked up again.

I think that it takes a very strong woman (inner strength) to be able to handle a man falling in love with her, without morphing into a monster (the process is a very potent process, it can poison a woman, really). A woman thinks she wants a man to fall in love with her for all the perks that come with it; but when a real love really does happen, when a real man shows his manhood; it's often too powerful a thing to endure without being poisoned. Hence, all the heartbroken men.

But, I do believe that there are strong women in the world today. A few. But there are. You could say, that the mark of a real woman, is a woman who can handle a man- a man falling in love with her. A woman who can recognize that, and keep it with her."

"The mark of a real man, is a man who can allow himself to fall deeply in love with a woman. But the reason why a man is often heartbroken, is because a woman can become overcome by the reality that she has made a man out of a boy, because it's just such an overwhelming process, a beautiful and powerful evolution.

Therefore, a man needs to fall in love with a woman who knows that men don't happen every day, and when a man does happen, that's a gift! A gift not always given, and one that shouldn't be thrown away so easily."

Kiana St Louis

DAY SIXTY-NINE: SOMEDAY

"There is only one happiness in this life, to love and be loved." –
George Sand

We're all stories in the end. Some of us are filled with pages dedicated to our experiences. We turn into the results of what people, things, and situations have made us. But I think we have to also make room for the pages that have yet to be filled. There's so much more to life and love than what we know and what we've been through There is so much hope in knowing that someday real love is promised to us. Tyler Kent White taught me that.

(Poetry on next page)

someday someone will love every inch of you – the fading sunset behind your eyes, the moonlight that dances through your hair, the sadness nestled in the creases of your palms. They're going to kiss all the parts you have kept hidden away and tell you how beautiful it all is.

Someday someone is going to say, "I love all of you, not just the parts that make sense, not just the parts you have shown me. I love the parts of you that I don't yet understand, the parts that weigh on your shoulders, the parts I only notice when I steal glances at you in the silence."

You will need to believe them, to believe that fairytales were not written for princesses in glass slippers, that they were written for women who have collected all the pieces of a broken heart and can't stand to put it together again. But most of all you will need to believe that they were written for you.

Someday someone will come to you with a happily ever after promise and slide it over your finger. Someday you'll realize you are not the lucky one, you are the deserving one. Someday you are going to take someone's breath away.

Someday you will realize just how stunning you really are, and you will fall to your knees. Just like you've made me, so many times before.

-Tyler Kent White

Kiana St Louis

DAY SEVENTY and DAY SEVENTY-ONE: THE GREAT LOVE DEBATE (pt3)

THE MEET UP.

I've begun to love these group interviews more than I expected. It's the perfect opportunity to hear thoughts from both sides, in this case, a young man and woman. It's even more exciting when your subjects don't know each other. There's always a hint of hesitancy when bearing all in terms of your love lives, and I understand that completely. Love and relationships - it's personal. But in the same breath, there's so much to learn from each other, and I was in awe of Rob and Jojo's fearlessness.

A few weeks ago, Rob (29), Jojo (23) and I met up at for a date night at one of my favorite Thai spots in downtown Brooklyn. We laughed, got serious, and talked about everything from break ups to make ups to people we wish we never met. Exciting stuff for sure. This is their story.

Kiana: So, tell me about your love lives. Are you two single? Dating? What's going on?

Jojo: Funny you ask (laughs) I legit planned to ask the guy I'm seeing that same question.

Rob: Wait, why do you have to ask him? Why don't you know?

Kiana: Right, good question.

Jojo: Rob, now I know we just met but come on bro. You know damn well you men are confusing as hell. I could easily be "dating" someone for months, only to later find out he's telling everyone else we're just friends.

Rob: Well, then that's the problem. What you think versus what the situation actually is will always be misconstrued. There's no reason you should be on different pages if you have grown-up conversation and are real about what's going on.

100 Days of Dating

Kiana: But, when is it ever that easy? Yes, communication is key. But we rarely actually speak on intent. That's where things get dicey. Not every man or woman is always up front about what they want. Even after they say it.

Jojo: Facts. It's a shame but it's a guessing game. I've been seeing this guy for about 6 months now. It's cool, we're vibing. He's taken me out on a few dates, we text everyday most times all day, and he's usually the person I'm either next to or on face time with when it's time for bed. However, he hasn't asked me to be his girlfriend.

Don't get me wrong; I'm not just waiting around for him to call the shots. But after the lemons life has thrown me, I'm just trying to figure out new ways to make my lemonade. So, I admit I'm a bit hesitant here with things, but the truth is, I do like him and if he asked me to be his girl, I'd say yes. But I just don't want to ask him about it or apply too much pressure. But at the same time, I'm not sure if I should entertain people. I hate dating (laughs).

Rob: Na, I feel you on that. You're trying to protect yourself but your feelings are already ahead of you. But I'm saying, why do women do that? Just tell the n***a how you feel. The absolute worst thing that happens is he's on a different type of time. But have you two even talked about the obvious? I don't think you should stop yourself from exploring other options if he definitely hasn't.

Jojo: I'm just tired of being the first to put myself out there. It's easy for you to just be like "Tell him how you feel", but yet again that's me cutting myself open. For once, I'd like a guy to be head over heels, confused, and trying to figure out how to tell me he wants more.

Rob: Right, I hear you. But unfortunately, that doesn't sound like the situation you're in.

Kiana: Rob, you clearly seem to have all the answers (laughs). Let's switch gears a bit. What's your story? Are you single? Dating?

Rob: (laughs) you see me right? Talking like I know what's going on. But na, I'm just trying to really understand women and how they think when it comes to things. When you get to be my age, you're young but you've seen a lot, done plenty, met plenty more and it can all be a bit exhausting. But to answer your question, I'm dating a beautiful woman who's got me hooked.

Jojo: Ooouu yes Rob! Tell us more.

Kiana: I have to admit the base in your voice, these dim lights, the way you just talked about this woman. I'm here for all of it. What's got you hooked?

Rob: Ya'll are crazy. So, we've been dating for about a year now, and I like to say that. Dating. I'm not sure why people are so keen on the whole "talking" thing but I "talk" to so many people throughout the day, so that isn't a safe enough term for me. I'm the type to claim what's mine. I admit, I haven't asked her to be my girlfriend yet, but I'm also the type to appreciate the right timing. For me, it wasn't about needing to date other women or test the waters or what have you, I just know the next person that I make *my* woman, will in turn be my wife. So I've been trying to make sure all the boxes are checked off.

But she's got all my boxes and then some. This girl man, she's just different. I know she's not into sports. She mixes up player's names and teams all the time (laughs), but I also know she tries to get into it because she knows I'm into it. And I appreciate that so much. She's not a cooker. (laughs) man, she burns water. But, she also never quits. She will YouTube, Rachel Ray, whatever she can if she knows I've had a bad day. She's funny as hell. She's not afraid to keep it real with me. She's definitely got her own. She knows how to control a room not with what she says but with how she acts. I can take her anywhere. Did I mention she's beautiful? She's also older than me, surprisingly. Only by like 2 years, but she's just got it going on and I appreciate that too. She makes me want to see how she's doing. She works so hard, too hard sometimes but I know those kids are everything to her - she teaches. I don't know, I'm rambling. But yeah.

100 Days of Dating

Kiana: Okay, so first of all, I'm in love with her. Secondly, Rob this sounds beautiful. I'm actually more in love with the fact that you're so openly in awe of her. Most men I know could tell me they're really feeling a girl but will also say "I don't know man, she's just cool." So, as I woman I appreciate that.

Jojo: Hell yeah! I'm about to introduce Dice to Ki and see what he say about me. (laughs)

Kiana: But you mention timing. Are you ever nervous that as you wait for your "perfect timing" you risk missing hers?

Rob: Yeah, I definitely have thought about that. I don't want to have her waiting on me. But I'm transparent Ki. I think I'm falling for her and I've told her my plans. I'm less afraid of her leaving me "because she's tired of waiting", because I don't make her feel like she's waiting. I'm in this with her and I try my hardest to let her know that. I'm not trying to sound like a sap now, but the reality is I go hard for the things I want. I went after my degree, my career, my car, and I'm going after her. I just need her to be a little patient with me. Something's coming.

Jojo: I wish more guys thought like you. I haven't heard something as genuine as this in.... ever! Why do you think guys are afraid to do what you're doing?

Rob: I don't think they're "afraid." I just don't think the young men you're dealing with are ready for that type of thinking and doing. Like I said, I'm old (laughs). I'm 30 in a few weeks, I played my games, hard. Don't get it twisted, I'm not proud, but I was a dog. But then I got tired. We all do after a while.

Jojo: Am I supposed to wait until this n***a gets tired? I'm not about to give him 6 more months to figure it out.

Rob: Na, I didn't say anything about waiting. Do your thing, kid. I know you don't want to be the first to say something, but that thought process would have you waiting for more than you think. He's not a mind reader, if you want more demand it. If he's not with it, fuck him.

Kiana: Preach.

Kiana St Louis

DAY SEVENTY-TWO:
NOT EVERYTHING YOU LOSE IS A LOSS

"If you cannot be a poet, be the poem."

Contributed poetry by: Erin Hanson

I was the type of person,

That held onto things too tight,

Unable to release my grip,

When it no longer felt right,

And although it gave me blisters,

And my fingers would all ache,

I always thought that holding on,

Was worth the pain it takes,

I used to think in losing things,

I'd lose part of me too,

That slowly I'd become someone,

My heart no longer knew,

Then one day something happened,

I dropped what I had once held dear,

But my soul became much lighter,

Instead of filled with fear,

And it taught my heart that some things,

Aren't meant to last for long,

100 Days of Dating

They arrive to teach you lessons,

And then continue on,

You don't have to cling to people,

Who no longer make you smile

Or do something you've come to hate,

If it isn't worth your while,

That sometimes the thing you're fighting for,

Isn't worth the cost,

And not everything you ever lose,

Is bound to be a loss.

Kiana St Louis

DAY SEVENTY-THREE: ADVICE FROM OPRAH

"For some reason I believed that if you fell in love it was a guaranteed thing that your path would cross with his, and I never wondered how it would feel to fall in love with a man whose future just couldn't include you." - Laura Pritchett

If a man wants you, nothing can keep him away. If he doesn't want you, nothing can make him stay. Stop making excuses for a man and his behavior. Allow your intuition (or spirit) to save you from heartache. Stop trying to change yourself for a relationship that's not meant to be. Slower is better. Never live your life for a man before you find what makes you truly happy. If a relationship ends because the man was not treating you as you deserve then heck no, you can't "be friends". A friend wouldn't mistreat a friend. Don't settle. If you feel like he is stringing you along, then he probably is. Don't stay because you think "it will get better." You'll be mad at yourself a year later for staying when things are not better. The only person you can control in a relationship is you. Avoid men who've got a bunch of children by a bunch of different women. He didn't marry them when he got them pregnant, why would he treat you any differently? Always have your own set of friends separate from his. Maintain boundaries in how a guy treats you. If something bothers you, speak up. Never let a man know everything. He will use it against you later. You cannot change a man's behavior. Change comes from within. Don't ever make him feel he is more important than you are... even if he has more education or in a better job. Do not make him into a quasi-god. He is a man, nothing more nothing less. Never let a man define who you are. Never borrow someone else's man. If he cheated with you, he'll cheat on you. A man will only treat you the way you allow him to treat you. All men are not dogs. You should not be the one doing all the bending... compromise is two way street. You need time to heal between relationships... there is nothing cute about baggage. Deal with your issues before pursuing a new relationship. You should never look for someone to complete you, a relationship consists of two whole individuals, look for someone complimentary ..not supplementary. Dating is fun... even if he doesn't turn out to be Mr. Right. Make him miss you sometimes, when a man always know where you are, and you're always readily available to him - he takes it for granted. Never move into his mother's house. Never co-sign for a man. Don't fully commit to a man who doesn't give you everything that you need. Keep him in your radar, but get to know others. - Oprah

100 Days of Dating

DAY SEVENTY-FOUR: I CHOOSE LOVE.

"Love is, above all, the gift of oneself." - Jean Anouilh

With all the crazy things going on in the world today, sometimes I feel silly faithfully writing about love. Maybe I should start a blog covering the not-so-quiet happenings in Libya where they're currently auctioning off slaves at the hands of Europeans. Or maybe I should write another book on the constant mistreatment and under value of people of color. Or a podcast dedicated to the corruption and misleading of our faithful government led by 45. Essentially, I could be writing or reporting my views on anything else, but I choose love because it's an obvious answer.

We don't love each other enough. We focus only on what makes us different; from the clothes we wear, to the music we listen to, our differences are put on a pedestal all in an effort to better label us and to divide us. Why else do we have economic classes? Yet, we fall right into it. Not enough of us question tradition. Not enough of us are curious and want change. Not enough of us choose love.

From worldly matters to that of the single heart, there is a yearning for peace, which has always been attainable. What are we afraid of? Is it vulnerability? There is so much strength in risk and opening ourselves up. The truest disservice is remaining silent.

"One of the best parts of being human is other humans. It's true, because life is hard; but people get to show up for one another, as God told us to, and we remember we are loved and seen and God is here and we are not alone. We can't deliver folks from their pits, but we can sure get in there with them until God does." - Jen Hatmaker

Kiana St Louis

DAY SEVENTY-FIVE:
I LOVE YOU, BUT I LOVE ME MORE

"When a woman becomes her own best friend life is easier." - Diane Von Furstenberg

Time and time again I've allowed love to cloud my judgments, knock me off balance, or drive me insane. I've been so consumed with trying to find happiness in someone else I've forgotten that happiness must first be born within myself. I've forgotten I must first accept who I am and request changes of myself that only *I've* demanded.

Every now and again I have to remind myself of self-love. There is a necessity of patience to endure any journey of healing. I've been rushing through the motions, trying not to feel things I know I must. I've given temporary men access to my life that have now become weights instead of wings. I've tried to force happiness and tell myself I'm ready to move on and move forward when in fact I need to stay still and truly deal with what I'm feeling so that when I finally move, it's never backwards.

However, despite the fact that I do have some more personal work to do, I have to also admit that in a matter of months I have come so far from where I once was - mentally and emotionally. I want to make sure I am analyzing my shortcomings, but also meditating on my successes. We must all learn to do this.

So many of us become stagnant in our growth as people and partners because we don't take the time to simply congratulate ourselves on our wins, regardless of how small they are. Sometimes whether we realize it or not, we need to be our own "pick-me-ups," we have to be the engine to keep ourselves running, we might even need to be our own ignitions to set our passions ablaze. All I'm saying is, we need to learn to love ourselves more than what feel like at the moment. We are not defined by the situations we go through but instead by the process we take to get through them.

I must learn to love me at *all* times, especially when I'm sad and lonely - for me that's when it counts the most. While love is a beautiful thing, I along with many men and women, apply such a pressure to finding romantic love that I think it's possible we may have overlooked the true essence of what it is we're really in search of. Love is patient, love is kind. Love has no color, love does not judge. Many are in search of an accepting, conscious, genuine, and consistent love. However, what we seek is already within us, we must learn to love it.

"If you have the ability to love, love yourself first." - Charles B.

Kiana St Louis

DAY SEVENTY-SIX: HER

"And that's when I know it's over. As soon as you start thinking about the beginning, it's the end." — Junot Díaz, This Is How You Lose Her

Contributed poetry by: Cosmicpull on DeepUndergroundPoetry.

Your life can be split up into two periods - before and after.

before is the calm, is the storm. it is a torrent that drags you around at its own pace.

before is measured in breaths taken, in heartbeats skipped, in texts sent.

before is measured in the hours you spend thinking about her smile.

before is-

before is gone.

but after?

after is the whisper of a town long abandoned.

it is the creak of wood, it is the slow decomposition, it is the dusty memorial to something once held precious.

it is the space ringing hollow where you once rearranged yourself to slot her in.

after is measured in the time since she's texted.

after is measured in the things you strike from your life lest they remind you of her.

after is the hours you spend wondering what you did wrong, what you could have changed.

after never ends. after leaves scars.

after is-

after simply is.

DAY SEVENTY-SEVEN:
WHY SOME MEN LEAD WOMEN ON

"Love will find a way through paths where wolves fear to prey."
— Lord Bryon

In doing some daily love writing research, I came across this article written by Corey Aaron on his very cool blog *Kram Comedy Speaks*. In this specific piece, he's answering one of the most important questions in the world: Why do men lead women on?

Maybe you're not actually being led on–

Okay, yes, some guys do sometimes lead chicks on but how does the saying go that I just came up with? Just because you think something doesn't make it true. Well that sounded much more original in my head. But yeah, just because you *think* you were led on doesn't mean you actually were led on at all. Somewhat analogous to my paragraph making fun of how dudes think all chicks want them, maybe you think you were led on simply because you wanted to be. Not that you were trying to be led on and subsequently abandoned, just that maybe you were finding significance where there was none and attributing feelings to certain actions when there weren't any. You liked the dude and maybe you liked him so much that you wanted to believe he liked you too so everything that he does is seen as a progression towards that end. Maybe the dude noticed this whole thing, realized it wasn't what he was going for and bailed simply to avoid further mess. I'm not saying this is true for all cases but I think this could be the case more often than we think. If humans are good at nothing else it's seeing what we want to see (even when contrary evidence is presented to us) so maybe that's what's happening in your specific case.

So what can you do? Be mindful of your interactions and really cue in on how the dude acts and the things he does. If one day you were picking out your future children's names and the next he disappears like he gave up NSA secrets then yeah, maybe you were led on. You're both nuts, but you as the chick have a stronger case. Is he just being kind of friendly and giving you attention since he probably doesn't get all that much female attention? Assuming you know any of his friends does he treat you like one of those or super special? There's a big truth that complicates everything I said in this paragraph, which brings me to my next point.

He's trying to put the D in the V–

You may not know this by now, but dudes enjoy getting laid. For many it's their utmost priority and some would probably give up the next 11 meals and a fortnight of sleep if it meant they got to bang right now. They'd of course regret that deal .00001 seconds after blowing their load and realizing how much they wish this chick would make them a sandwich but hey, we're not all that smart.

So dudes really like sex. Some chicks really like sex too but it seems like they're not willing to go through the extreme measures that some dudes take in order to procure the shag. Or perhaps they simply don't have to…I'll save that thought for another day. Anyway the fact of the matter is that many dudes will do and/or say pretty much anything in order to fuck whatever girl it is that they currently aren't fucking. And here's where the mess comes, from the chicka's point of view. If you're unaware I really hate to break this one to you, but some guys will even feign feelings in order to get you to allow him to stick his peen inside of one of your lady-holes. Jeez, who would do such a thing? As everyone knows, leading chicks on just to bang them was invented by Adolph Hitler so women's hearts would still be broken long after the Third Reich was a thing of the past. Now that the history lesson is over, let's relate this back to the original question.

Dudes sometimes lead chicks on just to bang them. I thought it would take longer to come to that conclusion. So yeah, if as a female you feel like you're constantly being led on (not just making it up because you really, really want that relationship) then it's probably because dudes are trying to bang you and you ain't givin' up the goods. In everything people do there's an at least subconscious assessment of risk vs. reward where we figure out how much we're willing to put into an endeavor weighed against what we're likely to get out of it. Applying this to our current problem, a good example would be that a dude may be willing to put in only a few text messages worth of work to try to nail down things with one chick whereas he might be willing to spend some time, say a few choice things or whatever and pretend to enjoy "Frozen" in order to get sex with another girl. Why? Well that depends. Maybe he doesn't find the first chick all that attractive whereas the second might be right up his alley looks-wise. There could be a million other reasons, but that's probably the most likely.

So you've been talking to a dude for a while, things seem like they're going nice and boom! He's gone quicker than Malaysia Flight 370. There's a solid chance he was just trying to get that D in and when you didn't oblige in whatever time frame he came up with he peaced. It's simply a matter of optimizing efficiency: the work he had to put in began to outweigh the banging of you. Sometimes you just have to cut your losses. This doesn't mean he was never actually interested in you as a person, but as they say, eventually you have to nut up or shut up. You didn't nut up, so he shut up the budding "relationship," or something like that.

"What do you have to gain from this?"

The answer is probably nothing, which is why the big bounce happened in the first place. Sure, there are some guys that get their rocks off from getting chicks to fall for them then fleeing like a hippie avoiding the draft (that would have been timely a good 45 years ago) but those are the same idiots that brag about getting a phone number before buying six carbombs and two jay-moo's.

So no, there really isn't anything to gain from leading a chick on except being able to retort "I could have banged her if I wanted to dude," and then ordering six carbombs and two more jay-moo's.

Where some women go wrong

The thing about people is sometimes they just change their mind. Yeah, it sucks that you were led on but it may be as innocuous as a change of heart. What are people supposed to do? If they wake up one day and they're no longer feeling whatever "it" is just be like "sorry mate, I'm no longer feeling this" before they've even gotten to the stage of an actual relationship? Sorry to break it to you but nobody really owes anybody anything unless there's some circumstance that changes that. If the dude you were talking to or whatever goes cold on the other end then unfortunately that's just the way it is. Just because you'd like an explanation doesn't mean you're owed one, which is something that I think most people inherently wouldn't agree with even if they say they do in their head after reading this. I get that it's nice but a courtesy is just that.

If you feel like you're being strung then take control of the damn situation. "Oh he's just playing some games but I know how he really feels." No, you're a moron both for thinking that and putting up with "games." If you're a girl and you're waiting around to be contacted then you're stupid too. "Oh but he might think I'm a desperate bitch." Well maybe you are, so if he thinks that then you're right and if you aren't desperate and he thinks that then he's retarded but either way, why would you want to be with this person? I'm a pretty big fan of doing what you want to do and not bending yourself to other people unless *you* want to so if you want to talk to the guy then do it, don't just wait for him to see what's going on with you at his convenience. If he's not into it then he'll let you know in some way (e.g. bouncing hard) but at least you're not compromising your desires to try to appeal to someone who owes you nothing and who you owe nothing to.

In male-female relationships people like to accuse the other party of playing games when things seem overly complicated or aren't going their way but the best way to beat the game is to clear the board. If you feel like you're being meddled with then speak up for yourself. A good "what the fuck" usually suffices. It may not work out but then at least you can say you didn't put up with any shit. Eventually things will end all happily ever after and you'll find just the right guy who doesn't view your reaching out as desperation and loves even the smelliest of your shits but until that day stop being such a pushover.

Women like to put the onus on men and then complain when we don't handle things the way they want to. Science shows men are inherently shittier communicators than women so if that's your problem then try communicating. If the response you get is silence then that's a pretty loud answer. Now you can move into the "but why" stage but that's stupid and I don't care about that right now.

My last thought on this topic is that as much as people hate being rejected they also really dislike rejecting others, generally speaking. Most people are too big of pussies to do something that will hurt someone's feelings directly so for them it's better to just let the other person be hurt by their inaction. I didn't murder that guy if I simply failed to pull the lever that would divert the train that ran over him! It's not exactly their fault I suppose. Some people are actually kind of nice and generally want to avoid hurting others so they sometimes don't do things that would be beneficial to a situation just because someone's feelings might be hurt. I get that I guess and I'm sure that's what happens in some instances.

100 Days of Dating

DAY SEVENTY-EIGHT: CLOSURE

Contributed poetry by Erin Hanson:

It's not the endings that will haunt you
But the space where they should lie,
The things that simply faded
Without one final wave goodbye.
Like a book with torn out pages,
Forgetting things you're sure you knew,
A question with no answer
And a song stopped halfway through.
So when your mind attempts to store them
Their crooked shape will never fit,
And forever in the corners
Of your consciousness they sit.
Jagged edges made from moments
You can't be quite sure were the last,
Slicing open thoughts that healed
As they attempt to slip right past.
You see, not knowing is what haunts you,
The memories that never mend,
For they are puzzles missing pieces
Of all the things that didn't.

Kiana St Louis

DAY SEVENTY-NINE and DAY EIGHTY: WHAT IS LOVE IN OUR GENERATION?

"Maybe we feel empty because we leave pieces of ourselves in everything we used to love." – Unknown

Cici B - she's tough. She's real. She's the fire I wish I had and the fire I am becoming. Reading her words makes me oddly emotional. Mainly because I'm welcomed again by the reality of how alike we are. I don't know her. Cici and I have never met. She's probably never heard of this project, or me, yet our likeness in love has ignited an unspoken unity. I know she pours out the way she has in a few of these different snippets of writing because she's been through heartbreak. She's known real love. She's felt things for someone she'll never be able to forget. I know somewhere she's still healing.

Out of many of the stories I've shared throughout this lyrical journey, I am most matched with her. I am reminded of my past relationship(s), I am reminded of the people who requested invitations to my life and then never showed up, and I'm reminded of my own healing. Why does love seem so hard? Why can't we just admit our faults, trust our hearts, and jump freely into whatever time has in store for us? Another reality: Even after all these stories, I still don't know lol. I've got 20 more days to go! This chapter is for me and Cici, this is part of our story.

"... And when he asked what it was that he could give to her that she'd never had before, her answer was so simple. "Consistency." She said. "If you wish to give me something that no other man has yet to give me - then don't give me mixed signals and emotions that leave me wondering - I'm tired of wondering. If you're gonna be with me, then be here. If you ever feel the need to leave, then stay gone. All I want from someone at this point, is consistency."

100 Days of Dating

"I am no longer in the business of giving people chance after chance, after fucking chance. I'm grown, you're grown, and we both know the difference between right and wrong at this point. Mistakes happen, of course, but when those mistakes become repetitive, you can't call them 'mistakes' anymore - now they're choices. YOUR choices. So no, I'm no longer in the business of giving people chance, after chance, after fucking chance. You get two strikes, and then you're out of here."

"I'm willing to compromise when it comes to many things - but not love man. Not love. I've done that too many times and it's taught me exactly what I want from what I don't want. And listen, it's not like the type of love I want is from a fairytale... no. The love I want is a very real thing. It's out there. And it has nothing to do with posting pictures or dropping everything to answer text messages immediately that aren't urgent - that shit is high school to me. What I want in love, is respect - even when arguments arise. I never want to cry my eyes out till I'm sick because of an argument again. I want a love that has commitment. Has tenderness. Has laughter. Has playfulness. Has passion. Has morals and above all else.. is always felt. Never again do I ever want to have to question whether or not the man I am giving all of myself to, loves me. And never again will I ever entertain a man who tells me that I'm asking for too much. I know what I want. What I want exists. And if one man doesn't want to give it to me then I won't break my head over it - he's simple not for me."

"One of the healthiest things I ever did for my life was hold myself accountable for the roles that I played in heartbreak. You know - fool me once, shame on you, but fool me twice then that shit's on me. It was so easy to sit around with my girls, and be coddled, and listen to all of the things I wanted to hear - "He's a piece of shit. You deserve better. It's not your fault. You didn't do anything wrong." And maybe all of those things were definitely true the first time around... but what about the second time? And the third time? And the fourth time?

How could I deserve better if I kept going back to the same piece of shit? How could it not be my fault when he'd already shown me who he was, but I chose to keep believing his words over his actions? How could I not have been the one doing anything wrong when I kept ending up at the same fucking dead end, heartbroken, with a face drenched in recycled tears? Come on. Seriously. Blaming the same man for doing the same shit over and over again, wasn't getting me anywhere. My choices had me sitting in the exact pike of shit that I deserved to sit in, and the only way to get out of it, was to start with holding myself accountable for MY OWN damaging behavior."

"A while ago, I promised myself that I would respect my heart, soul, and sanity by not sticking around for anyone's bullshit," I told him. "And I'll be damned if I break that promise to myself, for you." ---- Cici B.|TheCrimsonKiss

100 Days of Dating

DAY EIGHTY-ONE: YOU'RE NOT TOO MUCH, HE'S JUST NOT ENOUGH

"The most painful thing is losing yourself in the process of loving someone too much, and forgetting that you are special too." - Ernest Hemingway

I can't believe it took me so long to find this new blog I can't stop reading called, She*Said*. I don't know what I was doing before, but I feel like every second I wasn't reading these posts was a waste! Elizabeth, you are a woman after my own heart. It's so weird how I see bits and pieces of myself in other people's lives. While her story is coming from a woman's perspective, I think being "too much" is something both men and women have heard one time too many.

So often, we take people and situation-ships so seriously that we begin to take ourselves too seriously. We begin to over analyze everything that we do, what we say, essentially who we are in an effort to meet the likeness of the person we like... but where does that leave us? I'm tired of altering myself to fit some imaginary outfit that I didn't even pick out. It's about time we realize as people that the people we're "too much" for are simply not enough for us. Blogger, writer, and fellow lover Elizabeth Nelson, spelled this out perfectly, I couldn't have said it better. This is her story.

If you're a woman who has dated for any length of time, and who has ever been honest about what you wanted from a partner, I'm willing to bet someone has told you that you were "too much" at some point.

They've hurt your feelings and made you feel like it was your own fault for being too sensitive. They've disappointed you, then accused you of trying to make them feel bad. They've told you to chill out. They've asked you why you can't just accept things the way they are, and why you're always asking for more than they can give. They've made promises, then made you feel crazy and stupid for believing they'd keep those promises.

Kiana St Louis

Men don't even have to come right out and tell us we're too much in order for us to hear it. We hear it when they tell us they're not sure what they want. We hear it when they say they just want to have a good time and not talk about the future. We hear it when they say they're not looking to commit right now. We hear it when they sigh and shake their heads, when they don't return our texts, and when they tell us they need space. We've digested the message so thoroughly that we say it to ourselves anytime someone dismisses us, doesn't listen to us, or hurts us.

But what if, instead of believing we were "too much," we realized that these guys simply aren't enough? Because they're not. Any man – anyone, for that matter – who makes you feel bad about having feelings, standing up for yourself, having expectations in a relationship, or holding people to a standard of human decency, is an asshole.

There's nothing wrong with knowing what you want, and demanding it. There's nothing wrong with falling apart sometimes. There's nothing wrong with being weak and needy and not knowing what you want at all. You're allowed to say what you want, you're allowed to change your mind, and you're allowed to not feel bad or apologize for it.

Thirty-some years after having that fit at the dinner table, I'm finally shaking off the shame of being told that my anger was so devastating, I couldn't even fathom it. For years, I used to stare at myself in the mirror, wondering what it was my parents saw in my face that I apparently couldn't see. I'd make my angriest face, glaring at my reflection until I couldn't take it anymore and started to laugh. I still don't quite know what they saw in me, but I'm not scared of it anymore.

Sometimes, when we're fighting, my boyfriend sighs and shakes his head the same way my father did that night, and I know that whatever that look was, I've still got it. But if he thinks I'm too much, he'd better step up his game. Because I might be a lot, but I'm not too much. And I'll never try to make myself into less for anyone, ever again.

Contributed by: Elizabeth Laura Nelson

DAY EIGHTY-TWO and DAY EIGHTY-THREE: TO LOVE IS TO COMMUNICATE

You Can't Keep Secrets from Your Dignity

By: Fame Leanne King

Further my mind goes, than I believed it could fathom
Fathoms below even the deceased dreams chasm
Unpassionately growing through and between atoms
To learn
There is no whole truth in solely words
Blindfolded, if your mind isn't where the memory occurs
So it's sure
We'll never understand more than we're capable to confer
And it doesn't mean, you can't relate to the way I toss n' turn
In my sleep
That it isn't the same color we bleed
Or that we aren't perhaps equally 'deep'
Just that we hold some nature of privacy in our thoughts, from any other's gaze
Did I mention it was books of separate authors, though we're on the same page?
What I wish to relate today
Is I have been changing to date
I'm breaking, down just like anyone else
Draining my health
Enslaved by the chase of wealth
Smiling while we're high, but we'll retreat to our personal hells
The honesty is, I'm scared to delve into myself
Because I know where my truth gets ugly, and has no glamour
Not the 30 second commercial version of what it's like living with cancer
It's habits, actions and manner
Looming over my pride
Leaving a weakness in my stride
Making me feel tired before I've tried.

Kiana St Louis

Social Communication

By: Katie Biesiada

Hashtag done.
Hashtag I give up.
Hashtag tired.
Hashtag alone.

All we ever talk about anymore is hashtags and Instagram and texts and snapchat.

I'm done.

I miss the face to face contact.
The way someone's eyes light up or dim down in reaction to something.

I miss the way your hand feels when you place it on mine.

I miss your hugs.

And I miss your voice.

And I'm able to talk about anything with you over a text message, but I'm afraid that you don't want to talk to me, person to person.

I like to think that we have a great friendship, but I realize that we don't.

You FaceTime and call other people, but you won't do that for me.

I try to initiate more conversation than we have, but I feel like you hold back.

I pour some of my heart out into a message that I sent and your only response is an emoji.

I'm hurt.
As childish as it sounds, I'm hurt.

I'm broken and I feel like you keep taking pieces of me away.

100 Days of Dating

I'm broken and I wish you would actually talk and listen to me instead of typing it out.

I miss you because there's no one else and I'm sorry that there isn't.

I don't mean to burden you with everything that's wrong, but when you say that you're there for me, I expect you to follow through.

I miss you a lot.
And I need you to know that.
Because you mean so much to me.

And I know I don't mean as much to you...

Kiana St Louis

DAY EIGHTY-FOUR: MEN.

"Women were created from the rib of man to be beside him, not from his head to top him, nor from his feet to be trampled by him, but from under his arm to be protected by him, near to his heart to be loved by him." - Matthew Henry

This just in: Men aren't from Mars. Women aren't from Venus. Turns out, we're all from Earth - we have no choice but to deal with it. I say this because I've been having so many different fruitful conversations with both men and women on love, relationships, dating, cheating, marriage, etc., and there's been a common underlying theme. In conversation it seems everyone has pretty much held on the idea that they just simply don't understand the opposite sex and give up trying. People are content with "going with the flow" or "playing the field" or worst - matching petty behavior with petty behavior.

But how far do these actions truly get us?

Lack of true communication is at the core of a lot of failed relationships, failed dating experiences, or just failed love. Men do not clearly articulate their intentions when pursing women, and women fail to demand how they should be treated. If you've stayed with me this far, you've learned from a few willing men about how they think, why they react the way they do, or why they move how they do in general. I've learned that no one man is the same, however, many do share the same thought process, as do women. We're all in this love thing together; it's a risk for *everyone*. Yet, somehow, most reported heartbreaks are simply that of women.

I don't mean to pick on guys but I did want to touch on our human purpose. We were made love. We were made to reproduce, populate, and thrive. But how does that happen when we're (both men and women) too busy trying to see who cares the least? We need each other. When will we understand?

100 Days of Dating

MEN

By: Maya Angelou

When I was young, I used to
Watch behind the curtains
As men walked up and down the street. Wino men, old men.
Young men sharp as mustard.
See them. Men are always
Going somewhere.
They knew I was there. Fifteen
Years old and starving for them.
Under my window, they would pause,
Their shoulders high like the
Breasts of a young girl,
Jacket tails slapping over
Those behinds,
Men.

One day they hold you in the
Palms of their hands, gentle, as if you
Were the last raw egg in the world. Then
They tighten up. Just a little. The
First squeeze is nice. A quick hug.
Soft into your defenselessness. A little
More. The hurt begins. Wrench out a
Smile that slides around the fear. When the
Air disappears,
Your mind pops, exploding fiercely, briefly,
Like the head of a kitchen match. Shattered.
It is your juice
That runs down their legs. Staining their shoes.
When the earth rights itself again,
And taste tries to return to the tongue,
Your body has slammed shut. Forever.
No keys exist.

Kiana St Louis

Then the window draws full upon
Your mind. There, just beyond
The sway of curtains, men walk.
Knowing something.
Going someplace.
But this time, I will simply
Stand and watch.

Maybe.

100 Days of Dating

DAY EIGHTY-FIVE: WOMEN.

After dedicating the previous chapter to men and what women see, deal with, or fail to receive, I wanted to create an equal ground. I know there are so many times we feel men and women are too different to coexist, but as I mentioned before we're just missing basic understanding. Why do we feel like men never try? Why do men feel like women do too much? There's a barrier here, but after stumbling across Brendan Tapley's post on *Women's Day* I think I have a little more perspective as to why. I just had to share this with you. Here are 10 things men apparently wished women knew:

Here's the standard line on men: We're simple, straightforward, limited—and usually perfectly happy to leave it there. Why? Because it keeps your expectations of us low. But here's the single biggest thing women don't get about men: Masculinity is a complicated performance we agree to in order to be seen as men. Unfortunately, that performance is more designed to conceal than reveal us. For instance, it's easier and more "masculine" for us to talk about the great sex we had rather than describe the great conversation afterward. So, a woman ends up knowing the male script, but not the man. Breaking character, then, I give you (in random order) 10 things he wishes you knew about him.

1. Even Men Like Compliments Every Once in a While
Real guys, or so the story goes, don't need praise. Especially not about girlish things, like if those jeans show off our assets. But the truth is, men enjoy a little well-intentioned objectification. A squeeze of the biceps and a lingering stare when we reach for the top shelf—these remind us of what attracted you to us and appeal to our Darwinian sense of selectivity (i.e., what keeps you choosing us over the other monkeys). It also makes it OK, even desirable, to send a little objectification your way, too. And just to be clear, the praise doesn't need to be physical. In fact, it's important that women commend those things masculinity tends to belittle, like if we're good cooks or get passionate about foreign films. Tell us, too, when we've been a good father, a caring son or a helpful husband. Watch how much faster the toilet gets cleaned.

2. We Are Brutally Honest Because We Care

We know that, at times, tact can be the only four-letter word that doesn't describe us, but women need to rethink their reactions to male candor. Men lie and obfuscate with people they have no interest in. The art of BS—and indulging others with their BS—is how we get through the day. But with you, lucky you, we want to forget all that. We want to tell you why your mother bothers us and how you can solve the problem with your high-maintenance friend. In a relationship, honesty is a young man's mistake because the longer a man feels punished for it, the more he begins to censor himself. And that's when you really need to worry.

3. You Should Appreciate Our Reliability

Similar to honesty, a good man demonstrates his commitment to you by showing up. So it's more than a little irritating to hear about your fascination with the jerk who has mastered the art of illusion: He's there, but not really. It's a vicious cycle—the more men feel those guys get the benefits of your time and attention, the more incentive we have to become those guys. And that's bad for both of you since more of those guys turn your illusion into our delusion.

4. Love Means Never Having to Be Attached at the Hip

We acknowledge the importance of couple time. We'd even go so far as to say that, in the best relationships, love that is asserted each day deepens and extends. Lost in this, however, is the belief that time spent enriching oneself also enriches partnerships. In other words, going on a hiking weekend with the boys does not diminish the bond we share. Like women need the affirmation of their girlfriends, guys need the companionship of other men. This kind of solo time will refresh us and we'll come back with more for you.

5. We Respect You as Females—and Love What Makes You Women

It is sad to say that equality in our times means adopting the worst of both sexes: Men get more sexualized and women can be cruder. And while no fair-minded guy wants women to return to the 1950s sitcom (although coming home to a roast chicken and a stiff drink ain't bad as a fantasy), neither do we want the elimination of the feminine as a virtue. Don't be ashamed to hold on to those things that make you different from us, like how you care about smelling nice or reminding us of empathy. That isn't regressive; it's just beautiful. To see the exception, read #6.

6. Be the Boss in the Bedroom

Two words: Unleash yourself. Express your fantasies. Use your hands along with your…imagination. Show us who's boss and give us good directions—you already know we don't do well asking for them. Your explanations will heighten our intuition and your pleasure.

7. Our First Commitment Is to Ourselves

One of the biggest complaints by women (for the second, read #8) is that men don't commit. Right or wrong, men are raised to believe that a successful life hinges on self-fulfillment. Relationships, at first glance, seem to impinge on that. They make men nervous that the pursuit of happiness will become the path of missed opportunity. But men do come around to understand that true self-fulfillment depends on fulfilling another. What can you do in the meantime? Take a page from our script on this one and focus on your self-fulfillment, your own passions. This kind of healthy withdrawal will make pursuing you part of our happiness.

8. For Us, Seeing Is Believing

Do you want to know why men like sports? It's about pure measurable success. At the end of the game, no one can dispute the number of touchdown passes or homeruns. An athlete works toward a goal and is rewarded with concrete proof of his effort. What is the irrefutable proof of a successful emotional life? Here, the data is less tangible. Men fear endeavors where success is vague because failure seems a likely result. In case you hadn't noticed, we hate to fail. One way to take the failure out is to become his ally in those pursuits that bring him emotionally alive; his attempt at wholeness there will illuminate the great rewards of an emotional life elsewhere.

9. We May Lose Small Battles, but Always Remember the Wars We've Won

How important is putting the toilet seat down if the yard is mowed each week? Does it matter that an item was forgotten at the store when he checked off the rest? If he let the kid go to his friend's with a stained shirt but made sure to spend time on his science project, is there a point to mentioning it? Women should remember to give credit where credit is due.

10. Fathers Are Just as Important as Mothers

It can seem, at times, that the world elevates the feminine over the masculine and that the lessons men can impart are outmoded or regarded as Neanderthal. But when a bully is picking on your son, your husband showing him how to throw a punch is not nonsensical. Or if your daughter has an athletic talent, his testosterone-fueled guidance may teach her more than just competitiveness. Honoring what men know based on their experiences is just as valuable to the young as the insights of women. Freely sharing his wisdom prevents imbalance, both in those and us we seek to help.

100 Days of Dating

DAY EIGHTY-SIX and DAY EIGHTY-SEVEN: DO YOU BELIEVE IN SECOND CHANCES?

"The truth is everyone is going to hurt you. You just have to find the ones worth suffering for." - Bob Marley

It goes without saying that it's important to try to avoid causing people pain. Whether they're people you know or total strangers, hurting other people in any way is wrong.

Having said that, sometimes, we're the ones who get hurt. When people cause us pain in life, we handle it in different ways. We can get down and depressed about how we're made to feel. We can become bitter, hateful and resent them, or we can recognize we didn't deserve the pain and empower ourselves to overcome it.

It's important that we never let people bring us down mentally, emotionally or psychologically. In the same way you shouldn't hurt other people, you shouldn't let them hurt you either. You shouldn't give people the *power* or *opportunity* to hurt you.

But sometimes, it's not always in our own hands when it comes to people hurting us. It's important to have an open heart and be a loving and genuine individual. But we should also be cautious with the people we open our hearts to.

It's important to pick and choose who wisely we do all of the above for. Not everyone deserves your love, and everyone definitely doesn't deserve second chances after he or she has hurt you.

You need to decide who's worth fighting for, and who's worth giving a second chance to. Either way, you should protect yourself by going into these situations with caution.

When people hurt you through the things they say or do, you can either forgive them or let it go, bottle it up and implode your feelings, or be angry at them for what they've done. Why give someone that much power over your emotions when he or she doesn't deserve it?

Kiana St Louis

You should never let someone control you through the pain he or she has caused you. In other words, it's important to keep your guard up and protect yourself when you see that someone is hurting you, or can hurt you.

When people hurt you over and over again, you need to recognize that what they're doing is toxic. It's up to you whether or not you give someone an opportunity to harm you more than once-whether it be physically, emotionally, or spiritually.

When someone hurts you the first time, it's usually unpredictable and unexpected, but the same can't be said further down the line You need to be strong enough to recognize when someone isn't right for you in a relationship, or even as a friend, and end the situation as soon as possible.

You shouldn't put yourself in a situation that could cause you any level of pain, discomfort or stress. You need to love yourself enough to care how other people are making you feel. No one is *supposed to* be anyone's savior or superhero. If someone is hurting you too much, don't even try to be there for him or her.

True friends and healthy relationships should never be one-sided or compromise the integrity of your well-being. If you see that a situation is toxic, and you wind up being the one who keeps getting hurt, you should definitely close the door to that situation completely.

Remember: A true friend or partner in life would never want to cause you pain or hurt you in any way. Someone who actually cares about you will be selfless and loving. A true friend gives you hope and love, and knows the importance of good communication in your relationship.

Good communication never involves the intent of hurting someone. If anything, it involves learning how to talk and express yourself without hurting the person. If your friend, lover or partner in life isn't willing to communicate with you in a healthy way, you need to end that situation. You should seriously consider letting the door hit this person on the way out and taking back their key.

(Contributed by Anne Cohen from *Elite Daily*)

OR some might agree with Ranata Suzuki:

Second Chances

I do not believe that anyone who's ever loved us can drift so far from us that we could not reach out and pull them back if we honestly tried. At some point we must accept at least partial responsibility for what has transpired by admitting to ourselves that we do not simply lose people... on some level we let them go. Perhaps it was too difficult or too painful to try... or maybe the relationship seemed too short-lived or too broken to salvage... No matter the reasons it all fell apart, people can still fall back into each others arms for a second try at love if the feelings are still there... But it is not simply a matter of wishing for another chance - we are given so many chances to win back the people we've loved and lost, if only we'd see those opportunities for what they really are. It's not even a matter of crossing paths with them by pure chance or accidentally dialing their number because it's still in your phone - every single day we wake up is another chance to track down somebody we still have feelings for and convince them to give it another shot. But the funny thing about chances is - you have to take the chance... and the sad part is that most people are too scared, too stubborn, too stupid or too hurt from the first time around to take the chances they are given. So do I believe that we are given a second chance at loving the same person twice? Yes. I believe we are given many.
But I also believe that we usually screw them up.

Ranata Suzuki

www.feelmeforever.com

Kiana St Louis

DAY EIGHTY-EIGHT and EIGHTY-NINE: THE REBOUND GIRLS

"Don't pursue a heart that you're not ready to stay committed to." - @TrentShelton

Contributed poetry by: Stevette Gonzalez

Why can't they see me?
See past the pretty hair, cute face, long legs and thin waist.
They don't see me.
Rebound is what I'm made out to be.
They come falling back into my arms, heart big and warm.
I catch them.
I'm not too sure why I do, but the heart is worn, not at all new.
So why am I the rebound girl when there's so much I have to offer?
Smarts, talent and skin that's much softer.
I stand here questioning myself, but it ends with laughter.
I answer myself quite a bit faster...."It's not me, it's them"
All they really need is a friend.
Have I tried and tried to be there, and they still don't care.
Why? Because they don't see me.

Contributed poetry by: <u>Rhianecdote</u>

I think of the first guy who let me down
Just as his Ex came back to town
And though I can have a laugh
and joke with him now
I will never see him in the same light
ever since that night
Out of cowardice he thought it was alright
After knowing me for a good part of my life
To do me like he did
I guess I dodged a bullet...

But not for long
Tell em' how you really feel
And they run

100 Days of Dating

But when you can't be direct
You lose my **Respect**
And I don't think
That anyone has ever
Won it back

And when you can't be straight up
You forfeit my **Trust**
And I know for a fact
That nobody has ever
Gained that back
Sometimes I wonder if anyone ever will

And I don't know if this is due to my lack
of understanding, or any hurt that I feel
But I doubt it cause I was born to relate
Tread the empathy
But I find it winding and tiring of late
But what is the other option?
Hate?
No, I just wasn't made for that

So I seek to understand the reasoning
And see if this should lead
to an acceptance of the action
Whether it's a justification
For the jagged fragments I stand upon
of all that can be shattered in a fraction
cause we all make Mistakes right?

My prison is a prism of insight
I constantly have to negotiate
One I wish I could crack
But I guess if I'm Bound to the Rebound
I'll always bounce back.

DAY NINETY and DAY NINETY-ONE: THE GREAT LOVE DEBATE (pt4)

THE CONFERENCE CALL

A few weeks ago I sat with my two good friends Jason Kelly (27), and Brick (26). This is the first time I've had the chance to talk with just the boys on love, life, and intentions. Here is their story.

Kiana: So boys, tell me, how's your love life?

Brick: Define "love life."

Jason: (laughs) Damn Ki, we just jumping right in huh?

Kiana: Yes, J! Love life meaning your romantic encounters, special people in your lives, girlfriends, you know.

Brick: (laughs) Okay, okay. Let's do it. I'm single right now; I'm talking to a few different people seeing what works. I think I might want to be in a relationship or something soon, but I'm just figuring my shit out first.

Jason: I guess I'm somewhere around there too. Only thing is - I do have a shorty. We just started taking things seriously like a month or two ago, so far it's cool.

Kiana: I've heard that line before "figuring your stuff out." What exactly are men trying to figure out that gets in the way of simultaneously building a relationship?

Brick: I mean I can't speak on the lines you've heard from other men but I can say that I'm grinding right now. I'm the head of my household, it's important for me to make sure my sisters are good, money is coming in, and things are just in order before I'm out here making someone my girl.

Kiana: So what's your reasoning for talking to the few different people you mentioned earlier? You seem to have no intention on being anyone's boyfriend.

Brick: What's wrong with getting to know different people? There are mad people in the world, different circles, and situations. Just because I'm not trying to wife you doesn't mean we can't hang.

Jason: Man, that's how I used to think too. But to these women, you sound selfish bro.

Brick: How??

Jason: It's about intention. If you're not out here being real enough to tell these women that you're just taste testing, you're ultimately playing with them. I'm sure when you're ready you'll find what you're looking for and settle down at your own speed, that's what I did. But I kept it real with my girl, she didn't have to, but she waited for me. A few months later, here we are. But if the women you're talking think you're trying to build with them, you're inviting more issues for yourself.

Brick: I'm not lying to anyone. I haven't told anybody I'm trying to be with them and I'm damn sure not asking nobody to wait for me. So, if a shorty starts messing with me, knows wassup, and still wants to catch feelings that's kind of on her.

Kiana: Jason, tell us a little about your girl.

Jason: First, I just want to clear the air – I didn't ask her to wait for me, she chose to and then I chose her. Second, man I love that girl. She and I had been dating/messing around for a little while, but to be honest, at a point, I was in between jobs and my mom was sick…there was just a lot going on. I admit, instead of sharing this with her or my frustrations in general, I blocked her out. I didn't want her or anybody to really see me that low. I know, that wasn't fair but when shit is going on with you, you not really thinking about what's fair for someone else.

So, I felt like I had the world on my shoulders. Was drinking all crazy and messing with the around the way chicks. Damn thinking back, I know this sounds all over the place (laughs) but it's real. Craziest thing though, I remember coming back home after a wild night and Stacy was sitting on my steps. I had just been doing the absolute worst so I wasn't even trying to hear anything she was saying. But she stood up when she saw me and said she just wanted to lay eyes on me and make sure my heart was beating, we hadn't talked in almost a month. She knew I was going through something and she also knew she couldn't force me to open up to her, on top of that she wasn't trying to sit around and be with a confused n***a. She gave me an ultimatum: Stop drinking and try to save your mom or keep drinking and watch her die. The rest is really history to be honest.

Brick: Stacy sounds like one-of-a-kind bro, not every girl is built like that.

Kiana: Neither is every man. Jason had to be honest to her about everything. In order to find out who's built or not, people should have a chance to prove themselves.

Brick: Ah man I already see where this is going. Was this a group interview or an intervention? (laughs)

Jason: I'm weak!

Kiana: It's just a group interview, I promise! But life's an awful ugly place to not have someone. Be real with a woman and watch what happens. That's all a lot of us are in search for anyway, something real.

100 Days of Dating

DAY NINETY-TWO and DAY NINETY-THREE: RELATIONSHIP GOALS

"Men still think women will like who they are, not realizing: it's what they can do for a woman that sets the man apart." - Solange Nicole

Contributed poetry by: Court

*I want that waking up at 6 am to make you breakfast kind of love,
that my friends think I'm absolutely crazy kind of love
the kind of love that is reckless and addicting
that I don't care what you look like I just want to stay up all hours to share secrets kind of love
that every time I see you my heart throbs kind of love
that I see you upset and you don't have to say anything and I already know what to do kind of love
that stand next to me because I love you kind of love
that "you can have the cup with more coffee" kind of love
that you get my heart and the world gets the worst of me kind of love.
that you are my everything kind of love.*

*I just want you to bite my lip until I can't speak and can't scream anyone's name but yours.
I want you to touch the places that my ex forgot to touch.
I want you to let me scratch my brokenness into your back so that your moans can be the only thing that can fix me.
Let me make your body sing songs your lips don't know the words to.
Resurrect me so you can be all that I live for.
I want love.*

Contributed by: @Woodtheinspiration

Morning Word

You could be heaven sent and still be with someone hell-bent on keeping drama in your life. You are not doing anyone a favor remaining loyal to someone else who keeps you in draining situations. What if I told you that you still have the right to walk away from anyone walking all over you without you feeling guilty about it? What if I told you that love wasn't meant to make you feel like a prisoner surrounded by four walls of pain, but it was meant to make you feel alive and free like you just experienced emotional deliverance. Stop expecting cheap people to know your worth. Stop giving ungrateful people the very best parts of you. And stop acting like just because you signed up to be in love with someone, that means that you "have to" keep yourself tied to dreadful situations. When you see that someone you are involved with doesn't care about how they handle your heart, it becomes your responsibility to take it back and do what is best for YOU. You are not responsible for someone else hurting you, but you are responsible for how long you allow them to hurt you. And I want you to be happy again.
@woodtheinspiration

DAY NINETY-FOUR and NINETY-FIVE: SOULMATES

What we find in a soul mate is not something wild to tame it is something wild to run with. - Robert Brault

"Only once in your life, I truly believe, you find someone who can completely turn your world around. You tell them things that you've never shared with another soul and they absorb everything you say and actually want to hear more. You share hopes for the future, dreams that will never come true, goals that were never achieved and the many disappointments life has thrown at you.

When something wonderful happens, you can't wait to tell them about it, knowing they will share in your excitement. They are not embarrassed to cry with you when you are hurting or laugh with you when you make a fool of yourself. Never do they hurt your feelings or make you feel like you are not good enough, but rather they build you up and show you the things about yourself that make you special and even beautiful. There is never any pressure, jealousy or competition but only a quiet calmness when they are around. You can be yourself and not worry about what they will think of you because they love you for who you are. The things that seem insignificant to most people such as a note, song or walk become invaluable treasures kept safe in your heart to cherish forever. Memories of your childhood come back and are so clear and vivid it's like being young again. Colors seem brighter and more brilliant.

Kiana St Louis

Laughter seems part of daily life where before it was infrequent or didn't exist at all. A phone call or two during the day helps to get you through a long day's work and always brings a smile to your face. In their presence, there's no need for continuous conversation, but you find you're quite content in just having them nearby. Things that never interested you before become fascinating because you know they are important to this person who is so special to you. You think of this person on every occasion and in everything you do. Simple things bring them to mind like a pale blue sky, gentle wind or even a storm cloud on the horizon. You open your heart knowing that there's a chance it may be broken one day and in opening your heart, you experience a love and joy that you never dreamed possible. You find that being vulnerable is the only way to allow your heart to feel true pleasure that's so real it scares you. You find strength in knowing you have a true friend and possibly a soul mate who will remain loyal to the end. Life seems completely different, exciting and worthwhile. Your only hope and security is in knowing that they are a part of your life."

- Bob Marley

"People think a soul mate is your perfect fit, and that's what everyone wants. But a true soul mate is a mirror, the person who shows you everything that is holding you back, the person who brings you to your own attention so you can change your life.

A true soul mate is probably the most important person you'll ever meet, because they tear down your walls and smack you awake. But to live with a soul mate forever? Nah. Too painful. Soul mates, they come into your life just to reveal another layer of yourself to you, and then leave.

A soul mates purpose is to shake you up, tear apart your ego a little bit, show you your obstacles and addictions, break your heart open so new light can get in, make you so desperate and out of control that you have to transform your life, then introduce you to your spiritual master..."

- Elizabeth Gilbert from *Eat, Pray, Love*

DAY NINETY-SIX and DAY NINETY-SEVEN: DON'T TRY TO CHANGE HIM

"He's not perfect. You aren't either, and the two of you will never be perfect. But if he can make you laugh at least once, causes you to think twice, and if he admits to being human and making mistakes, hold onto him and give him the most you can. He isn't going to quote poetry, he's not thinking about you every moment, but he will give you a part of him that he knows you could break. Don't hurt him, don't change him, and don't expect for more than he can give. Don't analyze. Smile when he makes you happy, yell when he makes you mad, and miss him when he's not there. Love hard when there is love to be had. Because perfect guys don't exist, but there's always one guy that is perfect for you." - Bob Marley

I've been subject to trying to change someone before. I admit, that happened not because I wanted him to be better or different from the person I'd originally met, but I thought I was changing him to be the man he wanted to be. I thought I was helping. I could have helped the situation by making the choice of simply loving him for who he was or accepting his flaws and moving on. But I realize you can't do both. People shouldn't change people. If he's not the man you think meets your expectations, deal or leave. If she's not exactly meeting your requirements, deal or leave before children or other strings become attached. You always have a choice in love, remember to choose happiness.

Promise Yourself

Contributed by Christian D. Larson, Your Forces and How to Use Them

*To be so strong that nothing
can disturb your peace of mind.
To talk health, happiness, and prosperity
to every person you meet.*

Kiana St Louis

*To make all your friends feel
that there is something in them
to look at the sunny side of everything
and make your optimism come true.*

*To think only the best, to work only for the best,
and to expect only the best.
To be just as enthusiastic about the success of others
as you are about your own.*

*To forget the mistakes of the past
and press on to the greater achievements of the future.
To wear a cheerful countenance at all times
and give every living creature you meet a smile.*

*To give so much time to the improvement of yourself
that you have no time to criticize others.
To be too large for worry, too noble for anger, too strong for fear,
and too happy to permit the presence of trouble.*

*To think well of yourself and to proclaim this fact to the world,
not in loud words but great deeds.
To live in faith that the whole world is on your side
so long as you are true to the best that is in you.*

DAY NINETY-EIGHT and DAY NINETY-NINE: TO KNOW LOVE...

"With our love, we could save the world." - George Harrison

When Love Begins

Written by: Florence

*I always knew that love would come find me someday
but never did I know that it would be you who was headed my way
you caught me off guard and took me by surprise
but you simply captivated me, the same way you do when I look into your eyes*

*It's true that every good and perfect gift is from above
you were presented to me as a beautifully packaged gift full of humor, talent, intelligence, beauty and love
"it isn't finding the perfect person but learning to see an imperfect person perfectly"
we all have our flaws but when I view you through my eyes, perfection is all I see*

*From when you laugh to when you're upset, I still love the little things you do
especially hearing you laugh and seeing your nose wrinkle the same way mine does too
coming into this relationship has been hard at times but we've made it through
I know as long as we're on this journey together, there's nothing that we can't do.*

*Sometimes I wonder if what we have is too good to be true
too scared to get my heart broken and scared of the thought of losing you
but in the end, I trust in the author and perfecter of what I believe
because what we ask for in Him, we in return shall receive*

Kiana St Louis

"Where your treasure is, your heart will be also" is how the saying
goes
I may not know what tomorrow may bring, for God is the only one
who knows
the one thing I do know is that you are my one and only
a treasure in my heart that I want to devote my whole life to
completely

I know I don't need to prove my feelings to know they're true
because what I've known in my past, doesn't come close to the
experience I've shared with you
I've had the experience of being in relationships before
however, this is the first time I've been truly happy... I couldn't ask
for anything more
it's an honor to know that I am yours, as you are mine
and I trust God that He'll bring us together in His beautiful time

For now, I'll be waiting patiently for that day when we'll be
together
that precious moment in time when I'll say, "it's you that I want to
be with forever"
God made everything beautiful, precious and new
just as beautiful and precious as the day will be, when I look into
your eyes and say, "I Love You"

Contributed poetry by: Marcia A. Newton

Remember when we first did meet,
our hearts rejoiced and skipped a beat.
Remember our first kiss goodnight,
the hug we shared that summer's night.

Remember when we walked the beach
and all our dreams within our reach.
Remember how we used to be
when I had you and you had me.

Remember when we used to talk,
when we held hands and took long walks.
Remember how we spent our days
in warm sunshine and in the rain.

100 Days of Dating

Remember when our one desire
was take a chance and ignite the fire.
Remember the times that made our hearts melt
and all of the passion and desire that we felt.

Remember when you looked at me
and saw the one you love and need.
Remember when you reached for me
and knew that we were meant to be.

Remember when our love was new.
Remember the day we both said, "I do."
Remember the journey we started together.
Remember our love was always forever.

Remember the promise we made together,
to love and to cherish and to care for each other.
Remember the promise in good times and in bad
and to make each one happy rather than sad.

Remember when you held our child
and rocked the baby when I grew tired.
Remember the treasured times
like these when love grew into family.

Remember when the world was bright,
when we would laugh and hold on tight.
Remember when our hearts were broken,
when times were tough and words unspoken.

Remember when we grieved our loss
with parents gone and feeling lost.
Remember when our love endured
the pains and heartaches of the world.

What happened to the life we shared?
What happened to a love so rare?
What happed to the kiss goodnight,
the warm embrace, the love at night?

Did it all just happen? How do we right the wrong?
I know that in my heart your arms I do belong.

Kiana St Louis

Can we live our lives together just like it all began, and can we hold and cherish each other and remember our love again?

100 Days of Dating

DAY ONE HUNDRED: THE FINALE – MY STORY

"If you have the ability to love, love yourself first." - Charles Bukowski

We made it! 100 days later (give or take) and here we are! I am so excited to have finished this project, to have been able to learn so much from all of my willing participants, and I'm really proud of the progress I've made to heal. I would like to truly thank every person who shared his or her story through interview or poetry, this journey was for all of us.

2017 was a rollercoaster. Each up and down landed me in a new space, yet prepared me for the upcoming (and sometimes unplanned) life turns. I've learned lifetime lessons throughout the past few months from some of the bravest friends and family I have, and even strangers I've come to meet. Some people were hesitant but opened up past wounds in an effort to help those reading. Others shared secrets and stories they've never told a soul. This was a journey not only for myself but also for other pained lovers searching for answers.

As I've gone back and read, edited, and re read these stories again, I've found there is an underlying theme taped behind each chapter: Self-love. Whether people had been in relationships for years, newly connected, single, or just going with the flow, it was important for every man and woman to truly know and love themselves. It was in talking through all of the different situations that we realized one cannot give love unless we first love ourselves. While it may seem plain as day to most, a few of us have to really be out of a situation to see where we were.

Kiana St Louis

I admit, even in this new year of 2018 there are still so many unanswered questions left in the game of love. But I've learned that some lessons are guaranteed only through experience and sometimes you really have to go through tough times to truly appreciate them. Throughout this project, I've learned the importance of prioritizing my self-love and understanding *it's not selfish to love me* and put my feelings first. I've learned to trust myself and the decisions I make. I've learned to be fearless in letting people go, and truly understand that not everything you lose is a loss. I've learned to accept being single and know the difference between being alone and lonely. I've learned I am the master of my frequency and will continue to pour out the energy I hope to receive.

I am both a masterpiece and work in progress. I am strong but admit my weaknesses. Though life has taught me that people can be inconsistent, liars, and cheats, I am still eager to love and eager to live. I am not my experiences, but instead I am the result of all that I've been through. I am finally free. This is my story.

Tell me about your love life. Are you single? Dating? In a relationship?

It feels so funny to be on the other side of this! But, I'm really single. I have no interest in mingling much either. It finally feels a little good to only have to worry about myself.

What do you mean by "really single?"

This is the first time in a very long time that I am really just flowing. I don't talk to anyone, I'm not flirting with anyone, I'm not trying to figure anything out, I'm not wondering what a guy is up to, I'm not dating. I'm just single.

That's refreshing to hear, especially because you're saying all of this with a smile. But you mentioned not wanting to mingle, why is that?

I guess I'm just ready to re-learn myself, if that makes sense. Last year was super rough for me on the relationship side of things. I had a really bad break up with someone I thought I knew and was in a relationship with for 10 years. I tried to open myself to other people and it was a waste. I even started to kind of talk to someone but that got unnecessarily weird. I just want something stable. I don't want to wonder what I mean to a man, I don't want to feel like I'm doing too much, or he's doing too little, I just want to laugh and learn *from* and *with* someone. I want to be genuinely happy just by being with someone. That definitely hasn't happened yet and I partially think it's because I wanted it too badly.

But not anymore. I'm more focused on finding personal happiness than I am on finding a man for a relationship. I'm more concentrated on my energy and the vibes people give off than I am on settling down with just anyone. My failed love experiences have shown me that growth needed to happen, I was the common denominator. So, I figure if I flow instead of force, and shine my light, the right man will follow.

You mentioned you were talking to someone else. What happened there?

Not much actually and that was what was most frustrating about the situation. I never had someone repeatedly ask for my time, get it, and then act like they don't want it. He was by far one of the most confusing people I've ever met and probably one of my biggest disappointments.

We were talking/messing around for about 3 months, he made me feel very comfortable very easily and very early, which was something I liked. He made me feel like we were actually friends. After some time, we eventually became intimate and things changed, but not right away. The text messages, phone calls, and general effort slowly started to fade until he faded away completely. The last text message I have is a conversation he started about Black Panther and never finished. That was over a month ago.

I have no idea where he is, what he's up to, or let alone what the hell happened to us. But I don't care to. It's a process, it hurts, and I don't all the way understand it, but I'm learning some people are only in your life to help you get to another level. He came into my life right after my break up. I knew I was fragile, so I tried to play it safe, yet I still somehow caught a hairline crack. We weren't meant to be in a relationship, but he did help me get over my ex. So, I guess I should thank him for that.

10 years, man that's a long time. Tell us about that break up.

He was my high school sweetheart. I was 14 when we first met; I was a freshman and he was a senior. I thought he was bullying me at first (laughs) he was older and always had something to say - turns out he just liked me. Our relationship was wild. Because he was a senior I only had one year with him, every year after that was filled with time, space, and too much distance. To be honest, we should have just called it quits then. But we didn't. We kept it going, on and off, 2 kids (his kids), and 10 years later. He'd travel playing basketball overseas, while I finished college, joined the workforce and tried to fit into the adult life.

Last winter, things got crazy for the both of us from bills, to family issues, we both lost loved ones to cancer, it was just a mess. Usually when I'm going through a lot, I write and release to my closest friends, and at that time, to him. But for him, I guess he needed to close off completely. He didn't speak to me about his issues; in fact he didn't speak to me at all. He did speak to my friends though, which I thought was really weird. That taught me a lesson - if the person I'm with can't communicate to *me* in difficult times but manages to speak to other people, let alone MY friends, he's not for me.

But, fast forward, he stopped speaking to me in general and then I broke up with him. I was hurt for a long time because I didn't want to break up, but I also knew this guy was bugging and I couldn't be with someone that didn't want to talk to me. Fast forward some more, I called him one random drunk night (I don't regret many things in life, but this is for sure one of my biggest regrets. If I could go back in time, I would have never called). We spoke, kind of reconnected and continued to speak from there. We carried out this kind of unsure talking/dating thing for months until he spoke to my cousin and admitted he didn't want to be with me anymore after running up my credit card bill, but that's another story. He apparently felt like our story ended years ago but that I was the one holding on. To this day, he denies having ever said it, but I stopped believing him a long time ago.

I felt used, lied to, and cheated. I literally felt my heart fall into my stomach. The one person I loved with every part of me didn't love me back anymore. He used me, he stopped choosing me, and he never even apologized for it. I finally ended all communication, ties, and connection in October 2017. I had nothing left to give. I don't know where he is or what he's up to, and I don't wish to. If I were to see him today, I'd probably act like it didn't.

Sometimes we really just need to cut all ties and move on.

I've learned, sometimes that's the only way to save yourself.

So has this experience jaded you in any way? Do you not want to be in a relationship?

At one point it had. I remember almost wanting to give up on this personal project because of it. But not anymore, I still love the idea of love. I went to my cousin's wedding on New Year's Eve and opened the New Year witnessing love. I still believe in genuine love. I also believe that one day I'll get to have it too. I know I'm a really good woman. I am not perfect, nor to do I admit to be, but I still try and I know the right person will accept my efforts.

I'd like to be in a relationship, sure. But I think I have to do some more self-loving first. A lot of that last relationship messed with my confidence, my self-worth, and with my inner being. I have to find my balance again. I have to remember what its like to vibe with myself. I want to get my body right, my mind right, my money right, my relationship with God right and I hope in the midst of it all that someone will find me, especially because I'm not looking for him.

What was the most important lesson #100DaysofDating has taught you?

Great question. Hmmm, the most important lesson I've learned is to be unafraid to choose *Me*. My happiness, my goals, my type of love -- me. I'm a choice. I refuse to stay in an unhealthy relationship because of anything or anyone, I choose me. I refuse to let a confused man take any more of my time, love, or energy, I choose me. I refuse to let the fear of loneliness trap my mental state, or myself, I choose me. No matter how much I crave love, I choose to give love first to myself; I'm stronger that way.

Made in the USA
Columbia, SC
16 July 2018